Some of a person's mental states have the power to represent real and imagined states of affairs: they have semantic properties. *What minds can do* has two goals: to find a naturalistic or non-semantic basis for the representational powers of a person's mind, and to show that these semantic properties are involved in the causal explanation of the person's behavior. In the process, the book addresses issues that are central to much contemporary philosophical debate. It will be of interest to a wide range of readers in philosophy of mind and language, cognitive science, and psychology.

CAMBRIDGE STUDIES IN PHILOSOPHY

What minds can do

What minds can do

Intentionality in a non-intentional world

Pierre Jacob

Institute of Cognitive Science
CNRS, Lyon

CAMBRIDGE
UNIVERSITY PRESS

Published by the Press Syndicate of the University of Cambridge
The Pitt Building, Trumpington Street, Cambridge CB2 1RP
40 West 20th Street, New York, NY 10011-4211, USA
10 Stamford Road, Oakleigh, Melbourne 3166, Australia

First published 1997

Printed in Great Britain at the University Press, Cambridge

A catalogue record for this book is available from the British Library

Library of Congress cataloguing in publication data

Jacob, Pierre, 1949–
What minds can do: intentionality in a non-intentional world /
Pierre Jacob.
p.   cm. – (Cambridge studies in philosophy)
Includes bibliographical references and index.
ISBN 0 521 57401 3 (hardback) – ISBN 0 521 47436 6 (paperback)
1. Intentionality (Philosophy)   2. Philosophy of mind.   I. Title.
II. Series.
B105.I56J33   1997
128'.2–dc20   96-14157 CIP

ISBN 0 521 57401 3 hardback
ISBN 0 521 57436 6 paperback

TO MARIE-NOËLLE

Contents

Acknowledgments

From 1988 to 1994, I was fortunate to be a member of CREA (Centre de recherche en épistémologie appliquée) of Ecole Polytechnique and CNRS in Paris. For this period of time, CREA, a very lively research group led by Jean-Pierre Dupuy, provided me with a unique environment for the exchange of philosophical ideas in France.

I have used some of the material relevant to this book in some of the philosophy of mind courses which I have taught over the past few years in the doctoral program in cognitive science sponsored by University Paris 6, EHESS and Ecole Polytechnique. I started working on mental causation (the second part of this book) before working on the naturalization of intentionality (the first part). Some of the ideas involved in the first part of this book have been presented in the philosophy department at the University of Sienna (Italy), where I was invited to deliver four lectures by Gabriele Usberti in February 1995; at a workshop at the University of Hamburg (Germany) organized by Christian Stein and Mark Textor in March 1995; and in the Summer School on language and understanding at the International Center for Semiotics and Cognitive Studies in San Marino where I taught a course in June 1995. I am grateful to audiences there for their reactions.

Although I have several disagreements with them, this book owes a great deal to the work of Fred Dretske and Jerry Fodor.

Three friends deserve special credit for having provided – especially as part of our "Friday group" in Paris in the early 1980s – stimulating philosophical discussions and for criticizing drafts of my work over the past ten or so years: François Recanati, Dan Sperber, and Paul Horwich who read and discussed parts of the present book.

Many thanks to Ned Block for his extensive comments on the manuscript and for his support.

Acknowledgments

I am grateful to Luca Bonatti, Richard Bradley, Paolo Casalegno, Roberto Casati, Pascal Engel, Jerry Katz, Ruth Millikan, David Premack, Peter Railton, Georges Rey, Bob Stalnaker, and especially Jurgen Schröder for comments on parts of this book.

Discussions on various occasions with the following people have also been helpful: Daniel Andler, David Armstrong, Beatrice Bernazzi, Radu Bogdan, Jacques Bouveresse, Susan Carey, Peter Carruthers, Dick Carter, Donald Davidson, Martin Davies, Steven Davis, Dan Dennett, Jérome Dokic, Keith Donnellan, Frank Döring, Fred Dretske, Jean-Pierre Dupuy, Jerry Fodor, Gilles Fauconnier, Gary Gates, Allan Gibbard, Alvin Goldman, Samuel Guttenplan, Mike Harnish, Ray Jackendoff, David Kaplan, Frank Keil, Andreas Kemmerling, Jaegwon Kim, Max Kistler, Charles Larmore, Daniel Laurier, Keith Lehrer, François Lepage, Ernie Lepore, Barry Loewer, Nenad Miscevic, Kevin Mulligan, Karen Neander, Gloria Origgi, Elisabeth Pacherie, Claude Panaccio, Christopher Peacocke, John Perry, Jean Petitot, Philip Pettit, David Premack, Hilary Putnam, David Rosenthal, Philippe de Rouilhan, Jean-Michel Roy, Mark Sainsbury, Steven Schiffer, Michel Seymour, Peter Simons, Barry C. Smith, Charles Travis, Gabriele Usberti, Deirdre Wilson, Andrew Woodfield, Crispin Wright.

Introduction

This book is about semanticity or intentionality – about how semanticity or intentionality fit in a non-semantic, non-intentional world. Intentionality is one important feature of minds – of human minds, if not of other minds. It is what allows some of a human being's states of mind – the so-called "propositional attitudes" (such as beliefs and desires) – to be about (or represent) non-mental and mental things and states of affairs, some actual, some possible, and some impossible. In other words, having intentionality or being representations, an individual's states of mind have semantic properties. In particular, an individual's beliefs have truth-conditions: they can be true and they can be false (as the case may be). In contemporary philosophy, there are two broad approaches to intentionality: there is so to speak a top-down approach and there is a bottom-up approach.

What I call the top-down approach is embodied in the work of Davidson. The project is to characterize intentionality by starting with creatures – human beings – exhibiting systems of full-fledged propositional attitudes, possessing both the ability to speak a natural language and the further ability to attribute propositional attitudes to other creatures. From this top-down point of view, what is striking about an individual's full-fledged propositional attitudes is their holistic character. As Davidson (1982: 473) puts it, "one belief demands many beliefs, and beliefs demand other basic attitudes such as intentions, desires and . . . the gift of tongues." The top-down approach culminates in a "transcendental" argument for the view that "a creature cannot have thoughts unless it is an interpreter of the speech of another"; a creature cannot have beliefs unless it possesses both a language and the concept of belief (Davidson 1975: 157, 170). The reason why this argument is really fascinating is that, if correct, then it would justify a very strong form of anti-individualism: no creature could have thoughts unless it were a member of a social community.

1

The bottom-up approach, by contrast, starts with more modest creatures to which common sense and cognitive scientists are prone to attribute representational states or cognitive maps. Although bacteria, frogs, cats and dogs can neither speak a human natural language nor presumably attribute mental states to other creatures, still they can enter states having rudimentary intentionality, i.e., inner states representing aspects of their environment. Presumably, they can build maps of aspects of their environment even though they do not possess any concept of a map. Naturalistically minded philosophers (such as Dretske, Fodor, Millikan, and Papineau) are prone to emphasize the continuities between simpler physical and biological systems and creatures having full-blown sets of propositional attitudes, mastery of a human language and the ability to ascribe mental states to others. The bottom-up approach, as illustrated by naturalistically inclined philosophers, assumes that, if we want to understand some of the puzzling features of intentionality (such as the possibility of error or the capacity for misrepresentation), then our best bet is to start with the simplest, purest cases devoid of all the complexities and subtleties of the full-blown systems of propositional attitudes. On their view, we should not let our attention be diverted immediately by the achievements of the higher flights of human cognition. So we should first consider bacteria, frogs, cats, and dogs precisely because the ability to speak a human language and to ascribe mental states to others is far beyond them.

One can, I think, grant the advocate of the top-down approach that (to borrow a famous example from Malcolm) when a dog chases a cat, the dog's representation (correct or incorrect) of the cat's being up an oak tree differs from my belief that a cat went up an oak tree. For one thing, I have several different though related true beliefs about cats and about oak trees − such as that cats are feline mammals covered with fur and with paws on their feet; that oak trees have roots, branches and twigs and shed their leaves in autumn, and so on. I also no doubt have many false beliefs. Not only can humans have false beliefs, they can even have religious and/or superstitious beliefs about cats and trees whose "cognitive significance" would have been held dubious by logical positivists. Presumably, dogs do not have any such beliefs either about oak trees or about cats. Nor do I know how states of a dog's nervous system represent either cats or oak trees. Interesting differences between a genuine human belief that a substance is poisonous and a rat's disposition to avoid foodstuff which is poisonous have been thus described by Evans (1981: 131):

> The rat manifests the "belief" in only one way – by not eating – whereas there is no limit to the ways in which the ordinary belief that something is poisonous might be manifested. The subject might manifest it by, e.g., preventing someone else from eating the food, or by giving it to a hated enemy, or by committing suicide with it. These variations stem from the different projects with which the belief may interact, but similar variations arise from combining the belief with other beliefs. It might, for example, lead to a subject's consuming a small amount of food every day, when combined with the belief that the consumption of small doses of a poison renders one immune to its effects . . . It is of the essence of a belief state that it be at the service of many distinct projects, and that its influence on any project be mediated by other beliefs.

No doubt, the rat's disposition will serve fewer purposes than a human belief. From the fact, however, that they are less multipurpose or more single-purpose than human beliefs, it does not follow that either the state in the dog's nervous system or the rat's avoidance disposition lack aboutness, intentionality or semantic properties. Unlike humans, dogs cannot have religious beliefs about cats or about trees. Like human beliefs, however, the state in the nervous system of Malcolm's dog can be mistaken: it can, for example, misrepresent the location of the cat as being in the oak tree, when the cat is in fact in the neighboring maple tree. The fact that Malcolm's dog does not have the concept of belief, let alone the concept of truth, does not preclude him from misrepresenting features of his environment.

As Dennett (1983b: 69) – himself an advocate of the top-down approach – once wrote in an ecumenical tone of voice and in a slightly different context, "if you compare this [contrast between the two approaches] with the analogy of building a trans-continental railroad, you do start at both ends, and plan to meet somewhere in the middle." I do not know where the middle lies between the two approaches. Even though I endorse the bottom-up strategy of trying to find a naturalistic basis for intentionality and even though I am not convinced by the claim that a creature cannot have thoughts unless it has the concept of thought or belief, I do think that there is an important insight in the top-down approach favored by Davidson. Put in non-Davidsonian terms, the insight is that, underlying systems of full-blown human propositional attitudes, are two distinctively human cognitive capacities: the capacity for acquiring a human language and the capacity for forming beliefs about beliefs, beliefs about desires, desires about beliefs, desires about desires, in a word, the capacity for ascribing propositional attitudes to others. The idea, then, is that the arrival of brain structures with both linguistic and (as I will call them) "meta-representational" capacities (i.e., the ability to form propositional attitudes about propositional attitudes) must have been a turning point in the phylogenetic evolution of biological systems capable of entering states with intentionality (or semantic properties).

If one is a physicalist (as I am), then two questions arise: first, how can states of physical systems – bits of brain cells – have intentionality? Which of a system's non-semantic properties allow it to have semantic properties? Secondly, what aspect of a system's behavior can be explained by its possession of intentionality? What can the causal role of a system's semantic properties be? Because it deals with the above two complementary questions, the present book has two parts. The first part (chapters 1 to 4) examines the question whether the semantic properties of an individual's propositional attitudes can be derived from non-semantic properties and relations of the individual's mind. This is often called in contemporary philosophy of mind the task of naturalizing intentionality. The second part (chapters 5 to 8) tries to answer the question: can a physicalist recognize a role to the semantic properties of an individual's propositional attitudes in the causal explanation of the individual's intentional behavior? In Dennett's terminology, can an individual's propositional attitudes be "semantic engines"? If not, then a physicalist will be committed to the epiphenomenalism of intentionality – or of the semantic properties of an individual's propositional attitudes. This is the problem of mental causation.

In chapter 1, I characterize a position which I call intentional realism and acceptance of which, I argue, commits one to the twofold program of naturalizing intentionality and of showing that intentionality can be causally efficacious. In chapters 2–4, I argue for an informationally based teleosemantic approach to the task of deriving the semantic properties of an individual's propositional attitudes from non-semantic properties and relations of his or her mind. This approach assumes that information is a crucial ingredient of semanticity. Chapter 2 presents the leading ideas of informational semantics. In chapters 3 and 4, assuming the standpoint of informational semantics, I discuss three features of the semantic properties of an individual's propositional attitudes which ought to be accounted for by an informational approach to intentionality: the insensitivity of belief contents to their informational origins; the problem of intensionality (or referential opacity) and the problem of misrepresentation. I further distinguish two problems often confused in the literature: the problem of imperfect correlation and the problem of the transitivity of nomic dependencies. In chapter 4, I argue for a teleosemantic approach to the latter of the two problems, which, like Dretske's recent views, and unlike Millikan's purely teleosemantic approach, has an informational basis.

Chapter 5 discusses the "computational representational theory of mind" based on the language of thought hypothesis whose main advocate over the last twenty years has been Fodor. The language of thought hypothesis has two purposes: on the one hand, it is designed to solve the problem of compositionality of the semantic properties of an individual's propositional attitudes. On the other hand, it is designed to solve the problem of mental causation: mental symbols are supposed to have both semantic and syntactic properties. Syntactic properties, not semantic properties of mental symbols are expected to be causally efficacious. After examining conceptual issues raised by the language of thought hypothesis, I argue that it does not justify the thesis that the semantic properties of an individual's propositional attitudes are causally efficacious. In chapter 6, I argue that – contrary to recent claims of Fodor's – the alternative between semantic atomism and semantic holism is not exclusive and that consequently an intentional realist is not bound to accept semantic atomism. In chapters 7 and 8, I distinguish two reasons why the semantic properties of an individual's propositional attitudes might lack causal efficacy. I therefore distinguish two epiphenomenalist threats: the threat of preemption and the threat of externalism. The former – with which I deal in chapter 7 – arises because the semantic properties of an individual's propositional attitudes might be preempted by more basic physical (chemical or biological) properties of the individual's brain. The latter – with which I deal in chapter 8 – arises from the fact that the semantic properties of an individual's propositional attitudes are not local properties of the individual's brain. Dretske has, I think, recently provided the ingredients of a response to the threat of externalism – and has therefore sketched a justification of the thesis that the semantic properties of an individual's propositional attitudes are causally efficacious — that an individual's propositional attitudes are semantic engines. In chapter 8, however, I explain why I disagree with his sharp dichotomy between the role of the semantic properties of ontogenetically formed representations and the role of the semantic properties of phylogenetically formed representations. Finally, in chapter 9, I reflect on the differences between my mixed informational and teleo-semantic account of semanticity and Fodor's pure informational account. The former, unlike the latter, I argue, does not sever the link between semantics and psychology.

Part I: The naturalization of intentionality

1

What is intentional realism?

In this chapter, I would like to examine a realist view of the mind which I shall call *intentional realism*. At the heart of the version of intentional realism which I will discuss is Representationalism, i.e., the claim that the mind is primarily a representational system or that an individual's mind is a system whose job it is to deliver (or manufacture) representations of the environment for the benefit of the individual whose mind it is. Now, when we introspectively reflect upon our own human minds, we quickly discover that they are inhabited by two quite distinct sorts of states: propositional attitudes and experiences. Propositional attitudes, e.g., beliefs and desires, have what Brentano, reviving a medieval Scholastic word, called "intentionality." Conscious experiences, sensations or *qualia* are paradigmatic states about which it makes sense to ask Tom Nagel's (1974) celebrated question: what is it like to have them, to enjoy them or to be in them? *Qualia* are so-called because there is a subjective, seemingly intrinsic, *quality* characteristic of states such as smelling a perfume, hearing the sound of a cello, seeing a red rose, or tasting a strawberry.[1] This quality can only be experienced from a first person point of view or perspective. The representational claim seems true of propositional attitudes, not so obviously true of experiences.

In fact, there is a weak (almost analytic) reading of Representationalism: this is the claim that many of a mind's states – the so-called propositional attitudes – can be thought of as mental representations of (non-mental) states of affairs. There is a stronger reading of Representationalism which is the claim that understanding the

---

[1] For one of the clearest formulations of the view that experiential properties and intentionality raise two separate problems, see Field (1978). The latter is what he calls Brentano's problem.

representational (or semantic) properties of propositional attitudes can take us some way towards understanding aspects of conscious experiences. One of the challenges, therefore, faced by Representationalism is precisely to show that a theory of the semantic properties of propositional attitudes can throw light onto conscious experiences as well. This will be a topic for the next chapter.

Propositional attitudes are beliefs, intentions, desires, guesses, fears, hopes, etc. Philosophers call such states propositional attitudes on the linguistic ground that human beings ascribe them to one another by means of the utterance of a complex sentence containing a main verb expressing the person's attitude towards the propositional content expressed by (referred to or denoted by) the "that"-clause embedded under the main verb as in (1):

(1)   Anna thinks that Mars is one of the planets of the Solar system.

In (1) the verb "think" expresses Anna's attitude towards the proposi-tion expressed by the sentence "Mars is one of the planets of the Solar system." An individual's propositional attitudes are internal states of the individual.[2] To say that a person's beliefs are states internal to him or her is to say that somebody else cannot directly observe them. You can figure out some of my beliefs by listening to what I say or by attending to what I do. But you cannot experience my beliefs: you cannot see them, touch them, smell them, or hear them. Neither can I for that matter. I am, however, directly aware of the contents of some of my own beliefs to which I have special introspective access; some-times at least, I do not need to attend to what I do or listen to what I say to determine what I think.[3]

Whether or not "there is something it is like" to have them, the primary feature of propositional attitudes is that they are mental states

---

[2] To say that an individual's propositional attitudes are *internal* states of the individual is not to espouse an internalist (or anti-externalist) view of the contents (or semantic properties) of the individual's propositional attitudes. The controversy between internalism and externalism is about the semantic properties of an individual's propositional attitudes. To borrow an example from Davidson (1987), an individual's skin may have the property of being sun-burnt. The skin is part of the individual. The individual's skin, however, can only be sun-burnt if it stood in some causal relation to the sun, as opposed to some other source of energy.

[3] At least, this is true of my conscious beliefs. I am not directly aware of my unconscious beliefs.

with propositional content. As I said, they have the cluster of properties which Brentano called intentionality. They are *about* things and states of affairs, some real, some possible, some impossible. I may, for example, wish I were someone else or I may wish to ride a unicorn. These, I take it, are desires about impossible states of affairs. Beliefs too can be about impossible states of affairs: I may believe for instance that the greatest integer is a prime number. Some beliefs about actual, real existing things are true. Others are false: a false belief may wrongly ascribe to some actual thing a property which the thing does not have. Unlike a false belief about a possible though unrealized state of affairs, a belief about an impossible state of affairs might be said to be neither true nor false: it might lack a truth-value. Arguably, for the belief that *a* is *F* to be truth-evaluable, the presupposition that *a* exists must be satisfied. If it is not, then the belief that *a* is *F* is not truth-evaluable. This suggests that our beliefs may be mistaken in two ways.[4] What makes the representational thesis plausible – in fact almost trivial – in the case of beliefs is that they are representational states: they can represent states other than themselves, some non-mental, some mental. Beliefs can represent non-mental states of affairs such as the fact that Mars (which I take to be a non-mental entity) has the property of being one of the planets of the Solar system (which I take to be a non-mental property or relation). They can also represent mental states of affairs such as when Anna thinks that all her beliefs about Mars are true. I shall say that propositional attitudes have *semantic* properties.

In the present chapter, I am going to argue for the view I call intentional realism. In the last section, however, I will present a puzzle for intentional realism – a puzzle which will only be solved in the penultimate chapter of this book. The puzzle consists in trying to reconcile a thesis I call "the strong causal thesis" with two other plausible doctrines: an externalist view of the individuation of the semantic properties of an individual's propositional attitudes and the assumption that causal processes are local processes.

I.2 INTENTIONAL REALISM AND INTENTIONAL IRREALISM

As illustrated above, semantic properties are puzzling in a number of respects, some of them ontological (or metaphysical), others

---

[4] For more on the problems of misrepresentation, see chapters 3 and 4.

epistemological. At least, they should strike any philosopher – such as myself – who subscribes to a monist physicalist ontology as peculiar – if not weird or queer[5] – properties. The fact that propositional attitudes are about things and that they have semantic properties was one reason why Descartes embraced a dualist ontology. He could not see how purely physical things could have such properties. In effect, Descartes assumed that minds, unlike bodies, can exist without occupying space (or without being extended). His assumption was not merely that, whereas he could conceive of unextended minds, he could not think of unextended bodies. His assumption was rather that being extended is a necessary (or essential) property of bodies, it is not a necessary (or essential) property of minds. Alternatively, whereas thinking is a necessary (or essential) property of minds, it is not a necessary (or essential) property of bodies. He, therefore, posited a realm of immaterial, non-physical things or substances – minds composed of ideas – especially devised to be the bearers of semantic properties. The characteristic property (the main attribute) of all non-physical (non-extended) things was, according to Descartes, thought. On his view, therefore, only non-physical entities could be *about* physical things; only non-physical entities could be true or false.[6]

Now, when I say (as I did above) that I subscribe to a monist physicalist ontology, I merely mean to say that, unlike an advocate of substance dualism (or pluralism) of the Cartesian sort, I assume that bearers of semantic properties must be physical things: they must have physical properties too. Like things having chemical and biological properties, they must be decomposable into fundamental particles of the sort found in inorganic matter and recognized by basic physics.[7] How this rather weak constraint can be satisfied will

---

[5] "Queerness" is the word used by Mackie (1977: 38–42) to express a characteristic of values.

[6] Put in merely epistemic terms – as the assumption that a mind, unlike a body, could not conceivably be extended – Descartes' argument is open to the rebuttal that from the fact that water could conceivably lack the property of being H_2O, it surely does not follow that water is not H_2O. A contemporary version of the modal (*de re*) Cartesian argument is provided by Kripke (1972; 1982).

[7] If a Platonist were to insist that abstract entities too, for example, propositions, may have semantic properties even though they are devoid of physical properties, I would first point out that no system could "grasp" either a proposition or its semantic properties unless it had physical properties. I would secondly suggest that, on my view, propositions, unlike propositional attitudes and linguistic symbols, do *not have*

become clearer in a moment when I discuss *token physicalism*. Towards the end of the present chapter, I will unpack the ontological puzzle raised by the semantic properties of an individual's propositional attitudes as resulting from three plausible theses: externalism, the strong causal thesis, and the assumption that causal processes are local processes.

Not only do semantic properties raise ontological puzzles; they also raise epistemological puzzles. Both the ontological and the epistemological puzzles have driven many physicalists towards a rejection of intentional realism. Quine (1960: 220–21) ascribed to Brentano the thesis that the intentional (or semantic) vocabulary is irreducible to a non-intentional vocabulary – where I take the relevant issue of reduction to be mostly epistemological. Quine has linked Brentano's irreducibility thesis, which he accepts, to his own thesis of the indeterminacy of translation. Unlike Brentano, however, he concludes from the irreducibility thesis to the "baselessness of intentional idioms and the emptiness of a science of intentions" (*ibid*.: 221). Now, there is no doubt that Quine endorses physicalism, as his famous slogan makes clear: "no mental difference without some physical difference."[8] So his acceptance of Brentano's irreducibility thesis must be compatible with physicalism. Quine (*ibid*.) has drawn an epistemological distinction – which he calls "the double standard" – between the demands of daily life and the goal of "limining the true and ultimate structure of reality." Although Quine deems the use of intentional idioms to be inappropriate for the latter scientific goal, he concedes that it might be "practically indispensable" for our daily transactions with our conspecifics.

There are, it seems, two ways to reconcile physicalism and Brentano's irreducibility thesis: both are versions of what Boghossian (1990a) calls "intentional irrealism." The first version is the one which Boghossian (*ibid*.) labels the "error-theoretic" view; the other version

---

meanings or semantic properties, they *are* meanings or semantic properties. To a naturalistically inclined philosopher, it is a puzzle how a mind could grasp directly a proposition. A mind may, however, grasp the meaning or semantic property of a symbol. So why not identify the meaning or semantic property of a symbol with a proposition (or a constituent of a proposition)?

[8] See for example Quine (1977: 162–63). Insofar as he accepts the existence of classes, Quine is also a Platonist. He, therefore, faces the task of reconciling his Platonism with his physicalism.

is the one he labels the "non-factualist" view.[9] Both may be seen as arising from Quine's "double standard" view.

According to the error-theoretic version of intentional irrealism, any utterance of a sentence ascribing a semantic property to an individual's propositional attitude expresses a *false* proposition. The error-theoretic version of intentional irrealism has been called "eliminative materialism" and it has been explicitly advocated by P. M. Churchland (1981; 1984) and P. S. Churchland (1986). In P. M. Churchland's (1981: 1) words,[10] it is

> the thesis that our commonsense conception of psychological phenomena constitutes a radically false theory, a theory so fundamentally defective that both the principles and the ontology of that theory will eventually be displaced, rather than smoothly reduced, by completed neuroscience.

For two kinds of related reasons, and like many philosophers (including Baker 1988, Boghossian 1990a, Putnam 1988: ch. 4), I find the error-theoretic strand of eliminative materialism deeply unsatisfying: I find it unstable if not paradoxical. According to eliminative materialism, our folk concepts of propositional attitudes with their purported semantic properties are best compared to such concepts as the physical and chemical concepts of caloric and phlogiston and other alchemical concepts – i.e., concepts devoid of reference.[11] So the view is that there are no such states as propositional attitudes with semantic properties. When, however, the advocate of eliminative materialism puts forth his or her hypothesis that our concept of propositional attitude is much like, for example, the pre-Lavoisier chemical concept of phlogiston, he or she is presumably submitting his or her belief (that our concept of propositional attitude is much like the concept of phlogiston) so that we can assess it for truth or falsity. But if his view were right, then it is not clear that the whole procedure would make sense: it is not clear that it would be meaningful for the eliminative materialist to put forth his or her eliminative materialist belief and for us to examine its truth or falsity. At least, the eliminative materialist owes us an alternative account of the pro-

---

[9] As made clear by Boghossian (1990a), ethics has been the area in which both versions of irrealism have been most developed.

[10] See also P. M. Churchland (1984: 43; 1992: 420).

[11] P. M. Churchland (1981: 12–13; 1984: 44; 1992: 420).

cedure which does not presuppose that what he is doing is putting forth his own view (or belief) for us to examine its truth or falsity.

Interestingly, in the process of defending his hypothetical analogy between our concept of propositional attitude and the concept of phlogiston, P. M. Churchland (1992: 420) concedes that concepts of such artefacts as tables, chairs and mousetraps do possess a reference. I agree with Putnam (1992: 438–39) that this is a problematic concession to make for an eliminative materialist since the very existence of such artefacts depends on the propositional attitudes of their designers.

On the error-theoretic view of the ascription of semantic properties to an individual's propositional attitudes (presupposed by eliminative materialism), the utterance of a sentential structure of the form "x is P" (where "P" purports to express or refer to a semantic property) can never express a true proposition. Following Boghossian (1990a: 174), let us assume that if there are things having semantic properties, then there are things having truth-conditions. In other words, let us assume that the notion of truth-condition is one central semantic property. Then, one construal of the error-theoretic claim would be that all utterances purporting to ascribe some truth-condition to some representation or other must be false. What makes this position unstable or paradoxical is that on the one hand it claims that no utterance ascribing a truth-condition can be true. If this claim were true, then nothing could have a truth-condition. On the other hand, for any utterance ascribing a truth-condition to be false (as the error theory has it), then any such utterance must have a truth-condition. Something can only be false if it has some truth-condition. So the error theory seems committed to the uncomfortable claim that truth-condition attributing utterances must both have and not have truth-conditions.[12]

The essential claim made by the non-factualist version of intentional irrealism is the even more radical claim that predicates which

---

[12] Although this line of thinking has been challenged, I find it convincing. It has been challenged by, e.g., Devitt (1990) who makes a distinction between two notions of truth-condition: the notion of robust truth-condition and the notion of deflationary truth-condition. The idea then is that the eliminative materialist can use the deflationary notion of truth to say that all utterances ascribing some robust truth-condition are deflationarily false. For Boghossian's reply, see Boghossian (1990b). For a reply to Boghossian's reply, see Devitt & Rey (1991).

are supposedly or purportedly used to refer to (denote or express) semantic properties of an individual's propositional attitudes simply do not stand for any genuine properties at all. Arguably, not every meaningful predicate of a natural language expresses a genuine property.[13] So, for example, the question arises naturally whether ethical predicates – though meaningful – do or do not express genuine properties. This non-factualist version of intentional irrealism has been entertained quite explicitly by Stich (1983: 225–26):

> such predicates [as "is a belief that p"] typically do not express properties at all. What this suggests is that *there is no such thing as the property of believing that p*. The predicate "is a belief that p" does not express or correspond to a property. If this is right, then we have yet another reason for not thinking of folk psychological beliefs as state tokens, since a state token is the instantiation of a property by an individual during a time interval, and if there is no property, then there can be no state token. It is important to realize, however, that the nonexistence of belief *properties* and belief *state tokens* does not entail that *predicates* of the form "is a belief that p" are meaningless . . .[14]

Stich (1983) has developed his non-factualist version of intentional irrealism into a doctrine which he calls "the syntactic view of the mind" (to which I will come back in chapter 5). The reason I say that the non-factualist theorist makes a more radical claim than the error theorist is that it is presumably a precondition for an utterance to express a false proposition that its constituent predicate express in the

---

[13] It is, for example, controversial whether "witch," which is a meaningful predicate of English, expresses a genuine property in the sense that arguably it cannot have any genuine instantiation. Also it is controversial whether "round square" or "colorless green idea" are meaningful predicates which do not express genuine properties or whether they are meaningless.

[14] One particular reason Stich (1983) has for taking this non-factualist position is his view of belief-*ascription* based on similarity relations. So on his view, one strong reason why the predicate "is a belief that p," depending as it does on similarity relations which are contextual, does not express a genuine property would be that it cannot express one and the same property in all contexts. The predicate "is a belief that p", however, could still be meaningful and be instantiated: it would apply to different things in different contexts. Although I will not discuss here Stich's view of belief-ascription, in response to Stich, it might be pointed out that "is a belief that p" might express a disjunctive property. I will momentarily examine another less radical embodiment of the non-factualist position, i.e., Dennett's intentional stance.

first place a genuine property. To express a false proposition, an utterance must be apt for expressing truths.

One particularly interesting version of the non-factualist interpretation of intentional irrealism can be detected in one strand of the influential view which Dennett (1978; 1987c) has called the *intentional stance*. According to this anti-realist component of the intentional stance, which I want to briefly discuss, to attribute propositional attitudes to a physical system is *not* to disclose or reveal genuine semantic properties of the system. Rather, it consists in adopting a certain heuristic *stance* or attitude towards it which in turn serves pragmatic goals: not so much explaining the behavior of the system, as facilitating the prediction of its behavior.[15] In reference to the understanding of the behavior of chess-playing computers, Dennett (1971: 7) has said that "the decision to adopt the strategy is pragmatic, and is not intrinsically right or wrong."[16] So according to the anti-realist component of the intentional stance view, semantic properties of an individual's propositional attitudes arise from the stance taken towards the individual by an observer or an interpreter. The puzzling feature of the anti-realist component of the intentional stance position is that it seems to make a physical system *A*'s semantic properties relative to the stance of yet another physical system, *B*. But now when physical system *B* attributes propositional attitudes to *A*, what does *B* do if not express its own (higher-order) attitudes towards *A*'s attitudes? On the anti-realist component of Dennett's position, then, the semantic properties of *A*'s states are only a matter of *B*'s stance; but it does seem OK to endow *B*'s states with semantic properties. So the view seems to run in a circle or to be threatened by a regression. There is, however, a second ingredient of Dennett's doctrine which I will call "patternalism"[17] and which is not so clearly at

[15] Dennett's emphasis upon the predictive, as opposed to explanatory, role and value of the intentional stance is the reason why his position has been labelled "instrumentalistic." This is a point which distinguishes Dennett from Davidson, to which I come back in chapter 5.

[16] Arguably, as Dennett (1987b: 342–43) points out, not only is Quine (1960) an early advocate of eliminative materialism, but in recognizing the practical indispensability of intentional (or semantic) predicates in daily life (for predictive purposes), Quine (1960) is also an early proponent of the "instrumentalist" component of Dennett's own intentional stance view.

[17] Perhaps it would be better called "patternism"; but I prefer Rey's (forthcoming) pun "patternalism."

odds with intentional realism, as I will try to show shortly when I get to the view of the mind as a meta-representational organ.

I.3 THE ĐILEMMA OF THE INTENTIONAL REALIST

Unlike both an error theorist (or an eliminative materialist) and a non-factualist intentional irrealist, an intentional realist who subscribes to physicalism is, as I said above, committed to the view that the semantic properties of an individual's propositional attitudes are genuine properties of the individual's brain. In this chapter, I want to consider the task faced by an intentional realist who subscribes to physicalism. I will presently ascribe to intentional realism the following three theses: (i) the semantic properties of an individual's propositional attitudes are genuine properties of the individual. (ii) The semantic properties of an individual's utterances are derivative from the semantic properties of his or her propositional attitudes. (iii) The semantic properties of an individual's propositional attitudes must contribute to the production of the individual's intentional behavior.

According to physicalist intentional realism, a few evolved complex physical systems have minds. Human beings and a few higher animals do. But most physical systems – some of them quite complex – do not. Rocks, planets, stars, galaxies, oceans, maple trees, proteins, DNA molecules, viruses, alarm clocks, vacuum cleaners are not minded. They cannot occupy states having intentionality or semantic properties.[18] Conversely, according to intentional realism, semantic properties of states of systems with a mind are genuine properties of the system; they do not arise as the result of an interpreter's projection onto the system.

According to intentional realism, if semantic properties are genuine properties, then having a mind must make a difference – a causal difference. Minded systems must be able to do things which systems lacking a mind must be unable to do. If having a mind did not make a causal difference (in this sense), then, the intentional realist points out, what good would it do to have a mind? So at least, states of mind must be causes; they must have effects.

So the metaphysical research program of intentional realism is

---

[18] As I argue in chapter 9, some systems carry information about their environment; others have representational abilities; still others have meta-representational abilities.

twofold. On the one hand, it is incumbent upon the intentional realist to show that the fact that minds can occupy states with semantic properties can explain why systems having a mind can do things which systems without a mind cannot do. This is the problem of *mental causation*.[19] On the other hand, unless he is not a physicalist, the intentional realist must, in the words of Fodor (1987a), show "how an entirely *physical* system could nevertheless exhibit intentional states." Here is how the biologist T. H. Huxley expressed his puzzlement about the existence, not of intentionality, but of consciousness: "How is it that anything so remarkable as a state of consciousness comes about as a result of irritating nervous tissue, is just as unaccountable as the appearance of the Djin, when Aladdin rubbed his lamp."[20] If we replace "state of consciousness" by "representational state" or "intentionality," then Huxley raises the very issue which gives rise to the program of *naturalizing* intentionality or the semantic properties of mental states.

Arguably, the problem of mental causation and the problem of naturalizing intentionality pull in opposite directions and the intentional realist might well face a dilemma one horn of which has been well spelled out by Fodor (1987b: 97):

> I suppose that sooner or later the physicists will complete the catalogue they've been compiling of the ultimate and irreducible properties of things. When they do, the likes of *spin*, *charm*, and *charge* will perhaps appear upon their list. But *aboutness* surely won't; intentionality simply doesn't go that deep. It's hard to see, in face of this consideration, how one can be a Realist about intentionality without also being, to some extent or other, a Reductionist. If the semantic and the intentional are real properties of things, it must be in virtue of their identity with (or may be supervenience on?) properties that are themselves *neither* intentional *nor* semantic. If aboutness is real, it must really be something else.

---

[19] Notice that it is slightly misleading to refer to *the* problem of mental causation here. Later in this chapter, I will distinguish a weak from a strong causal thesis. Later still, in chapters 7 and 8, I will argue that an intentional realist faces two epiphenomenalist threats: the threat of preemption and the threat of externalism. Besides, strictly speaking, one ought to distinguish the problem of showing that intentionality can play a causal-explanatory role in the production of an individual's intentional behavior from the further problem of showing that creatures with a mind can do things which creatures without cannot do. In chapters 5, 7 and 8 of the present work, I can only claim to deal with the former, not with the latter, problem.

[20] Quoted by Block (1994: 210) and Humphrey (1992: 218).

This is the Reductionist horn of the intentional realist's dilemma. On the one hand, the intentional realist is a physicalist. So minds must be nothing but complex physical systems whose queer semantic properties must not be supernatural properties. At best, they must be explainable on some physical basis. At least, they must be explainable on the basis of some non-intentional, non-semantic properties and relations.[21] On the other hand – and this is the anti-Reductionist horn of the dilemma – the intentional realist is a realist about minds. Minds do possess genuine semantic properties; which is to say that their having semantic properties must make a causal difference. But this second line of thought drives the intentional realist into emphasizing the uniqueness of minds in the physical world whereas the first line of thought pulls in the opposite direction of deemphasizing the uniqueness of minds among other natural physical systems.

Arguably, without some additional assumption, this dilemma is not inevitable. For – as will appear later in this chapter (section 1.5) – not all versions of physicalism are committed to reductionism about the mental. A token physicalist (as opposed to a type physicalist) may subscribe to the idea that all things – minds included – must be composed of fundamental elementary physical particles without requiring that the semantic properties of an individual's states of mind be reducible to, or definable in terms of, the physical, chemical, and biological properties of the individual's brain states.[22] What can, however, be called the naturalistic perplexity, combined with physicalism and intentional realism, does give rise to the above dilemma. What I call the naturalistic perplexity is, in Fodor's (1984: 32) terms, "the worry . . . that the semantic (and/or the intentional) will prove permanently recalcitrant to integration in the natural order." A philosopher worried by the naturalistic perplexity will reject what Field (1972) called "semanticalism," i.e., the view that semantic facts are primitive and irreducible, in the way a vitalist assumes that biological facts are primitive and irreducible, i.e., not explicable in physical, chemical,

---

21 As Schiffer 's (1987: 10) "eighth hypothesis" has it, "[these] semantic and psychological facts are not irreducibly semantic or psychological but can be revealed to be facts statable by sentences devoid of semantic or psychological terms . . ."

22 As will emerge in section 1.5, the job of the notion of supervenience is precisely to license a physicalist non-reductive view of the relation between the semantic properties of an individual's states of mind and the physical properties of his or her brain states.

non-biological terms. The idea that our naturalistic proclivities ought not to tolerate that semantic facts be primitive irreducible facts has been expressed by Dennett (1971) as the idea that to endow a device's internal states, structures or events with content is "to take out a loan" of intentionality.[23] So if you take out a loan of intentionality, you must repay your debt. The naturalistic perplexity – the debt incurred – would be, if not relieved, at least attenuated, if it were possible to say in a non-semantic (non-intentional) vocabulary what it takes for a system with physical, chemical and biological properties to have semantic properties. This would contribute towards minimizing the deficit of the intentional realist.[24]

This issue is indeed closely related to the issue of the reducibility of a system's semantic properties to its non-semantic (physical, chemical, biological) properties. There are two broad ways one can think about reduction in this context. On the one hand, there are several famous examples of reductions achieved in the sciences: water turned out to be identical to H_2O molecules; gold turned out to have atomic number 79; lightning turned out to be nothing other than electrical discharge; (mendelian) genes turn out to be nothing but DNA molecules. Such identities are nomic in the sense that what is claimed is that nothing would be water unless it were composed of H_2O molecules; nothing would be gold unless it had atomic number 79; nothing would be a gene unless it were composed of DNA molecules, and so on.[25] On the other hand, when philosophers think of reducing semantic properties to non-semantic properties, they have in mind providing necessary and sufficient non-semantic conditions for the possession of semantic properties. Since Quine's (1951) attack on the analytic/synthetic distinction, it is commonly held by philosophers that the attempt to provide necessary and sufficient conditions on almost any concepts – i.e., to analyze or define almost any concept – is doomed to failure. So perhaps philosophers who embark on the project of naturalizing intentionality should only aim at providing

---

[23] Actually, Dennett (1971) speaks of a "loan of intelligence." But I'm concerned with intentionality, not intelligence as such.

[24] When he writes that "intentionality won't be reduced and won't go away," Putnam (1988: 1) obviously disavows what I call the naturalistic perplexity. He must either think that an intentional realist incurs no debt; or that if he does, he should not worry about reimbursement.

[25] For a little more on nomic necessity, see the next chapter.

sufficient non-semantic conditions on the possession of semantic properties.[26]

Be that as it may, given the intentional realist impulse to bridge the gap between semantic properties and non-semantic (physical, chemical and biological) properties, the dilemma of the intentional realist is, I think, genuine. Furthermore, it is, in my view, quite productive in contemporary philosophy of mind. Presumably, the way to resolve the tension is to point out that a mind is nothing but a physical (chemical and biological) system, only a physical (chemical and biological) system with a complicated organization. The burden, then, lies in unfolding the appropriate notion of organization.[27]

I.4 THE PRIORITY OF THOUGHT OVER LANGUAGE AND THE COGNITIVE TURN

I said above that the substance dualist (of a Cartesian sort) believes that only non-physical things can have such queer properties as semantic properties. As a matter of fact, it would be an obvious mistake to assume that only propositional attitudes have semantic properties. Words and other linguistic symbols too have semantic properties. To an ontological substance dualist, it is of course controversial whether propositional attitudes *are* physical objects − or states of physical objects. I suppose, however, that it is uncontroversial that words and linguistic symbols are physical objects. At least, as will emerge momentarily (in section 1.5), one may assume that word *tokens* and linguistic *tokens* − if not types − are physical objects with physical properties. Now, the parallelism between the semantic properties of some beliefs and the semantic properties of some linguistic symbols is striking. And it has indeed struck many philosophers. My belief that, for example, Sienna is north of Rome has truth-conditions. And so does my utterance of the English sentence "Sienna is north of Rome" which I may use to express my belief. Both are true iff the relation *x is north of y* holds of two Italian cities, Sienna and Rome.

The intentional realist thesis I now wish to consider is the thesis of the priority of the semantic properties of thoughts (or propositional

---

[26] Fodor (1990b: 51) for one undertakes the weaker task of providing sufficient non-semantic conditions on semanticity.

[27] This is where functional and computational notions become relevant to our project. See chapters 5−7 for discussion of these notions.

attitudes) over the semantic properties of linguistic symbols (or utterances). More generally, the thesis assigns priority to the semantic properties of thoughts over the semantic properties of any other thing having semantic properties.[28] So if pictures are taken to have semantic properties, then their semantic properties too must derive from the semantic properties of propositional attitudes of the people who produced them. This thesis, which was put forward by Grice (1957; 1968; 1969), as it applies to the semantic properties of linguistic symbols, is endorsed by all philosophers of mind who subscribe to intentional realism but who disagree about much else: Searle, Fodor, Dretske, to mention only a few. It is often referred to as the view that mental states possess *original, underived* or, misleadingly, I believe, *intrinsic* intentionality.[29] Linguistic symbols, by contrast, are said to have derived intentionality. As Haugeland (1981a: 32) put it,

> [linguistic symbols] only have meaning because we give it to them; their intentionality, like that of smoke signals and writing, is essentially borrowed, hence *derivative*. To put it bluntly: computers themselves don't mean anything by their tokens (any more than books do) – they only mean what we say they do. Genuine understanding, on the other hand, is intentional "in its own right" and not derivately from something else.

The contrast between original and derived intentionality is a thesis rejected by most philosophers who dislike intentional realism such as Quine, Davidson, the Churchlands, Stich, Dennett, and Putnam possibly because they have no sympathy for the reductionist idea that semanticity must have an underived source.

I now want to take the present occasion to draw your attention to a revealing feature of our present situation in analytic philosophy. The thesis of the priority of language over thought was, I think, characteristic of the so-called *linguistic turn*. There were, I believe, two main

---

[28] I ascribe the thesis of the priority of the semantic properties of thoughts over the semantic properties of utterances to intentional realism because, on my view, intentional realism involves a reductionist element. I don't think that the considerations below prove the truth of this thesis; but I think their convergence makes it plausible and I assume it is true.

[29] As will appear later, it is, on my view, misleading to call, as Searle (1992) does, genuine or primitive intentionality intrinsic intentionality, for it suggests that the intentional realist priority of thought over language is inconsistent with an externalist (extrinsic) view of content (or semantic properties) – which it should not be.

forces driving the priority of language over thought. One was the behaviorist impulse. The other one was the view that anything worth calling a thought must be linguistically expressible. The second view, which has been called "the principle of effability" by Katz (1981: 226), says that "each proposition (thought) is expressible by some sentence in every natural language." I take it some such principle is involved in the following passage from Dummett (1978: 442):

> Thoughts differ from all else that is said to be among the contents of mind in being wholly communicable: it is of the essence of thought that I can convey to you the very thought I have, as opposed to being able to tell you merely something about what my thought is like. It is of the essence of thought, not merely to be communicable, but to be communicable, without residue, by means of language.

For such a principle as the principle of effability to be true, every thought – every propositional attitude worth calling a thought – must be expressible by some sentence of every natural language. If this principle were true, then verbal communication could proceed without any inferential process: each thought could be "coded" into the linguistic meaning of some sentence of every natural language.[30] As we shall see shortly, this view has been explicitly (and I believe successfully) challenged by contextualist philosophers and linguists.

Let us take the two grounds for the priority of language over thought one at a time. Unlike my beliefs, which are unobservable, my utterances are publically observable. When you listen to me, what you hear are my utterances, not my beliefs. It may even seem that, even in the first-person case, we sometimes find out what we think by attending to what we say. As the British writer E. M. Forster once put it, "How can I know what I think until I see what I say?"[31] Logical behaviorism was the philosophical attempt to analyze propositional attitudes into speech dispositions.[32] The logical behaviorist attempt to reduce propositional attitudes to speech dispositions was given up

---

[30] Arguably, decoding the linguistic meaning of an utterance is an inferential process whose input is the sound structure of the utterance. According to generative grammar, it is a computational process. So by "inferential process" in the text, I mean the process mapping the content communicated by an utterance from the linguistic meaning of the sentence uttered.

[31] Quoted in Dennett (1987: 113).

[32] For an early penetrating critique of philosophical logical behaviorism, see Putnam (1963).

when it was found out that the latter are neither necessary nor suffi-cient for the former. On the one hand, given that I believe that snow is white, I will be disposed to utter the English sentence "Snow is white" only if I know English, if I further intend my audience to know that I believe that snow is white, and so on. So being disposed to utter a sentence is a necessary condition for having a belief conditional on having many other complex unobservable mental states. On the other hand, I might be disposed to utter the English sentence "Snow is white" and either disbelieve that snow is white or be agnostic as to the color of snow, if, for example, I concurrently believe that, by uttering "Snow is white," I might save my life or the life of somebody I love. So the proposal seemed hopelessly circular.

Besides, whether or not non-human animals and human babies can think and have propositional attitudes, they certainly cannot speak a human (natural) language. But now, if having a thought or a proposi-tional attitude did reduce to (or consist in) having a disposition to utter a sentence of a natural language, then non-human animals and human babies would then on *a priori* grounds be precluded from entertaining thoughts and propositional attitudes. This might be undesirable especially if one assumes that the acquisition (or learning) of a natural language by a human baby does require him or her to think and have a few propositional attitudes to begin with.[33]

As I said earlier, intentional realists subscribe to the priority of the semantic properties of thoughts over the semantic properties of lin-guistic symbols. The priority of language over thought was characteristic of the linguistic turn. Its most eloquent contemporary representative is Dummett (1973: 362) according to whom it would be wrong to assume that assertion is "the expression of an interior act of judgment; judgment, rather, is the interiorization of the exter-nal act of assertion." The converse priority is characteristic of what I

---

[33] I take the work of generative grammarians to be relevant to what I call the cognitive turn since, on their approach, linguistics is part of psychology: the various syntactic and semantic abilities of a mature speaker of a natural language depend on his or her tacit knowledge of the grammar of the language, which in turn depends on his or her tacit knowledge of universal grammar. Furthermore, the task of linguistics is to contribute to solve the inductive problem of language acquisition: How, on the basis of primary linguistic data, does a human child manage to construct the grammar of the language spoken by members of his or her linguistic community? See Chomsky (1975; 1980a, b). For a different Platonistic view of linguistics, see Katz (1981).

would like to call the *cognitive turn*. The most convincing kinds of consideration in favor of the priority of thought over language derive, I think, from Grice's twofold program. The first step of Grice's program consists in trying to derive the semantic properties of linguistic symbols from the semantic properties of the propositional attitudes of individuals who use them. The second step of Grice's program consists in his general views about human communication.

The first step of Grice's (1957) program is what Schiffer (1987) has called "Intention-Based Semantics" (or IBS for short). The first step of the Gricean program is to reduce the semantic to the psychological. IBS purports first to offer a definition of speaker-meaning in terms of psychological (and behavioral) concepts or in terms of a speaker's propositional attitudes (intentions, beliefs and desires). More specifically, the first goal of IBS is to define speaker-meaning in terms of a speaker's intentions to trigger or produce propositional attitudes and/or action in a hearer. The idea, then, is to define the notion of speaker-meaning without appeal to the semantic properties or meanings of any linguistic expression used to express the speaker's propositional attitude. It purports secondly to define the semantic property or meaning of a linguistic expression as "certain kinds of correlations between marks and sounds and types of acts of speaker-meaning" in Schiffer's (1987: 242) own terms.

The central feature of Grice's view of human communication is that knowledge of the grammatical rules of a natural language is only one ingredient in human communication: it is neither a necessary nor a sufficient condition. It is not necessary because not all human communication is verbal communication. Whether in verbal or nonverbal communication, Grice (1957) argued, the task of the audience is to determine the communicator's intentions. So for non-verbal communication to succeed, the audience must ascribe a mental state to the communicator on the basis of non-linguistic cues. Imagine, for example, a couple at a party – or at some other social gathering. The woman may, for example, communicate to the man her desire to leave the party by pointing to her watch, or by ostensively moving her eyes in the direction of the exit, or by making gestures exhibiting her desire to go to sleep. From the fact that knowledge of the grammar of a natural language is not necessary for communication, it does not follow immediately that the principle of effability is false. For it is open to an advocate of this principle to argue that the relevant notion of thought must be tied to what is verbally communicated.

However, as several linguists and philosophers of a contextualist persuasion have argued, knowledge of the grammatical rules of a language is not even a sufficient condition of successful communication, for two complementary reasons.[34] And if this is correct, then, I think, one serious ground for the defense of the priority of language over thought based on the effability principle disappears. To argue this, I will assume that, in verbal communication, there is an intuitive distinction to be drawn between what is explicitly expressed (or communicated) and what is implicitly communicated by an utterance. This is the distinction between what a speaker *says* and what the utterance means (the overall content which is communicated by an utterance and which includes both what the speaker said plus the *implicatures* of her utterance). To illustrate the distinction between the content explicitly expressed and the implicatures of an utterance, I will refer to a joke told by Dennett (1987: 76): the Newfie joke. Newfies are Newfoundlanders and they are often the target of ethnic jokes made in Canada.

> A man went to visit his friend the Newfie and found him with both ears bandaged. "What happened?" asked the man, and the Newfie replied, "I was ironing my shirt when the telephone rang." – "That explains one ear, but what about the other?" – "Well, I had to call a doctor!"

As this joke makes plain, understanding it requires recovering a lot of information which is *not* explicitly expressed (or grammatically encoded) by the words uttered. For instance, the Newfie does not say that he applied the iron upon either of his ears. Nor does he say that the iron was hot and that he burnt both ears, and so on and so forth. So much of the understanding relies on inference based on shared knowledge between speaker and hearer.

As made clear by work done in pragmatics, following Grice, such as Carston (1988), Recanati (1989; 1993), Sperber & Wilson (1986), we can at least distinguish two kinds of information implicitly communicated by an utterance. And in the framework I am about to sketch, all of the implicit information which I just said was required to

---

[34] Among the contextualist authors involved, I include Fauconnier (1985), Perry (1986), Sperber & Wilson (1986), Travis (1985; 1989).

understand the Newfie joke belongs to the second level of meaning. So, given the existence of a level of linguistic meaning, there are three levels of meaning involved in verbal communication two of which depend on contextual information.

First of all, the information explicitly expressed by an utterance is generally richer than the linguistic meaning (or the semantic structure) of the sentence uttered. In other words, what is said – the proposition explicitly expressed – by an utterance is under-determined in many respects by the linguistic meaning (or semantic structure) of the sentence uttered.[35] For an example, consider my utterance of (2):[36]

(2)   John gave Mary his key and she opened the door.

I assume that the linguistic meaning (or semantic structure) of the sentence-type (2) depends on the meanings of its parts and on syntactic rules – something delivered by the grammar of English. Presumably, part of what you take me to be saying by an utterance of (2) involves the following three features: (i) the first conjunct describes an event which happened before the event described in the second conjunct. (ii) The personal pronoun "she" is coreferential with "Mary." (iii) The event described by the second conjunct consists of the opening by Mary of a salient door with the key referred to in the first conjunct as the key John gave Mary. Notice in particular that the sentence-type (2) does not contain the prepositional phrase "with the key John gave her." None of these three features is part of the linguistic meaning (or the semantic structure) of sentence (2). None of these three features can be determined by the grammar of English alone. However, these three features are presumably part of the complete thought (or belief) which I expressed by my utterance of (2) and which you are likely to ascribe to me on the basis of my utterance of (2).[37]

---

[35] Fauconnier (1985), Recanati (1989), Sperber & Wilson (1986), Travis (1985) argue convincingly that the under-determination of the proposition explicitly expressed by an utterance goes far beyond the mere fixing of the reference of indexical expressions and involves resolving a great variety of ambiguities, among them the conditions of satisfaction of vague predicates. The contextualist view that the proposition explicitly expressed by an utterance is much under-determined by the linguistic meaning of the sentence uttered was not held by Grice himself.

[36] This example is from Carston (1988).

[37] It is a topic of controversy whether resolving all the indeterminacies involved in the linguistic meaning (or semantic structure) of an utterance is required for the utterance

Secondly, by uttering a sentence, not only do I express explicitly a propositional content – something I say – but I may also convey implicitly or indirectly some further propositions (possibly under a different attitude than belief). Suppose I utter (3):

(3)   It's hot in here.

I may express my belief that the temperature is too high relative to some scale and to some relevant purpose.[38] But you may also take me to be conveying my wish or desire that someone in the audience would open the window (notwithstanding my possible improper use of the definite description "the window" in a room which may contain more than one window, not to speak of other windows in other rooms in other buildings in the universe). But in uttering (3), I certainly did not say explicitly that I wished someone would open the window. In my utterance, I did not mention any window. Nor did I refer to the act of opening one. So for you to ascribe to me the desire that someone open the window on the basis of my utterance of (3), you must have reached this conclusion by some spontaneous process of inference.[39]

Both the enrichment of the linguistic meaning of the sentence-type uttered into the proposition explicitly expressed and the inferential process which delivers the content implicitly (or indirectly) communicated by an utterance strongly suggest that any model of verbal understanding should ascribe priority to thought over language. But now, following the lead of some recent work of Sperber (1993), I will go one step further and consider the complexity of the process involved in the understanding of such a simple utterance as (3). Presumably, we may agree that one of the premisses on which

to express a complete proposition (something truth-evaluable) or not. Consider just two examples from Sperber & Wilson (1986: 189): "I have had breakfast" and "I have been to Tibet." In the first case, is the speaker saying that he has had breakfast at least once in his life? Arguably, this much might be part of the linguistic meaning of the utterance. And it is truth-evaluable. See Recanati (1989; 1993) for discussion.

[38] Notice that the scale and the purpose relative to which the temperature is high must be part of what is explicitly expressed by my utterance of (3) and it cannot be part of the linguistic meaning of the sentence-type (3).

[39] Following work in pragmatics, I assume here that the intuitive distinction between what is said by an utterance and what the utterance conversationally implicates can be drawn by using such notions as Grice's cancellability of conversational implicatures.

anyone in the audience bases his or her spontaneous reasoning is something like the following:

Premiss P:
Pierre Jacob said "It's hot in here."

When we look at this premiss, we can see that it contains a quotation of my utterance of (3). In that sense, the first premiss is itself a (mental) representation of a linguistic representation. Now what conclusion does the audience reach at the end of the process? The content of the conclusion involves my desire that someone open the window. But the conclusion involves more: it must involve a representation of my intention that the audience believe that I wish someone would open the window. Suppose we agree that the audience concludes that I intend him or her to believe that I wish someone would open the window. In the representation of the content of the audience's conclusion, the first person pronoun refers to someone in the audience:

Conclusion:
Pierre Jacob intends [me to believe [that he wishes [that someone would open the window]]]

Now, I want to draw your attention to the number of levels or the complexity of embeddings of representations involved in this conclusion. You, in the audience, must be able to represent my own – speaker's – intention which itself involves three levels.

Let us take stock. I am arguing that human minds are meta-representational organs. Beliefs are mental states. If A has a belief about, for example, the fact that object a has property F, then B's belief-report about the content of A's belief is an utterance whereby B tries to convey what A believes for the benefit of yet a third person, C. A might express his belief by uttering a sentence of his language whose truth-condition is that a is F. B's belief-report contains a sentence of her language whose truth-condition too is that a is F. But now, by uttering her belief-report about the content of A's belief, B has expressed her own higher-order belief about the content of A's belief. If one assumes with Representationalism, as I do, that A's belief that a is F is a representation of the fact that a is F, then one may suppose that B's belief about A's belief (about the fact that a is F) is a higher-order representation of A's representation of the fact that a is F. In general, one may call "meta-representation" a (higher-order) representation of a representation (of a state of affairs).

If we take premiss P of the above reasoning to be a (first-order) meta-representation, on the basis of the fact that it is a representation of (a linguistic) representation, then the conclusion is a higher-order meta-representation. Human beings excel at communication (verbal and non-verbal). If the foregoing reflections are on the right track, then the ability to understand verbal behavior presupposes an ability to attribute rather complex states of mind to other people. In that sense, our human minds are not only representational systems; they are meta-representational systems. Now, if one assumes, as I do, this meta-representational picture of verbal understanding, then one must, I think, grant the priority of the semantic properties of propositional attitudes over the semantic properties of linguistic symbols. The meta-representational picture of verbal understanding is, therefore, an argument for the intentional realist thesis that the semantic properties of utterances derive from the semantic properties of propositional attitudes. I concede that the above considerations about human communication do not establish the thesis that the meanings of linguistic expressions derive from the semantic properties of the propositional attitudes of speakers who use them. I do think, however, that the neo-Gricean (meta-representational) view of human communication concurs with Grice's reductionist program to vindicate the intentional realist thesis of the priority of the semantic properties of an individual's propositional attitudes over the semantic properties of linguistic symbols.

Whether or not one agrees with Davidson (1975: 170; 1982: 478) that a creature cannot have a belief unless it has the concept of belief, the view that human minds are meta-representational devices can, I think, accommodate one aspect of Davidson's (1975: 157; 1982: 477) claim that "a creature cannot have thoughts unless it is an interpreter of the speech of another." Many distinctly human thoughts are thoughts about thoughts, beliefs about beliefs, beliefs about desires, desires about beliefs, desires about desires. One could not have such higher-order thoughts about thoughts unless he or she had meta-representational abilities.

Furthermore, on the assumption that the mind is a meta-representational device, one can, I think, reconcile what I earlier called the second ingredient of the view Dennett calls the intentional stance and intentional realism. Dennett (1981a) has contrasted two perspectives one might take on propositional attitudes: *realism* and *interpretationism*. In Dennett's (*ibid*.: 14–15) words:

> [The former] likens the question of whether a person has a particular belief with the question of whether a person is infected with a particular virus – a perfectly objective internal matter of fact . . . [The latter] likens the question of whether a person has a particular belief to the question of whether a person is immoral, or has style, or talent, or would make a good wife.

As I said above, the intentional stance stands in sharp contrast with intentional realism by stating the priority of the stance towards a physical system over the system's possession of states with semantic properties. What Dennett here calls interpretationism could also, as I pointed out above, be called "patternalism" by reference to his famous (1991a) view that, only from a certain stance or point of view – the intentional stance – can *patterns* of propositional attitudes and *patterns* relating propositional attitudes and intentional behavior be discerned. And this latter component of his intentional stance doctrine is an insight which fits well with the realist view of the mind as a meta-representational organ. The insight is that only a creature with the meta-representational ability to form beliefs about beliefs could solve the delicate task of interpreting the semantic properties of the propositional attitudes of another creature. This epistemological insight, I think, does not force anyone, however, to embrace the puzzling ontological view that semantic properties are all a matter of stance.

1.5 TOKEN PHYSICALISM AND THE WEAK CAUSAL THESIS

Remember: one task of the intentional realist is to show that minds make a causal difference. The second thesis I wish to ascribe to intentional realism is the thesis that propositional attitudes are *causes*. Now, I want to distinguish a weak and a strong reading of the second intentional realist thesis – the causal thesis. On the weak reading, the thesis merely asserts that propositional attitudes can be causes. On the stronger reading, the thesis asserts that semantic properties of propositional attitudes are causally efficacious properties.

I start with the weaker thesis. Propositional attitudes can cause other propositional attitudes. And they can be causes of intentional behavior. So, for example, I intend to drink a glass of orange juice and I believe that there is some orange juice in the ice-box. This is why I perform this complicated sequence of physical motions: I move my limbs so as to cross the living room until I reach the kitchen. I pull the door of the ice-box wide open with my right hand. My desire for a glass of orange juice together with my belief that there is orange juice in the ice-box drive me out of my armchair and move me across the room: propositional attitudes are causes of intentional behavior. Suppose I discover, to my surprise, that there is no orange juice in the ice-box. Instead, there is grapefruit juice. Then, not only do I drop my belief that there is orange juice in the ice-box and acquire the belief that there is grapefruit juice instead. I also turn my intention to drink a glass of orange juice into an intention to drink a glass of grapefruit juice. My new belief that there is just grapefruit juice in the ice-box has caused me to delete (or to get rid of) my older belief that there is orange juice there. My new belief that there is grapefruit juice in the ice-box has also made me convert my previous intention to drink a glass of orange juice into a new intention to drink a glass of grapefruit juice. My new belief causes me to acquire new mental states.

Now, I think that the ontological doctrine known as *token physicalism* provides a satisfactory account of the weaker reading of the causal thesis. I earlier claimed that what is characteristic of a monist physicalist ontology is the rejection of the view that only non-physical things (or states of non-physical things) can have semantic properties. Interestingly, token physicalism is a view according to which physical things having physical properties can have – or at least are not precluded from having – semantic properties.

As I noticed, propositional attitudes are not the only kind of physical objects with semantic properties: words and other linguistic symbols too have semantic properties. Now, following Peirce's famous distinction, we may distinguish between *types* and *tokens* of linguistic symbols. By assumption, different tokens of the English word "dog" are said to belong to the same abstract word-type. By virtue of being a token of this type, every token of the English word "dog" refers to the class of dogs or stands for the property doghood. Every token of "dog" has the semantic property that it has by virtue of falling under its type. Every token of "dog" differs from any other token of the same type by some of its non-semantic properties: for example, its spatio-temporal properties. If not types – which are abstract things or universals – tokens of words and linguistic symbols have causal properties. Some tokens of the word "dog" are written symbols (or inscriptions). Others are spoken symbols (or utterances). Inscriptions of the word "dog" have, for example, optical properties which can be detected by a camera (as well as by a human eye). Utterances of the word "dog" have acoustic properties which can be detected by a tape-recorder (as well as by a human ear). Distinct inscriptions of the same word-type may have distinct optical properties. Distinct utterances of the same word-type may have distinct acoustic properties.

Arguably, not every utterance (or inscription) of a linguistic symbol should be identified with a token of the symbol in question. The reason for this is that two distinct utterances (or inscriptions) may consist in two distinct uses at different times of one and the same token. As contemporary phone-recording systems well illustrate, one and the same token of the linguistic type of words "I am not home right now. But if you leave your name and number, I will call you as soon as I get back" can be used on many different occasions in different (aborted) phone conversations. Utterances (or inscriptions) are, therefore, more concrete than tokens because they are more sensitive to time differences. Having registered the distinction between linguistic tokens and utterances (or inscriptions) for the sake of clarity, I propose to largely ignore it because, on my view, the type/token distinction is mostly relevant for problems of mental causation; and linguistic tokens, though less concrete than utterances (or inscriptions), have all the physical properties required for causal interactions.

All the distinct tokens of the word "dog" having different physical properties have, therefore, one and the same semantic property: they all stand for, denote, or refer to, the class of dogs. Or perhaps I should say that they all express (or denote) the property of being a dog. A rather natural (physicalistic) view of how different tokens of the word "dog" can all share the same semantic property is to assume that one and the same semantic property – the property of denoting the class of dogs (or the property of being a dog) – is multiply realized by each token's possession of its own peculiar physical properties. This, then, is a case of multiple realization of a higher-order property – the semantic property of all tokens of the word "dog" – by distinct more basic physical properties of distinct tokens of the word "dog." Now, symbol tokens typically enter causal interactions in the processes whereby they are detected (or perceived) by physical devices such as a camera, a tape-recorder, a human eye or ear. *Prima facie*, such physical devices pick up physical properties, not semantic properties, of symbol tokens. Therefore, it seems natural to assume that linguistic symbols enter causal interactions by virtue of their physical properties, not their semantic properties.

Particular mental states have characteristic mental properties: for example, belief states have contents or semantic properties. Type physicalism is the view that what is common to all instantiations of a kind of belief is a physical property. Many different individuals may at one time or another (or the same individual at different times) have the same belief, for example, the belief that Sienna is north of Rome. According to type physicalism, when different individuals are said to believe that Sienna is north of Rome, they are all in a brain state with one and the same physical property. What all instances of the belief that Sienna is north of Rome have in common is the physical property of the brain state all individuals are in when they have this belief.

Token physicalism assumes that the type/token distinction can be extended from linguistic symbols to mental states. So different belief tokens can fall under one and the same belief type. For example, if two individuals believe that Sienna is north of Rome, then each individual's belief is a unique belief token. Different tokens of the belief that Sienna is north of Rome can therefore fall under the same type of belief.[40] On the standard version of token physicalism, the mental relates to the physical as the semantic property of a linguistic symbol relates to its physical properties. An individual's belief token is said to be identical to one of the individual's brain-state tokens. This is the content of the token physicalist identity thesis. For an individual to harbor a particular token of the belief that Sienna is north of Rome is for him or her to be in a particular brain-state token. By virtue of the identity between mental state tokens and brain-state tokens, mental

---

[40] Arguably, the above distinction between linguistic tokens and utterances (or inscriptions) of a token could be mirrored at the level of thoughts (or propositional attitudes). We might say perhaps that an individual's belief token which was, for example, perceptually formed has then been stored in the individual's memory. The same belief token might then have been activated twice in two distinct thought (or belief) episodes: once in the perceptual encounter (which triggered its tokening); another time in an inferential process when the belief token was retrieved from memory and used as a premiss in an inference.

state tokens can be ascribed physical properties since it is uncontroversial that brain-state tokens have physical properties. Just as linguistic symbols are supposed to enter causal interactions by virtue of their physical properties, similarly mental state tokens enter causal relations by virtue of their physical properties.

Unlike type physicalism then, token physicalism does not assume that the semantic (or mental) property of an individual's belief token is identical (or reducible) to some physical property, let alone to some physical property of the individual's brain. None the less, it assumes that the semantic property of a belief token *supervenes* upon some physical property or other. A set of semantic properties Ψ is said to supervene on a set of underlying or subvenient properties Φ if no semantic Ψ-property would be instantiated unless a subvenient (physical) Φ-property were coinstantiated; and whenever one and the same subvenient (physical) Φ-property is instantiated, one and the same supervenient semantic Ψ-property is coinstantiated too.[41] So no instantiation of a supervenient semantic property Ψ will be distinguishable from the instantiation of a different supervenient semantic property Ψ' unless the subvenient property in virtue of which Ψ is instantiated differs from the subvenient property in virtue of which Ψ' is instantiated. It is not required, however, that the instantiation of one and the same subvenient Φ-property underlie each and every instantiation of a single supervenient Ψ-property. As noted by Kim (1994b: 582), claims of supervenience consist of a claim of covariance together with a claim of dependency. Token physicalism only requires that the instantiation of some physical property or other underlie every instantiation of any semantic property. So if the instantiation of some semantic property consists in the tokening of an individual's propositional attitude in the individual's brain, then token physicalism requires that the subvenient property be some physical property, not that the underlying property be a physical property of the individual's brain. Perhaps the subvenient property will be a composite property involving some physical prop-

---

[41] See Kim (1982; 1984; 1994b). The notion of supervenience seems to have been first introduced in ethics by Hare (1952) whose view was that ethical predicates (or properties) supervene on non-ethical predicates (or properties). He meant that no two individuals could be alike in all their descriptive (natural) or non-ethical properties and unlike in some ethical respect. Davidson (1970) introduced the idea of supervenience in the philosophy of mind.

erty of the individual's brain together with some physical property in the individual's environment.

Token physicalism is widely accepted today among monist physicalists. Davidson's anomalous monism and psychofunctionalism are versions of token physicalism. One of the basic premisses used by Davidson to derive anomalous monism is the thesis that propositional attitudes can be causes of physical events (as when I move my left arm because I intended to) and effects of physical events (as when I form a belief as a result of my perception of some physical event). According to psychofunctionalism, propositional attitude tokens are brain-state tokens characterized by their causal roles: they are causally related to inputs, other mental state tokens and behavioral outputs. The basic idea underlying psychofunctionalism (first expressed, I believe, by Putnam) is the idea that mental (or semantic) properties of tokens of an individual's propositional attitudes are higher-order properties of first-order physical properties of an individual's brain.[42] So for example, the property of being analgesic is a functional property of various substances having different chemical properties. Analgesic substances typically suppress pain into persons who absorb them. Being analgesic is a property which consists in the possession of one or another chemical property within a disjunctive class of chemical properties. On this view, for a brain-state token to have some semantic property is for it to possess some physical property or other. The point I wish to emphasize presently is that the reason for the wide acceptance of token physicalism lies in the fact that it secures a causal role for propositional attitudes. So it accommodates the weak reading of the causal thesis of intentional realism.

1.6 EXTERNALISM AND THE STRONG CAUSAL THESIS

I now turn to the strong reading of the causal thesis according to which, not only are propositional attitudes causes, but their semantic properties are causally efficacious. Reconsider again my trip from my armchair to the ice-box in the kitchen. It is made up of a sequence of complicated physical motions: my legs took me across space; then, by moving appropriately the fingers of my right hand, wrist, forearm and

---

[42] For much more detailed discussion of psychofunctionalism and the notion of a functional property, see chapters 5–7 of the present work.

arm, I pulled the ice-box open. Many different muscles and muscle fibers must have contracted and then relaxed upon receiving chemical and electrical signals from my brain and central nervous system and propagated along nerve fibers. The reason all of this occurred within me is that I wanted a glass of orange juice and I thought there was orange juice in the ice-box.

I assume that my belief and my desire are causes of my behavior: they managed somehow to drag me out of my armchair. This is the content of the weak causal thesis.[43] But, rightly or wrongly, common sense also takes it that the semantic properties of my belief and desire were causally efficacious in producing my behavior. Had I not had a desire and a belief, each with a specific content – had I not wanted a glass of orange juice and had I not believed that there was some in the ice-box – then I would not have embarked on this trip to the kitchen. I have many other beliefs, not to speak of desires. I, for example, believe that whales are mammals and that my name is "Pierre Jacob." However, unlike my belief that there is orange juice in the ice-box, neither my belief that whales are mammals nor my belief that my name is "Pierre Jacob" are relevantly involved in the causal explanation of what I did when I got up, went up to the kitchen and pulled the ice-box open. So what I believe – the content (or semantic property) of my belief – matters to what I do when I do what I do for reasons or intentionally. This is what I mean by the strong causal thesis – the thesis that the semantic properties of propositional attitudes are causally efficacious in the production of intentional behavior. Nor, I think, can we simply deny that the explanation in question is a causal explanation. Not, at least, if we subscribe to intentional realism. In any case, I will assume that Davidson (1963) has effectively dealt with the view that reasons can't be causes and that reason explanations are not causal explanations.[44] How could the semantic property of my belief be involved in the process of muscle contraction and relaxation? How could the

---

[43] In this chapter, I assume the truth of the weak causal thesis. Later, in chapter 8, when I discuss the "componential" view of behavior, I will reexamine the weak causal thesis and argue that what an individual's propositional attitudes cause is not the individual's behavior proper but his or her physical motions.

[44] In chapters 7 and 8, I will make explicit several distinctions: between causal relations and causal processes; between causal and non-causal explanations; between causal relations and causal explanations.

content of my belief be efficacious in the propagation of electrical and chemical signals from my brain to my muscles?

Two quite natural assumptions make the strong causal thesis puzzling. One assumption is that causal processes are *local* processes. Following current philosophical jargon, I will call the other assumption *externalism*.

Externalism, to which I subscribe, is the view that the semantic property of an individual's propositional attitude is a relational (extrinsic) property of the individual's brain. It depends on relations between the individual's brain and objects, properties and relations in his or her environment. As Putnam (1974) has put it, two microphysical twins whose brains would be physically indistinguishable might none the less have propositional attitudes with different contents – different semantic properties. On the one hand, I find it conceptually useful to distinguish what I call externalism from anti-individualism.[45] According to the former, the semantic property of an individual's belief may depend upon the individual's *non-social*, physical, chemical or biological environment. According to the latter, famously defended by Burge (1979; 1982; 1989),[46] the semantic property of an individual's belief may depend upon what other members of his or her linguistic or social community think. On the other hand, I agree with Dretske (1993b) that there is a distinction to be drawn between what I shall pompously call a "transcendental" version and a non-transcendental version of either doctrine. According to transcendental anti-individualism, no state of an individual would qualify as a (genuine) thought – an individual could not be credited with thoughts – unless the individual belonged to a linguistic or social community. According to transcendental anti-individualism, then, Robinson Crusoe could not form genuine thoughts. According to mere (non-transcendental) anti-individualism, the contents (or semantic properties) of some, many, most or all of an individual's propositional attitudes depend on his or her social or linguistic community.

Presumably, Burge (1979; 1982; 1989) should be interpreted as arguing for a non-transcendental version, not for what I call a

---

[45] In his Jean Nicod lectures, delivered in Paris in the spring 1995, Davidson distinguished what he calls perceptual externalism from what he calls social externalism.

[46] Burge also argues for externalism.

transcendental version of, anti-individualism. So should Putnam's (1974) notion of the "linguistic division of labor." Notice that, if thought is essentially informational (as envisaged in chapter 2), then "transcendental" externalism might be vindicated by informational semantics. Notice also that vindicating "transcendental" anti-individualism would require more than pointing out that most or all of an individual's actual propositional attitudes depend upon the individual's social environment. It would require showing that no state of an individual could constitute thinking unless the individual belonged to a social or (linguistic) community. One of the reasons why Davidson's (1984) views on radical interpretation are so fascinating is that they might constitute a road towards transcendental anti-individualism. They might suggest reasons why only if they could be recognized as such by an interpreter could mental states of an individual constitute genuine thoughts. For an individual A to have genuine thoughts about cows, Davidson (1991) argues, not only must she stand in (perceptual) relation to genuine cows (not fake cows); but she must also stand in relation to another creature B himself standing in relation to the very same genuine cows: A must be able to detect and interpret B's cow-reactions and vice-versa B must be able to interpret A's cow-reactions. Davidson (1991) calls "triangulation" the set of relations holding between two thinking creatures and the common object of their genuine thoughts. What is distinctive of Davidson's notion of triangulation is the requirement that for A to form genuine cow thoughts, she must have the ability to recognize B's cow reactions.[47]

If externalism is right, then the semantic properties of beliefs do not supervene on the physical properties of an individual's brain. Think of a photograph of Monica Vitti. Suppose Monica Vitti had an identical twin sister. Consider two photographs: one of which is a picture of Monica Vitti and the other of which is a picture of her identical twin. The two pieces of paper might be physically and chemically indistinguishable. However similar the two pictures might be, still only one piece of paper would be a picture *of* Monica Vitti: only the one which

[47] To assume that triangulation in Davidson's sense is a necessary condition for having genuine thoughts is to be both a transcendental externalist and a transcendental anti-individualist. In his Jean Nicod lectures, delivered in Paris, in the spring 1995, in particular in his second and third lectures, Davidson further elaborates on the notion of triangulation.

was the end-product of a process at the beginning of which Monica Vitti sat in person. This suggests that the property of the photograph of being a picture of Monica Vitti does not supervene on the physical properties of the piece of paper. Alternatively, consider two canvases. They might be physically and chemically indistinguishable. Suppose, however, that only one of them is a genuine Picasso painting whereas the other is a copy. This shows that the property of the canvas of being a genuine Picasso painting does not supervene on the physical properties of the canvas. Being a genuine Picasso painting is a historical property of the canvas involving a relation to Picasso's own hand.

Now, the assumption that causal processes are local processes strongly suggests that only local properties of a cause can be causally efficacious in the process whereby the cause produces its effect. As McGinn (1989: 133) has expressed the locality assumption:

> what happens at the causal nexus is local, proximate and intrinsic: the features of the cause that lead to the effect must be right where the causal interaction takes place . . . The causal powers of a state or property must be intrinsically grounded; they cannot depend upon relations to what lies quite elsewhere.

I will conclude this chapter by making explicit the conflict between three ideas: externalism, the strong causal thesis, and the locality assumption. If externalism is correct, then the semantic properties of an individual's beliefs are not local properties of the individual's brain. My belief, for example, that there is orange juice in the ice-box derives from complex relations between my brain and items in my environment. The semantic property of my belief is a highly relational (extrinsic) property of my brain. It does not supervene on the physical, chemical, biological properties of my brain. The puzzle, then, raised by the strong causal thesis is to understand how such an extrinsic, non-local property of my brain can be involved in such local processes as the propagation of electrical and chemical signals through nerve fibers whereby muscle contraction and relaxation are controlled. To make the puzzle vivid, consider among many an example of Dretske's (1988: 79):

> a soprano's upper register supplications may shatter glass, but their meaning is irrelevant to their having this effect. Their effect would be the same if they meant nothing at all or something entirely different.

The soprano's sound may well have a (derived) meaning. The sound may well be one causal factor in the process of glass-breaking. But the property of the sound involved in the breaking of the glass will clearly be its acoustic property, not its semantic property. It is incumbent upon an intentional realist who subscribes to the strong causal thesis to show that the semantic property (the content) of my belief that there is orange juice in the ice-box is not as epiphenomenal in pulling me out of my armchair as the semantic property of the sound is in the shattering of the glass. Neither the strong causal thesis nor the tension between it, externalism and the locality assumption will be directly addressed however until chapters 7 and 8 of this book in which I hope to show how the semantic properties of an individual's propositional attitudes can be causally efficacious in explaining his or her intentional behavior.

2

Introduction to informational semantics

2.1 INFORMATIONAL SEMANTICS: A BOTTOM-UP STRATEGY

One of the two tasks facing intentional realism, I claimed in the first chapter, is to show how the semantic properties of an individual's propositional attitudes can arise, if not out of completely non-semantic, non-intentional properties and relations, at least out of less than fully semantic, less than fully intentional properties and relations. The task amounts to analyzing the notion of aboutness or representation. What underlying non-semantic properties and relations may confer upon a system its ability to represent (or be about) other things and states of affairs? This is what the naturalization of intentionality consists in.

There are three main approaches to this task, two of which rely on an informational approach, one of which is purely teleological. Though I do believe that an informational approach must be supplemented by teleological concepts in order to offer a satisfactory solution to some of the puzzles of intentionality, I do, however, think that information is a genuine ingredient of intentionality. Vindication of my claim that a mixed informational and teleological approach can solve (some of) the puzzles of intentionality will have to wait until the third and fourth chapters.

In this chapter, I will present the basic ideas of the informational approach. Informational semantics – as I will call the approach – has been developed by a number of philosophers – including Barwise & Perry (1983), Dretske (1981), Evans (1982), Fodor (1984; 1987b), Israel & Perry (1990), Stalnaker (1984), Stampe (1977). The guiding idea of informational semantics is that the semantic properties of an individual's propositional attitudes derive primarily from the informational relations between the individual's mind and his or her environment. Although informational semantics bears some affinity to causal theories of reference (such as Kripke's and Putnam's), as I will shortly explain, it does not restrict itself to actual causal relations. Accepting the standpoint of intentional realism, I will assume that the target of informational semantics, unlike that of the causal theories of reference (in the hands of Kripke and Putnam) is at heart the contents of thoughts – only derivatively the contents of linguistic symbols. This is important since the task is to try and capture the semantic properties of thoughts which do not presuppose the existence of language and linguistic capacities, let alone a linguistic community. One naturalistic feature common, I think, to all informational semanticists is that they proceed from the bottom-up. For this reason, I will call them *bottom-uppers*. They want to understand how the subtle features of minded creatures fit in, mesh with, and can be integrated with, our views of other physical and biological systems.

In terms of the distinction drawn in chapter 1 (section 6), informational semanticists may be called "transcendental" externalists:[1] in virtue of their informational approach, they may be committed to the view that an individual's thoughts presuppose objects, properties and relations from his or her environment. An individual's internal state would not count as a genuine thought unless the individual's mind stood in informational relations to objects, properties, and relations from his or her environment. An individual could not think at all unless he or she stood in various informational relations with objects, properties, and relations from his or her environment. Informational semanticists might in addition be anti-individualists and assume that the contents of many, most or all of an individual's thoughts depend on what other members of the individual's social (or linguistic) community think. But nothing in the informational approach per se will commit them to (what I earlier called) "transcendental" anti-individualism, i.e., to the view that an individual could not think – could not engage in thinking – unless he or she were a member of a social (or linguistic) community or that Robinson Crusoe could not form genuine thoughts.

---

[1] As I said in chapter 1, a mere "non-transcendental" externalist claims that the semantic properties of many if not all of an individual's propositional attitudes depend on relations between the individual and objects, properties, and relations in his or her environment. A "transcendental" externalist subscribes to the stronger view that an individual could not engage in thinking at all if he or she did not stand in relation to objects, properties, and relations in his or her environment.

There is, therefore, a significant difference of emphasis between the bottom-up approach of informational semantics to the semantic properties of an individual's propositional attitudes and Davidson's (1975: 157) interpretation strategy as embodied in his famous thesis that a creature would not have thoughts unless it could interpret another's speech. An informational semanticist would presumably object to such a strong "transcendental" anti-individualistic thesis. He might, however, agree with the weaker view that only creatures able to form higher-order thoughts about thoughts can engage in interpretation at all. He can, in other words, accept – indeed welcome – the view that the arrival of meta-representational abilities constitutes a genuine threshold in the phylogenetic evolutionary ladder of systems capable of entering states with semantic properties.

The relevant notion of information at stake in informational semantics is the notion involved in many areas of scientific investigation as when it is said that a footprint or a fingerprint carries information about the individual whose footprint or fingerprint it is. In this sense, it may also be said that a fossil carries information about a past organism. The number of rings in a tree trunk carries information about the age of the tree. The fact that a piece of paper stained with litmus turns red in contact with a particular liquid carries information about the fact that there is some acid in the liquid. In this sense too, molecular biologists talk of genetic information being carried by a piece of DNA, copied into RNA and serving as template for the synthesis of proteins in a cell. An X-ray carries information about, for example, a broken leg. The height of the column of mercury in the glass-tube of a thermometer carries information about temperature. A gas-gauge or a speedometer in an automobile carries information respectively about the amount of gas in the gas-tank and about the speed of the vehicle. A clock carries information about time. A compass-needle carries information about the direction of geomagnetic north. In all these cases, it is not unreasonable to assume that the informational relation holds between an indicator and what it indicates (or a source) independently of the presence of an agent with propositional attitudes – even in those artefactual cases in which an agent assembled the artefact in the first place. Once the informational relation is in place, it holds whether or not some information-processing device picks up the information.

It is important to emphasize – as, for example, Evans (1982: 123–4) and Peacocke (1983: 6–7) have done – the differences between the information-theoretic notion of information underlying the above scientific uses of the term "information" and the commonsense notion which is intrinsically linked to the contents of an individual's propositional attitudes. What I just called the commonsense notion of information is at the root of the Fregean view of propositional content.

To see the contrast at work in the philosophy of language, let us consider the utterance of a simple sentence such as (S) containing a singular term in subject position:

(S)   Hesperus shines.

In contemporary philosophy of language, there is a controversy over the following question: What is the proposition expressed by the utterance of (S)? According to Fregeans, the contribution of the name "Hesperus" to the proposition expressed by an utterance of (S) is the mode of presentation of the referent of the name, the sense (or *Sinn*) of the name. On the Fregean view, the proposition expressed by an utterance of (S), therefore, contains a mode of presentation of the planet, Hesperus. According to the anti-Fregean so-called "theory of direct reference," the proposition expressed by an utterance of (S) does not contain any mode of presentation of the referent of "Hesperus"; it merely contains the planet. Whereas the Fregean view identifies the proposition expressed by an utterance of (S) with the object of the thought or belief expressed by the utterance, the theory of direct reference identifies it with the state of affairs which is the truth-condition of the utterance. In support of their view, and following Frege's (1892) lead, Fregeans point out that a rational competent English speaker who holds (S) true may well hold (S') false in spite of the truth of the identity (I):

(S')   Phosphorus shines.
(I)   Hesperus = Phosphorus.

Fregeans conclude that an utterance of (S) and an utterance of (S') must have different cognitive significance or different informative value: they carry different informations. According to the theory of direct reference, substitution of "Phosphorus" to "Hesperus" in (S) does not alter the content or truth-condition of (S): given that "Hesperus" and "Phophorus" are coreferential, if an utterance of (S) is true, so is an utterance of (S'). Similarly, according to informational semantics, replacement of a singular term by a coreferential term does not alter the informational content of an utterance. The notion of information underlying the Fregean view of propositional content is based on the cognitive notion of what an agent endowed with propositional attitudes can learn. A rational competent English speaker may assent to an utterance of (S) and dissent from an utterance of (S') if he or she does not know that (I) is true. He or she cannot doubt the truth of (I'):

(I')   Hesperus = Hesperus.

Nor can he or she normally find it informative. He or she, however, is likely to find the truth of (I) informative. The cognitive notion of information in which the Fregean view of propositional content is rooted cannot, therefore, be used without circularity in the current naturalistic project. Within the philosophy of language proper, the Fregean link between the notion of information and what an agent with propositional attitudes finds informative is not the only available view, since advocates of the anti-Fregean theory of direct reference are prone to emphasize the fact that two distinct utterances with the same truth-conditions – such as (S) and (S') – do convey the same information in a relevant sense of "information."[2] Unlike the Fregean cognitive notion, and like its anti-Fregean competitor, the information-theoretic notion used in science is expected to be independent of the presence of agents with propositional attitudes.

My presentation of informational semantics will rely on Dretske's (1981) classical work, one important feature of which is its roots in *reliability* theories of knowledge in epistemology. Reliabilism in epistemology (as developed by Armstrong, Dretske, Goldman and Nozick) takes the nomic dependency of a belief state about the environment upon the environmental condition the belief is about as a crucial ingredient of the justification of the belief, i.e., what makes the belief state a state of knowledge. Informational semantics uses many of the tools of epistemological reliabilism to capture, not the justification of a belief, but its content – its semantic property. Not all of an individual's beliefs are justified or qualify as states of knowledge.

---

[2] For such a non-Fregean notion of information within the philosophy of language, see, for example, Kaplan (1978), Richard (1990), Salmon (1986).

All of an individual's beliefs, however, have some content – some semantic property – or other. The task of informational semantics, therefore, is more basic than reliabilist epistemology since it aims at explaining naturalistically a property which all beliefs – justified or unjustified – have. Besides, it aims at explaining naturalistically a property which not only beliefs have but also all other propositional attitudes have. In this and part of the next chapter, I want to see how many features of the semantic properties of beliefs informational semantics can capture. Although the reliabilist ingredient of informational semantics is controversial (and has been disputed),[3] I will argue in chapter 4 that it is justified on evolutionary (adaptationist) grounds.

At the beginning of the first chapter, I mentioned the fact that propositional attitudes are not the only inhabitants (or citizens) of our human minds: conscious experiences, sensations or *qualia* too are mental states. They too have content – albeit non-conceptual content. The non-conceptual content of experience is a topic much discussed by contemporary philosophers. I think this topic can benefit from informational semantics. Given the existence of conscious experiences, I said that Representationalism – i.e., the claim that the mind is primarily a representational system – faces a challenge: it is incumbent upon Representationalism to demonstrate that it can throw light not just onto propositional attitudes but onto conscious experiences as well.

After presenting the basis of informational semantics and trying to alleviate the worry that it might surreptitiously reintroduce intentionality by the back door, I also want to show that one of the benefits of informational semantics is that it can help us meet the challenge faced by Representationalism. Actually, I think informational semantics has the resources to corroborate a stronger claim: the claim that only a system capable of having genuine beliefs can have experiences. As I see it, the thesis that information is a genuine ingredient of intentionality derives some support from the fact that informational semantics throws some light onto conscious experiences and hence vindicates the representationalist strategy. In particular, one of the two reasons why I will advocate in chapter 4 an informationally-based teleosemantic approach to intentionality, as opposed to a purely teleological approach, as advocated by, for example, Millikan (1984; 1993),

---

[3] In particular by Millikan (1989b; 1990b).

is that, on my view, informational semantics helps explain some features of conscious experiences. The other reason is that informational semantics provides a good account of the intensionality of belief contents (about which more in chapter 3).

2.2 INFORMATION AND NOMIC DEPENDENCY

In this section, I want to consider the conditions under which it is permissible to say that some physical object r (e.g., a fingerprint on a piece of paper) carries information about some other object s (e.g., the identity of the person who imprinted his or her fingerprint on the piece of paper). When does the fact that state r (r for receptor) of system S has property G carry information about or indicate the fact that some object s (s for source) has property F? Let r be some internal state of system S. State s's being F is some environmental condition (or state of the world).[4] Clearly, the information or indication relation is going to be a relation between states or facts.[5] The general idea is going to be that the indication relation between state r of receptor system S and what it indicates, i.e., the fact that object s is F (the source) is the converse of some sort of causal relation between the fact that object s is F and the fact that state r has property G. We could abbreviate the appropriate underlying relation by saying that c (the fact that s is F) causes e (the fact that r is G).

The seminal idea here is Paul Grice's (1957) contrast between *natural* meaning and *non-natural* meaning. Smoke (or the presence of smoke) naturally means (or indicates) the presence of fire. But of course the word "fire," not the word "smoke," non-naturally means (denotes or stands for) fire. The word "smoke" non-naturally means smoke or the presence of smoke, not fire. Whether Grice was right about assuming a sharp contrast between the meanings of words and the way effects naturally mean (or indicate) something about their causes I shall leave open for the moment. What is relevant now is that

---

[4] As a matter of terminology, I will always use "r" for receptor to refer to a particular state of a physical system receiving some information; "s" for source to refer to some physical entity in the receptor's environment; "G" to stand for some property of r and "F" to stand for some property of s so that in my informational framework there must exist a nomic dependency between instantiations of G and instantiations of F.

[5] This point is explicitly recognized by Israel & Perry (1990: 3) whose principle (A) is that "facts carry information."

Grice's notion of natural meaning (or indication) seems to be the converse of some sort of causal relation. If fire stands to smoke in some causal relation or if smoke is caused by fire, then the idea would be that smoke (being an effect of fire) carries information about (or stands in some indication relation to) its cause, i.e., fire.

The goal is to reduce semanticity to non-semantic notions. The strategy presently envisaged is that the informational (or indication) relation is an appropriate basis for the reduction. This implies that the relevant informational relation is itself an *objective* relation in the sense that it holds whether or not any cognitive intentional system processes the informational relation. Dretske says that information is an objective commodity. If it turns out that the informational relation is the converse of some causal relation, then of course the appropriate standpoint of an informational semanticist on the causal relation itself is that of metaphysical realism. If it turns out that the informational relation is the converse of some nomic relation between properties – one of which is instantiated by the indicator and the other of which is instantiated by what is indicated – then the appropriate standpoint of informational semantics is to assume that the nomic relation between properties holds objectively. The informational or indication relation, for example, may *underlie* some epistemic relation, i.e., an *evidential* relation. If smoke stands to fire in some indication relation, then on the basis of this relation, an agent with propositional attitudes might take the presence of smoke to be evidence for the presence of fire. The evidential relation – which is an epistemic or explanatory[6] relation – presumably holds between belief states: between an individual's perceptual belief that smoke is instantiated and his or her inferred belief that fire must be, therefore, instantiated. But on the naturalistic view assumed here, although the indication relation may underlie an epistemic (inferential or explanatory) relation between belief-states, it cannot be identified with it.

On the basis of the intuition underlying Grice's notion of natural meaning, let us try to capture the informational relation between effect *e* and cause *c* by means of (1):

(1)   *e* carries information about *c* iff *c* causes *e*.

---

[6] Rightly or wrongly, I assume here an epistemic non-ontic (non-ontological) view of explanation.

(1) says that the existence of a causal relation between c and e is a necessary and sufficient condition for e to carry information about c.

Whether or not the fact that c causes e is a necessary condition for e to carry information about c is controversial. One interesting example of Dretske's (1981: 38–39) suggesting that a causal relation between indicator and what is indicated may not be necessary is the following. Imagine two television receivers B and C both causally connected to a sending station, A. Supposing that B and C both causally depend on A, although there is no causal relation between B and C, then there might still exist an informational link between B and C: you might learn about events at C from knowledge about events at B. But there is no causal link between B and C. The fact that events at both B and C have a common causal ancestry in events happening at A may suffice to ensure an informational link between B and C.

The reason why the existence of an actual causal relation between a signal and what it indicates is not sufficient for information is that *possible* causal relations or *counterfactual* dependencies also contribute to determining informational relations.

It is conceptually helpful here to accept the standpoint of communication theory, i.e., the theory of the transmission of information. From this standpoint, when we examine the informational relation between a source s and a signal r, we start with what happened at the source. Suppose that the relevant fact at the source is that s was F. For this to be the case, other (alternative) possibilities at the source – such as the fact that s might have been H – must have been *eliminated*. In this sense, the obtaining of this very state of affairs at the source – the fact that s was F – generated information. Some of this information may not be transmitted from s to r. Given the total information generated at the source by s's being F, we may ask how much of it is still present in r's being G. In effect, this is to ask how much r's being G depends on s's being F. The information generated by the obtaining of s's being F at the source and not carried over by r's being G is the *equivocation* of r. When we consider in turn the total information carried by r, we may distinguish two parts: the part which is supplied by s via the causal link between r and s and the part which is not coming from s. The latter is called the *noise*. The main reason why the existence of an actual causal relation is not sufficient for information is that signal r may be *equivocal*. Although s did cause r, part of the information generated by s's being F may not be present at r. The equivocation of a signal arises from the fact that knowledge of the actual causal process connecting the source and the signal may reveal nothing of alternative possible causes of the signal.

The existence of an actual causal relation is, therefore, not sufficient for the informational relation because the existence of alternative possible causal processes leading to the tokening of the signal is relevant to the information carried by the signal. Let us try, then, to capture the contribution of possible causal processes to the information carried by a signal *r* by means of the notion of the nomic dependency of the latter on a source *s* as in (2). So conceived, nomic dependency involves a relation between state types, not tokens.

(2)   The fact that *r* is *G* (e.g., the fact that the height of the column of mercury of thermometer τ is such-and-such) indicates (or carries information about) the fact that *s* is *F* (e.g., the fact that the temperature of the liquid in which thermometer τ is immersed is so-and-so) if and only if the fact that *r* is *G* depends nomically on the fact that *s* is *F*.

The topic of nomic dependency (or law) is a difficult topic in the philosophy of science. I shall assume here that nomic dependencies can be *ceteris paribus*; and I shall assume some intuitive distinction between nomic dependencies and mere accidental generalizations based primarily on the fact that the former, unlike the latter, are *referentially opaque*, in the following sense.[7] Consider first the true merely accidental generalization (Γ):

(Γ)   All Fs are G.[8]

If (Γ) is true and if replacement of predicate "F" in (Γ) by coreferential (or coextensional) predicate "H" leaves the truth-value of (Γ) unaffected, then we may say that (Γ) is referentially transparent or that "F" in (Γ) occupies a referentially transparent position. Consider now claim (Λ):

(Λ)   It is a law that all Ps are Q.

---

[7] I'll come back to the notion of referential opacity or intensionality in chapter 3, section 2 in the context of belief contents.

[8] I shall assume that the logical form of such a generalization is a universally quantified conditional of the form "$(\forall x)(Fx \rightarrow Gx)$" where the bound variable ranges over (concrete) individuals. In the case of a law, it is a matter of some controversy to determine the range of the bound variable.

Suppose (Λ) is true. Then, even though predicate "R" may be true of, or apply to, (all and only) the objects to which predicate "P" applies or of which predicate "P" is true, replacement of "P" by "R" in (Λ) may nevertheless turn (Λ) from a truth into a falsehood. Replacement of "P" by coreferential predicate "R" in (Λ) does not preserve the law-likeness (or nomicity) of "All Ps are Q." The position occupied by "P" in (Λ) is, therefore, referentially opaque (or intensional). In other words, the expression "it is a law that . . ." in (Λ) is a referentially opaque (or intensional) context. I will also assume that laws, unlike accidental generalizations, support counterfactuals. This is a standard assumption in the philosophy of science.[9] It is, however, somewhat controversial, since it is true of strict laws, i.e., of laws such that if the antecedent is true, then the consequent must be true without exceptions. If a law is not strict, then given the truth of its antecedent, its consequent will be true only if further conditions obtain. If there are, as everybody acknowledges, non-strict laws, then they may not always support their relevant counterfactuals in the required way. What is controversial is whether there exist strict laws, i.e., laws such that the instantiation of the property mentioned in the antecedent guarantees that the property mentioned in the consequent will be instantiated no matter what.[10] I will, however, assume presently that claims of nomic dependency of the form "The fact that r is G depends nomically on the fact that s is F" entail counterfactuals such as "r would not be G unless s were F." If so, then acceptance of (2) entails acceptance of (3):

(3) If r would not be G unless s were F, then the fact that r is G indicates the fact that s is F.

As Dretske (1981: 245) has put it, there must be "a nomic (lawful) regularity . . . which *nomically precludes r's* occurrence when s is not F." We might capture Dretske's remark by means of (4):

(4) The fact that r is G indicates the fact that s is F if and only if it is nomically necessary that s is F, given that r is G.

---

[9] See Goodman (1955), Hempel (1965) and Davidson (1980) for classical endorsements of this assumption.

[10] Davidson is a well-known advocate of the view that there are strict laws of basic physics. Kistler (1995) contains an interesting criticism of this view. See chapters 5 and 7 for further discussion.

The fact that the height of the column of mercury in the thermometer coincides with numeral *30* indicates that the temperature of the coffee (in which the thermometer is immersed) is 30°C if and only if it is nomically necessary that the temperature of the coffee is 30°C given that the height of the column of mercury in the thermometer coincides with numeral *30*.[11] What underlies the informational relation is what Godfrey-Smith (1992) has called "head-world" reliability by contrast with world-head reliability and which could as well be called "indicator-world" reliability.[12] What is required by head-world (or indicator-world) reliability is that *s* be *F* (the temperature be 30°C) if *r* is *G* (the height of the column of mercury in the thermometer coincides with numeral *30*), not that every instantiation of *F* by *s* always yields a tokening of the indicator state *r* (with property *G*). Head-world reliability says: the internal state *r* of system *S* would not be tokened unless condition *s* in the world were *F*; the height of the column of mercury in the thermometer would not coincide with numeral *30* unless the temperature were 30°C. It does not stipulate that each and every time *s* is *F*, *r* is *G*; it does not stipulate that each and every time the temperature is 30°C, the height of the column of mercury in the thermometer coincides with numeral *30*. Another way to put the view is to say that *s* being *F* in the world (the temperature's being 30°C) is a necessary, though not a sufficient, condition for the tokening of internal state *r*'s being *G* (for the height of the column of mercury in the thermometer to coincide with numeral *30*). So there is room for cases of so-called "false negatives": cases in which *r*'s being *G* fails to be triggered in the presence of its normal cause (of which more in chapter 4).

Dretske (1981) himself has expressed his head-world reliability view of the informational relation as the requirement that the conditional probability P (*s* is *F/r* is *G*) = 1. This probabilistic formulation raises two kinds of problems which I will merely state but cannot examine here: one problem is the value 1 assigned to the conditional probability. The other problem is the appropriate interpretation of probability. The subjective interpretation is not suitable for the naturalistic reduction of intentionality since probability is then relative to

---

[11] Of course the nomic dependency involved here is *ceteris paribus*: if the thermometer is broken, then even though the height of the column of mercury in the thermometer coincides with numeral *30*, it may be the case that the temperature of the coffee is not 30°C.

[12] Since not all indicators need be states of some head.

an agent's beliefs. So the subjective interpretation of probability would not satisfy the naturalistic condition. The propensity interpretation does not seem right because the signal could hardly have a propensity to derive from a source. Finally, the problem with the frequency interpretation is that, on this interpretation, an event could fail to occur even though it has probability 1. I will merely assume that these problems can be bypassed on the nomic interpretation of the informational relation along the lines of (2)–(4). This is a point Fodor (1990b: 58) has much emphasized. In his terms, "the basic idea of informational semantics" is that

> the content of a symbol is determined solely by its nomic relations. To put it roughly but intuitively, what laws subsume a thing is a matter of its *subjunctive* career; of what it would do (or would have done) if the circumstances were (or had been) thus and so. By contrast, a thing's actual history depends not just on the laws it falls under, but also on the circumstances that it happens to encounter . . . only nomic connections and the subjunctives they license count for meaning.[13]

2.3 THE PROBLEM OF THE RELATIVITY OF INFORMATION

For stylistic reasons, I will now often talk of the informational relation between *r* and *s* (instead of talking of *r*'s being *G* and *s*'s being *F*), where *r* is, for example, the height of the column of mercury in the glass-tube of a thermometer and *s* is the external temperature. Up to this point, I have fictitiously assumed that what underlies the informational relation is a one-one nomic dependency of a signal *r*'s being *G* upon a source *s*'s being *F*. But this is a simplifying assumption. For two complementary reasons, this assumption must be revised. One reason is that what information *r* carries about *s* may differ according to what *other* information *K* is already available to the receiver. This is the

[13] On behalf of informational semantics, Fodor (1994: 90) writes: "What a thought represents is largely independent of its *actual* history if the informational version of externalism is true. Thoughts of cats are thoughts *of* cats not because cats *do* cause them but because cats *would* cause them under circumstances that may be largely or entirely counterfactual." And as Israel & Perry (1990: 3) put it: "What underlies the phenomenon of information is the fact that reality is lawlike; that what is going on in one part of reality is related to what is going on in some other part of reality, by laws, nomic regularities, or, as we shall say, constraints."

problem of the relativity of information to previous information already available. The other reason is that, if r carries information about s, then not only does r depend nomically upon s (in the sense that r would not be G unless s were F), but it depends on many other conditions C as well. This is the problem of the dependency of a signal r upon auxiliary conditions, which Dretske (1981) calls the problem of channel conditions.[14]

I start with the problem of the relativity of information to information already available which is well illustrated by an example of Dretske's (1981: 78–81). Consider four shells and a peanut located under one of them. Suppose A alone has already turned shell 1 and shell 2 and has found both of them empty. B has not. Then, A and B check over shell 3 and find it empty. Finding shell 3 empty does not supply A and B with the same information. Or does it? Finding shell 3 empty informs A that the peanut is under shell 4. It only tells B that the peanut is under shell 1, under shell 2 or under shell 4. So what information is contained in one and the same signal (no peanut under shell 3) varies according to what information was already available to A and B.

If we want to take into account the relativity of information contained in a signal to what a receiver already knows, as we must, then we ought to amend (4) into (5):

(5)   The fact that r is G indicates the fact that s is F relative to K if and only if it is nomically necessary that s is F if (r is G and K) and it is not nomically necessary that s is F if K.

Once the information contained in a signal is thus relativized to information K already available to the receiver, it may seem that it is only one small step to conclude that the naturalist project is doomed. What accounts for the difference in information derived by A and by B from one and the same signal is that, prior to the occurrence of the signal, there are things A knew which B did not. If so, and assuming that knowledge is some kind of reliable true belief, then the information contained in a signal turns out to be relative to some kind of belief (or propositional attitude). If information presupposes belief, then we cannot naturalize

---

[14] In his important criticism of informational semantics, Loewer (1987: 290–91) does not draw the distinction between the two problems: the problem of the relativity of information to information already available to the receiver and the problem of channel conditions. This failure, on my view, somewhat weakens his criticisms.

the latter in terms of the former. However, even though we must recognize the relativity of information, we do not have, I think, to concede that the information contained in a signal is relative to an agent's propositional attitudes. We may still argue that what the information contained in a signal is relative to is just *information* – information already available to the receiver of the signal. Dretske (1981: 80) suggests that the relativity of information should be understood on the model of the relativity of the velocity of a signal, or the simultaneity of events, to a frame of reference. This kind of relativity does not threaten the objectivity of the commodity under consideration. Similarly, relativizing new information to information already available does not threaten the objectivity of the former. What the relativization imposes, however, is the need for some non-relative notion of information as an inductive basis for the definition of relative information.

2.4 THE PROBLEM OF CHANNEL CONDITIONS

I now turn to the problem which, following Dretske (1981: 107–34), we may call the problem of "channel conditions." Any measuring instrument whose internal states (r's being G) are nomically and reliably correlated with some environmental condition-type (s is F) carries information about the environmental condition s. So the position of a pointer on a voltmeter will carry information about the voltage drop across the resistor in an electrical circuit. The position of the pointer of a gas gauge in an automobile will carry information about the amount of gas in the gas-tank of the automobile, and so on. The position of the pointer in the voltmeter, however, does not merely depend upon the voltage drop across the resistor. It depends, among other things, on the leads which connect the voltmeter to the circuit. Now, the leads are composed of wires having a determinate resistance. Nor does the position of the pointer of the gas gauge in the automobile depend merely on the amount of gas in the tank. It also depends on electricity flowing through the automobile. Let us call C these auxiliary conditions – which Dretske calls channel conditions. The state of the signal (the fact that r is G) depends, not merely upon the state of its source (the fact that s is F), but upon channel conditions C as well.[15]

---

[15] Conditions which Dretske (1981) calls channel conditions are what Stampe (1977) calls *fidelity* conditions and Stalnaker (1984) *relevant normal* conditions.

In fact, the problem of channel conditions should be broken down into two distinct issues. One sub-problem is simply the problem of providing a distinction between source and channel conditions. If we cannot supply such a distinction, and given that a signal r depends not just on a source s but on channel conditions C as well, then why not say that r carries information about conditions C rather than about the source s – or at least about C as well as s?

The other sub-problem is this: the fact that r carries information about s depends upon conditions C. But if the informational relation between r and s depends in turn upon conditions C, then the informational relation itself is now at risk of being undermined. Auxiliary conditions C are conditions of proper transmission – or flow – of information via (or through) the measuring device; they are conditions of proper functioning of the measuring device. If they do not hold, then the device is malfunctioning. If the device is malfunctioning, then the pointer might be in one position – r might be G – and still not carry the information it is supposed to carry – that s is F. Any signal would then turn out to be equivocal. Although there might well exist a nomic dependency between normal (or standard) states r of a measuring instrument and some environmental condition s, still the nomic dependency itself depends on critical conditions C. Given that r seems to carry information about s, how do we know that conditions C prevail? If conditions C happen not to prevail, then, contrary to appearances, the fact that r is G will not in fact indicate the fact that s is F. So the second sub-problem raised by channel conditions is the skeptical doubt that we may never know that a signal r does in fact carry information about a source s.

Both problems are, I think, genuine problems for informational semantics. Both have been explored by Dretske (1981). Let us take them one at a time.

The former is the problem of distinguishing what the information is *about* and the channel *over* which the information is transmitted and received. It is in fact reminiscent of the problem in the philosophy of science of distinguishing laws (which are part of an explanatory theory) from auxiliary assumptions (boundary conditions and idealizations) needed to apply laws in particular cases.

Dretske's strategy for dealing with the distinction between source and channel conditions seems to me to be the right one. The idea is that a source, unlike channel conditions, has genuine alternative possible states. To say that a source has genuine alternative possibilities is just to repeat the point that for *s* to be *F* (for this state to obtain), alternative possible states of *s* (as that *s* might have been *H*) must have been eliminated. And of course, elimination of alternative possibilities at the source involves the generation of new information at the source. Channel conditions *C* are conditions over which the information contained in signal *r* about *s* flows or is transmitted to some receiver. To say that conditions *C* have no genuine alternative possible states is to say that the fact that they hold (or prevail) fails to generate any new information not already available to the receiver.

Now, we face the question: How do we know whether conditions *C* do or do not have genuine alternative possibilities? This in effect is the question: How do we know whether our measuring instrument (or indicator) is *reliable*? As emphasized by Dretske, the name of the solution to this problem is: *calibration*. How do we determine the resistance of the wires connecting our voltmeter to the electrical circuit? How do we know whether the battery in our car generates electricity? In both cases, we calibrate our instrument. Calibration informs us that channel conditions are sufficiently stable so that they do not have relevant alternative possibilities. If so, calibration informs us that channel conditions are not likely to generate new information. During calibration, we use known values of some relevant magnitude to get information about the instrument itself. Two things are worth noting about the process of calibration: First of all, it is an empirical process. So the question whether some condition *C* is stable enough – invariant enough – to lack genuine relevant alternative possibilities and, therefore, to qualify as channel conditions for some process of information transmission, is an empirical question, not a purely conceptual one. Second, the measuring instrument cannot simultaneously carry reliable information about source *s* – that, for example, *s* is *F* – and carry the information that it is reliably doing so. A measuring instrument, for example, a clock or a thermometer, cannot carry reliable information respectively about what time it is or what the temperature is and simultaneously carry the information that it is respectively a reliable watch and a reliable thermometer. In order to determine whether clock *K* or thermometer *T* is reliable, we need to know antecedently what time it is or what the temperature is. So, presumably we need the information supplied by some other clock *K'* or thermometer *T'*.

This last remark brings us, I believe, to the second of the two sub-problems raised by channel conditions – the problem of the skeptical doubts. Given that the informational relation depends upon channel conditions, can we ever *know* that signal *r* carries information about source *s*? What, I think, dramatizes this problem is precisely the fact that an instrument must either carry information about some source *s* or carry information about its own reliability. But, as I said above, it cannot do both at the same time. The avenue open to the informational semanticist at this point, I think, is to take a strong *externalist* position (in the sense in which externalism is a position in epistemology). What the informational semanticist *qua* externalist epistemologist may do is make a sharp distinction between levels of information, i.e., between some lower-order information and the higher-order information that the lower information is reliable. Accordingly, a signal *r* may carry information about source *s* without carrying the higher-order information that the information about *s* which it carries is reliable information. This in general is the externalist ploy in epistemology. The internalist in epistemology claims that no reliable information can constitute an agent's knowledge unless the agent has the higher-order information that the lower-order information is reliable.[16] The externalist just denies the constraint: information may be reliable without carrying the information *that* it is reliable. Knowledge just is reliable information. The higher-order information that the information which constitutes knowledge is reliable, though crucial for calibration, is superfluous for knowledge. So the fact that state *r* of a measuring device cannot simultaneously deliver reliable information about source *s* and deliver the (higher-order) information that the information it delivers about *s* is reliable does not prevent the information it delivers about *s* from being reliable.

2.5 INFORMATIONAL SEMANTICS AND CONSCIOUS EXPERIENCES

In the remainder of this chapter, I want to argue that informational semantics can throw some light upon conscious sensory experiences. By so doing, informational semantics contributes a step forward

[16] See, for example, Lehrer (1991) as an instance of the internalist strategy in epistemology. Lehrer (1991) argues that unless the higher-order information that the lower-order information is reliable is available, we do not have a case of knowledge.

towards understanding what is somewhat misleadingly called "the" problem of consciousness. This problem which, by Fodor's standards, and unlike the problems raised by intentionality, looks intractable, is, in Fodor's (1994: 82) terms, the problem of "how anything material – for that matter, how anything at all – could be conscious."

For two reasons, it would be more accurate to talk of the problems of consciousness. The first reason is that the predicate "conscious" applies at least to two sorts of entities: a *person* may be conscious and a person's mental *states* may be conscious. The notion involved in a person's being conscious is that of "creature consciousness": a person may be conscious if he or she is not asleep, not drugged or not in a coma. The more enigmatic notion, however, is that of a conscious mental state or state consciousness. According to the so-called "higher-order thought theory" of conscious states, a person's mental state S (a belief or a sensory experience) is a conscious state if the person whose state it is is conscious of it in virtue of having formed a (higher-order) thought about it.[17] So according to the higher-order thought theory of conscious states, the notion of state consciousness is to be analyzed in terms of the notion of "creature consciousness." The second reason is that, as Block (1994; 1995) has emphasized, a person's mental state may be "*A*-conscious" if it is *accessible* to the person for verbal report and for guiding intentional action. Or it may be "*P*-conscious" if it has a phenomenal or sensory property, if, in other words, there is, in Nagel's terms, something it is like to be in that state. Unlike the latter, the former seems obviously to be a cognitive notion. I find the higher-order thought theory of conscious states congenial first because it fits nicely with what I called in chapter 1 the meta-representational view of the mind and second because it accounts nicely for the difference between conscious and unconscious mental states. Some of my beliefs, not all, are conscious: for one of my beliefs to be a conscious belief, I must have a higher-order thought about it. Consider one of my sensory experiences in virtue of which I am conscious of a thing and/or a property. Not all states necessary for my being thus conscious of (or for my experiencing) a thing or a property, however, need be conscious states. For one of those sensory states to be a conscious state, I must

---

[17] The main advocate of the higher-order thought theory of conscious states is Rosenthal (1986; 1993a; 1993b).

have a higher-order thought about it. In other words, I may be conscious of things and properties either by having a sensory experience or by having a thought about them. But neither the experience nor the thought need be a conscious state.[18]

Informational semantics can, I think, shed light on one of the problems raised by the existence of conscious mental states, i.e., the Nagelian problem of how anything physical could have olfactory, visual, auditive or tactile conscious (modality-specific) states, i.e., experiences and sensations. This is then the problem of how a state of a physical system can come to be *P*-conscious (in Block's sense). The reason I say only one of the problems raised by the existence of conscious mental states can be so identified is that there are presumably several ways one could be transitively conscious of something without undergoing a modality-specific sensory experience. One could, for example, be transitively conscious of something by having conscious conceptual thoughts and/or propositional attitudes about it. And it is not clear that for all such conceptual thoughts, there is something it is like to entertain them. Furthermore, understanding how a physical system could be in modality-specific information-carrying states may not exhaust all the facets of the Nagelian problem of what it is like to undergo a conscious experience. Still, there must be something it is like to be in a modality-specific informational state. So an informational approach to the problem of how a physical system may enter modality-specific informational states may shed some light upon the Nagelian problem.

Now, simplifying somewhat, the first option open to a monist physicalist faced with the problem of conscious experience is to take an eliminativist stance and deny that an individual's subjective conscious experience (or sensation) – in whatever modality – constitutes a genuine property of the individual (or of the individual's brain). If a

---

[18] The higher-order thought theory of conscious mental states accounts quite nicely for the accessibility notion of state consciousness: one of my beliefs is a conscious belief if I am conscious of it. On Rosenthal's version of the higher-order thought theory, it is supposed to account for phenomenal consciousness too. I think, however, that it is implausible to require that only creatures able to form higher-order thoughts about lower-order sensory states can have states such that there is something it is like to be in such sensory states. Sensory states via which a person is creature-conscious of things and properties which are not conscious states in the higher-order thought theory sense I propose to call states of consciousness.

monist physicalist takes a realist stance towards the property of having a given subjective conscious experience, then three avenues seem open to him or her.

He or she may, as McGinn (1991) does, catalog this problem among what Chomsky (1975; 1980a) calls unsolvable "mysteries" by contrast with solvable problems. In virtue of the cognitive limits of the human mind, the problem of conscious experience would then turn out to be "cognitively closed" to the human mind (McGinn's expression) and bound to remain a mystery. Assuming that the human mind does not have the cognitive capacity to understand the problem of conscious experience does not imply the eliminative view that conscious experiences are not genuine properties.

Starting from the initial assumption that minds are inhabited by two kinds of states – states with intentionality and states with qualitative content – it is quite natural (even if not inevitable) to try and provide a reductive account of one of the two kinds of states in terms of the other. A monist physicalist who takes a realist stance towards the problems of consciousness, while rejecting the mystery view, could thus adopt one of the following two strategies.

He may, as Searle (1992) has argued we should, try to derive a solution to the problems of intentionality from a solution to the problems of consciousness. This strategy follows from Searle's thesis of the priority of consciousness over intentionality.

Alternatively, he may expect a solution to the problems of consciousness from a solution to the problems of intentionality. Claiming, as I just did, that the higher-order thought theory can throw light on the accessibility sense of state consciousness and claiming, as I am going to, that informational semantics can take us some way towards understanding phenomenal conscious experiences is to travel along the last route.

Although being conscious does not reduce to having a conscious experience, I will assume that one characteristic way in which an individual may undergo a conscious experience – or be conscious – is by having a sensory experience. In this sense, conscious experience is primarily sense experience: what our senses tell us about our environment. It's quite clear, as Dretske is fond of reminding us, that one's sense experience differs from one's belief: what one experiences is an object s which may happen to have property F; what one believes is *that s* is *F*.[19] Evans (1982: 123–24) has expressed this distinction as the principle of "the belief independence of the state of the informational system." I shall give two examples of non-conceptual content, one from visual experience, the other from auditory experience.

Consider first an example from Peacocke (1983: 12). Suppose you are standing on a road stretching from you in a straight line and you see two trees on the side of the road, one a hundred meters from you, the other two hundred meters from you. Suppose your experience represents both trees as being the same height. It is also a feature of your visual experience that the nearer tree will occupy more of your visual field than the more distant tree. Such a feature can be constitutive of your experience without your having the ability to conceptualize it. If so, the feature in question will be part of the content of your experience; it will be non-conceptual content. A person's visual experience can, therefore, visually represent things in a certain way even though the person enjoying the experience does not possess the concept of the way things are thus represented.

As an example of the non-conceptual content of an auditory experience, consider, for example, the experience I had one day upon hearing a particular note produced by my wife's pressing a particular key – say, the C of the third octave – on a particular piano – a Bechstein. Even though I did not recognize which note it was, there was, of course, something it was like to experience the sound. It obviously differed from my belief that the sound produced on the Bechstein was a C of the third octave – a belief I acquired only after my wife told me which note was the sound. On the one hand, a creature – a human infant or a non-human animal – lacking the required concepts might experience the sound. Lack of the relevant concepts, however, would prevent anyone from forming the belief. On the other hand, a person having the relevant concepts may acquire the belief without experiencing the sound, if, for example, somebody trustworthy informs him or her of the relevant fact.

The differences between conceptual and non-conceptual content (especially of visual experiences) have been much discussed by con-

---

[19] Perhaps allowance should be made for experiences *that* so and so (seeing that so and so or hearing that so and so). In this case, these experiences would be mixed states having some of the qualitative features of the experiences of objects and some of the propositional features of beliefs. But my present concern is to emphasize what distinguishes experiential states from beliefs.

temporary philosophers (e.g., Bach 1987, Evans 1982, McGinn 1983, McDowell 1984, Peacocke 1983, 1989, Recanati 1993) under the guise of the contrast between descriptive and non-descriptive (or *de re*) modes of presentation. As Crane (1992c: 143) has put it, "for any state with content, *S*, *S* has non-conceptual content, *P*, iff a subject *X*'s being in *S* does not entail that *X* possesses the concepts that canonically characterize *P*." Peacocke (1992a: 105 sq.) – whose views have evolved since *Sense and Content* (1983) – proposes to capture the non-conceptual content of a visual experience by means of the notion of a *scenario* where a scenario is a set of "ways of filling out the space around the perceiver . . . The idea is that the content involves a spatial *type*, the type being that under which fall precisely those ways of filling the space around the subject which are consistent with the correctness of the content." The correctness conditions for the scenario will in turn be specified relative to an origin (e.g., the centre of chest of the perceiver) and a set of axes (up/down, left/right, forward/back). Unlike states with conceptual contents which are inferentially related to one another, states with non-conceptual contents, even though they may have correctness conditions, are not so inferentially related to one another.

If we now think of the non-conceptual content of an auditory experience, a related difference between the non-conceptual content of my sensory experience of a sound and the conceptual content of my belief that the sound was a C of the third octave is that, the latter, not the former, inclined me towards *intentional* behavior: only after I had formed the belief did I feel the impulse to say that the sound perceived was a C of the third octave. Assuming that the sound comes from my right-hand side, my acoustic experience of the sound might cause me to turn my head rightwards, i.e., towards the direction from which the sound is coming. But, unlike my uttering a sentence to the effect that the sound I heard was a C of the third octave, my turning my head rightwards in the direction of the sound would be automatic or reflex, non-voluntary intentional behavior, i.e., not under the control of my beliefs and desires.[20] As I will explain momentarily,

---

[20] Notice that there is a sense in which the control exerted by my beliefs and desires upon my intentional voluntary behavior is *conscious* control, whereas the control exerted by my conscious sensory experiences upon my intentional non-voluntary instinctive behavior is non-conscious (or unconscious) control. I do not think, however, that there is anything paradoxical in claiming that non-intentional behavior is under the

informational semantics offers an account of this difference in terms of the difference in how one and the same piece of information is coded.

To start with, consider first how informational semantics contributes to solving the problem of determining "the object of perception" – what sense experience is an experience *of*. I shall concentrate on visual perception. The main problem raised by the objects of perception is the *distality* problem. Godfrey-Smith (1989: 536) calls it the "horizontal axis" problem, where the "horizontal axis" codes the distance between a representation – a percept – and the various links of the perceptual process, such as the proximal stimulus and the distal stimulus. This is a problem which plagues purely causal accounts of the content of sense experience. Consider the visual experience of seeing an elephant. What we visually experience are properties of the elephant, not properties of receptors on our retina. The firing of receptors on the retina, though, is the proximal stimulus: it is a necessary step in the causal chain leading from the elephant to the visual experience, without which no visual experience (of the elephant) would occur. Why do we see the elephant, not the firing of receptors on our retina? When we experience the color of an object under various lighting conditions, the color attributed to the object by our experience does not change with the lighting conditions. Our visual experience of the shape and size of an object does not change as we change the distance and position of our head relative to the object. What Dretske (1981: 162), following current psychological practice, refers to as constancy mechanisms are responsible for the fact that different proximal retinal stimulations underlie one and the same visual experience: the sensory experience remains constant in response to different proximal stimulations.[21]

non-conscious control of a conscious sensory experience. For more on the pair of distinctions between intentional and non-intentional behavior, and between intentional voluntary and intentional non-voluntary behavior, see chapters 7 and 8.

[21] Among perceptual constancies, Gleitman (1986: 207–11) mentions lightness constancy, size constancy, shape constancy. The problem, as he puts it (*ibid.*: 207), is that "to see the real world is to see the properties of real objects: their color, form, and location, their movement through space, their permanence or transience. But we have noted previously that organisms cannot gain experience about the distal stimulus directly; all information about the external world comes to us from the proximal stimulus patterns that distal objects project upon the senses. Of course, the same distal

Fodor (1983: 60) has put this point in the following way:

The *typical* function of the [perceptual] constancies is to engender perceptual similarity in the face of the variability of proximal stimulation.
Proximal variation is often misleading; the world is, in general, consider-
ably more stable than are its projections onto the surface of transducers.
Constancies correct for this, so that, in general percepts correspond to
distal layouts *better than* proximal stimuli do.

If this is correct, then the informational approach has an explanation of why the object of perception is a distal stimulus, not a proximal
event. Before showing how informational semantics can account for
constancy phenomena, however, I want to briefly dispel a possible
objection to informational semantics based on the existence of visual
illusions. Whether informational semantics is refuted by visual illusions is important since – as will emerge fully in chapter 3 – visual illusions are cases of misperception or misrepresentation and one thing
we want to do is to account for the possibility of misrepresentation on
an informational basis. Consider such famous visual illusions as the
Müller-Lyer illusion (figure 1).

   Fodor (1983) argues that the very fact that in A, the segment on the
left still *seems* longer than the segment on the right to someone who
knows that the two segments are equal is evidence that the information-processing involved in visual perception is modular, i.e.,
informationally encapsulated or independent of one's beliefs.
Gregory's (1966: 131–63; 1970: 79) explanation for such a visual illusion (which is generally accepted) is that we can think of each segment
as the bidimensional projection of a three-dimensional physical
object. We can think of the segment on the left as the two-dimen-
sional projection of the interior intersection of two walls of a room
with the ceiling on top and the floor at the bottom (as is illustrated by

object will produce different proximal stimulus patterns, but the perceptual system
somehow 'sees through' the different masks. It responds to the permanent features of
the real object regardless of the illumination that falls on it and the distance and
orientation from which it is viewed. The best proof is provided by the *perceptual
constancies*. A crow looks black even in sunlight; an elephant looks large even at a
distance; and a postcard looks rectangular even though its retinal image is a trapezoid,
unless viewed directly head on. In all of these cases, we manage to transcend the
vagaries of the proximal stimulus and react to certain constant attributes of the distal
objects such as its shape and its size."

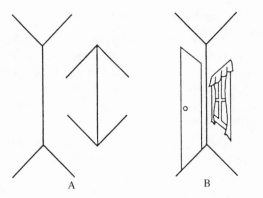

A   B   C

Figure 1 From Gleitman (1986: 210)

diagram B). We can think of the segment on the right as the bidimensional projection of the outside corner of a building with each wall
receding away from the observer (as illustrated by diagram C). On this
view, the segment on the left – the interior corner of a room – is then
interpreted as the projection of the part of the room which is furthest
away from the observer, whereas the segment on the right – the outer
edge of a building – is interpreted as the projection of the building
which is closest to the observer. The visual system then compensates
for the assumed difference in distance separating the observer respectively from the interior corner of the room – the left segment – and
the outer edge of the building – the segment on the right – by taking
the former to be larger than the latter: the allegedly more distant
segment is taken to be longer than the allegedly closer segment.

    Now, the problem for informational semantics is to explain how
on informational assumptions, the two segments can be seen as
unequal. Given that the two segments *are* equal, the visual percept
must carry the information that they are equal. So how can the existence of the Müller-Lyer illusion be reconciled with the informational claim that the visual percept must carry the information that
the two segments are equal? What, I think, the informational semanticist may say is that, prior to the having of the visual illusion, there is
a pre-illusory simpler or lower level of visual information-processing
– which Dretske (1969) called non-epistemic (non-cognitive) or
simple seeing – where what one sees are two segments which happen
to be equal. At this non-epistemic level, the two segments (which

68

happen to be equal) are not seen *as* anything – so they are neither seen as equal nor as unequal. The having of the visual illusion then requires some more information-processing: seeing the two segments *as* unequal involves a certain amount of what Dretske (1969) called epistemic (or cognitive) seeing. Still, a further effort of cognitive processing is required in order to form the *belief* that, although they look (or seem) unequal, the two segments are in fact equal. If, as I think we should, we assume that when we see the two segments as unequal, the content of our perceptual state may be non-conceptual in Peacocke's sense (as space being filled in a certain way), then we will distinguish a non-conceptual notion from a conceptual notion of epistemic seeing.[22]

Let us now turn to the fact that the object of perception is a distal object, not a proximal stimulus. The crucial point is that different possible proximal events – different from the actual one – *might* have served as an intermediate link in the chain from the distal stimulus to the experience. What our sense experience r's being G carries information about is what it is reliably correlated with in the sense of (4) above. Our visual experience r would not be G unless the distal stimulus s were F. The former nomically depends on the latter in the sense that if r is G, then s is F. The information that the distal stimulus s is F, therefore, is information carried by r's being G with no equivocation. r's being G, however, is equivocal with respect to the firing of receptors on the retina. Although one particular proximal event did serve as an intermediary cause in the process yielding the tokening of visual experience r, still other proximal events – the firing of different receptors on the retina – might have caused one and the same visual experience r. Sometimes one proximal event, sometimes another proximal event is an intermediate cause in the perceptual process. The informational account, therefore, unlike a purely causal one, explains why the content of a visual experience screens off or filters out the proximal event and why the informational relation holds of the experience and its distal, not its proximal, stimulus.

---

[22] This can be quite readily captured in terms of the distinction soon to be examined between analogical and digital coding of a piece of information. I discussed this approach to accommodating the Müller-Lyer visual illusion within informational semantics with Cristina Meini who wrote a predoctoral memoir on this topic at CREA in the Spring 1995.

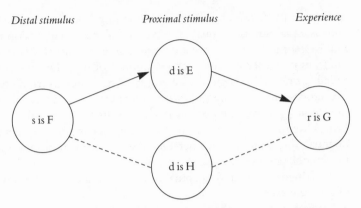

Figure 2 From Dretske (1981: 157). The solid lines indicate actual causal relations; the broken lines indicate possible non-actual causal relations.

I will now close the present chapter with a sketch of how informational semantics may vindicate the representationalist claim according to which the right strategy is to try and derive properties of conscious experiences from semantic properties of propositional attitudes (and not vice-versa). I will argue that informational semantics suggests that only a system capable of forming beliefs can have conscious experiences.

Dretske claims that one and the same state of affairs – that s is F – can be coded in two distinct ways: it can be coded *analogically* or *digitally*. A signal r codes analogically the fact that s is F if and only if the fact that s is F is not the most specific information about s contained in r. Alternatively, if the fact that s is F *is* the most specific information carried by r about s, then the information that s is F is digitally coded by r. The distinction can be illustrated by a great number of examples. A picture will usually carry analogically the information which an utterance carries digitally. For example, the information that a blue ball lies in between a red ball and a yellow ball can be the most specific information (about the balls) carried by the utterance of the English sentence "A blue ball lies between a red ball and a yellow one." So this information is carried digitally by the utterance. The same information, however, will be analogically carried by a colored picture since a colored picture cannot convey this information without carrying information about particular shades of red, blue, and yellow. While a black and white picture will not carry information about the shades of red, blue, and yellow, it cannot carry the information that a blue ball lies between a red ball and a yellow one without carrying information about the sizes of the various balls, and about which one of the red and the yellow ball is to the right and which one is to the left of the blue ball. Notice that by carrying digitally a piece of information, a signal will carry analogically less specific information. By virtue of carrying the information that *s* is a square, *r* will carry analogically the information that *s* is a rectangle and that *s* is a parallelogram.

It might be objected to the distinction between analogical and digital encoding that no carrying-information structure ever codes any definite piece of information analogically. Consider a colored snapshot *r* of a red ball. Snapshot *r* will carry the information that the ball is red digitally, if this is the most specific information about the ball that is coded by the snapshot. So we may say that the snapshot carries digitally the information that the ball is red and that it carries analogically the information that the ball is colored. However, a ball cannot be just red without being a particular shade of red. Suppose then that the ball is actually crimson.[23] If *r* carries the information that the ball is crimson, does it carry the information that the ball is red analogically or digitally? If *r* carries the information that the ball is crimson, then given that the information that the ball is crimson is more specific than the information that it is red, *r* carries the former information digitally and the latter information analogically. So it seems that the snapshot carries the information that the ball is red both digitally and analogically. What this merely shows is that the distinction is not a classificatory distinction: a structure does not code a piece of information analogically or digitally per se, but relative to a set of alternatives.

Following Dretske, we can then, I think, rely upon the distinction between analogical and digital encoding of one and the same piece of information in order to account for the needed distinction between the non-conceptual content of an experience and the conceptual content of a belief. Both an experience and a belief may carry the information that *s* is *F*. An experience of an *s* (which is *F*) will carry analogically the information that *s* is *F*, whereas a belief that *s* is *F* will carry the same information digitally. When my wife

---

[23] The relation between being crimson and being red or between being red and being colored is the relation holding between what traditional philosophers called a *determinate* property and a *determinable* property. See chapter 7.

pressed a key on a Bechstein, I first had an experience and then I acquired a belief. Both the experience and the belief carried the information that s was F – that the sound was such and such. But they carried this information in different ways. The information that s is F is the most specific information the belief carried about the sound. It said nothing else about it. The information that s is F was carried as part of the overall information the experience carried about s. In the experiential state, the information that s is F is *nested* (Dretske's word) in the information that s is P where to be P, s must be F and H and Q, just as the information that s is a rectangle is nested in the information that s is square.[24]

The information that the flower s in front of an eighteen-month-old child is a daffodil F is nested in her visual experience of the flower: she visually perceives the flower; but she cannot identify it as a daffodil. She cannot code digitally this piece of information which is carried analogically by her sensory state. Discussing what he calls demonstrative identification, Evans (1982: 146) has called the insensitivity of (informationally based) perceptual experiences to beliefs "the belief-independence of the information-link." This very same insensitivity has been of course much discussed by Fodor (1983) as the contrast between *modular* input systems and central thought processes.

Now, we might think of the transition from an experience of an s which is F (a sensory or perceptual state) to a belief (a conceptual state) that s is F as a process of classification, categorization, recognition or identification (of the fact that s is F). On the informational semantic view, we may capture this transition as a process of *digitalization*. A process of digitalization in turn is a process of *abstraction, extraction* or *elimination* of information. On the semantic informational view, going from a sensory experience carrying analogically the information that s is F to the conceptual state of believing that s is F (of recognizing s as an F) consists in *extracting* the austere information that s is F from the profuse and more specific information carried by the sensory state, for example, the information that s is P. The idea is rather Lockean: the sensory state analogically carries the information that s is F by virtue of carrying the information that s is P (where s is P if it is F,

---

[24] Analytic (mathematical, logical or conceptual) as well as nomic relations between properties may underly the nesting relation between two pieces of information.

H and *Q*).[25] In order to recognize (or categorize) this *s* as an instance of *F*-ness, the information that *s* is *F* has to be disentangled (divorced or abstracted) from the information that *s* is *P*. Extracting the information that *s* is *F* from the information that *s* is *P*, therefore, involves *loss* of information: it consists in the elimination of the information that *s* is *H* and *Q*. "Until digitalization has occurred," says Dretske (1981: 182), "nothing resembling classification or the subsumption under concepts has occurred."

At the heart of the informational account of the distinction between sensory and conceptual content, based on the distinction between analogical and digital coding of information, is, therefore, the assumption that information-processing involves a loss of information. Following Miller's (1956) classical paper, it has been widely assumed in cognitive psychology that more information is available in the input to the perceptual process than in the output: there is a limit on a human being's ability to recognize (or identify) "unidimensional" stimuli, which is not to say that there is the same limit on a human being's sensory sensitivity to (unidimensional) stimuli.[26] Miller's point is that there is a limit on the number of items which are available for a subject's immediate recall (or which can be stored in immediate memory). In a very influential experiment performed and reported by Sperling (1960), subjects were exposed to tachistoscopic presentations of rectangular arrays of nine letters (3–by-3) for 50 milliseconds. Typically, subjects could only report correctly four or five of the nine letters. When, however, Sperling signalled a particular row for attention with a tone occurring 150 milliseconds after the display was removed, then subjects reported letters in

---

[25] To say that the information that *s* is *F* is already present in the experience by virtue of the fact that the experience codes the information that *s* is *P* and *s* is *P* if it is *F*, *H* and *Q*, is not to say that one forms the belief simply by having the experience, since to form the belief one must still extract the information that *s* is *F* out of the information that *s* is *P*. One may perfectly well be in a state carrying the information that *s* is *P* without being able yet to extract (or digitalize) the information that *s* is *F*.

[26] Unlike unidimensional stimuli, which differ from one another in only one respect, multidimensional stimuli (such as objects, faces, words) differ from one another in many ways. In his paper on "Some Limits on our Capacity for Processing Information," Miller (1956) argued that the number seven can be thought of as an indication of the human capacity to make absolute identificatory judgments on unidimensional stimuli.

the relevant row with 100% accuracy.[27] Neisser (1967: 17–22) has interpreted Sperling's experiment as evidence for what he calls "iconic storage" (of information) in short-term memory: although they cannot all be retrieved, all letters are stored in some iconic form. The point is that since subjects cannot know in advance which row will be signalled for attention, they must be able to store information about every letter in the display in some preattentive format, even though they can only recall or identify half of the letters in the display. Iconic storage is what I have called analogical coding. The letters which can be retrieved (or identified) are coded digitally. In other words, there is, as Lindsay & Norman (1972: 329), among many, have emphasized, a "discrepancy between the amount of information held in the sensory system and the amount that can be used by later stages of analysis." In a word, if the transition between a percept (e.g., of a dog) and a concept (of a dog) is to be thought as of information-processing, then it is a process of selective elimination of information.

Notice that, on the one hand, by accepting the distinction between analogical and digital coding of information, I am not saying (and do not want to suggest) that *all* of an individual's concepts must result from a process of digitalization or extraction of information. As will appear in later chapters, I distinguish between a concept and the property a concept is a concept of.[28] As I just said, the digitalization view is quite Lockean. On my view, it applies to those of an individual's concepts of properties to which the individual may be experientially related. It does not apply to concepts of properties of which the individual cannot be experientially (or non conceptually) aware. I, therefore, endorse the conditional claim that if an individual has an experience of a property, then the digitalization view can account for the transition between the individual's experience, and his or her concept, of the property. I do not, therefore, have to presuppose that every property which has been in the past and will be in the future conceptualized by scientific theorizing must be analogically encoded in an individual's sensory experience. Nor am I bound (as will appear in chapter 8) to deny the existence of innate conceptual representations.

[27] Incidentally, experimental work on visual attention reported by, for example, Treisman & Gelade (1980) suggests that letters can be detected preattentively as separable features and may perhaps qualify as what Miller (1956) called a undimensional stimulus.

[28] See chapter 3 (section 3) and chapter 5 (section 2).

On the other hand, if the difference between a conceptual representation and a sensory representation of the fact that s is F is to be cashed in terms of the difference between digital coding and analogical coding of the fact that s is F, then the notion of a maximally fine-grained experiential state would seem to be precluded. If the sensory content of a sensory experience is non-conceptual content and non-conceptual content is information analogically coded, then there will presumably be no room for a notion of a maximally specific sensory experience. A conscious sensory experience will then be a state with a graded continuous finegrainedness attached to it. I think an informational semanticist can embrace this conclusion and live with it.

Consider the information that a signal r carries digitally. Dretske proposes to call it r's *semantic content*. The important feature of the notion of the semantic content of a signal, for the purpose of naturalizing the semantic properties of beliefs – a feature to which I will return in the next chapter – is that it differs from the mere informational content carried by a signal. If a signal r carries the information that s is F and if the information that s is H is nested (either nomically or analytically) in the information that s is F, then it follows that r carries the information that s is H. But if the information that s is F is r's semantic content, then even if the information that s is H is nested in the information that s is F, the information that s is H is *not* r's semantic content. The reason is simple: if the information that s is F is r's semantic content, then r carries the information that s is F digitally. If so, then r cannot carry digitally the information that s is H: it carries the information that s is H analogically. A signal's semantic content has a uniqueness which mere informational content lacks.

A physical system – for example, a thermostat or an electrical cell – may be capable of receiving and coding information without being able to digitalize it. A system incapable of converting information carried analogically into information coded digitally cannot occupy states having semantic content (in the sense defined above). *A fortiori*, it cannot have beliefs. Informational semantics makes two claims here. The first claim is that a state's having semantic content is a necessary, not a sufficient condition, for being a belief (about which more in the next chapter). The second claim is that, unless a system can enter states having semantic content, it cannot have conscious experiences: unless it is able to digitalize information, its states carrying information analogically are not conscious experiences. The difference between a mere information-processor and a mind is that a mind can, and a mere information-processor cannot, subject those of its states which carry information analogically to a process of digitalization. Unless a system can undergo (or submit itself to) this process of digitalization, its states carrying information analogically do not qualify as conscious experiences. Unless it could be digitalized, a piece of information analogically carried by some internal state of a system does not qualify as a conscious (or sensory) experience.

On the view I am taking here, there are then two aspects to a system's capacity to enjoy conscious experiences. On the one hand, conscious experiences are distinct from propositional attitudes. Not only does the non-conceptual content of a conscious experience differ from the conceptual content of a belief as information coded analogically differs from information which has been digitally extracted from the former. Also – as the sound example illustrates – entertaining a belief, unlike enjoying an experience, disposes one towards intentional voluntary behavior or voluntary action. Although my acoustic experience of the sound produced on the piano carried analogically the information which was later digitally coded in my belief that the sound was a C of the third octave, only after I had formed the belief was I able to say of the sound which note it was. And saying something is intentional voluntary behavior. To say, as I just did, that beliefs, unlike conscious experiences, are linked to intentional voluntary behavior is not to deny that conscious experiences can be linked to intentional non-voluntary behavior (or behavioral dispositions).[29] On the other hand, a system which would encode a piece of information analogically without the capacity for retrieving it for cognitive use would, on the present view, be incapable of enjoying a conscious experience. This is an aspect of conscious experience explored in depth by Evans (1982: 158) who argues that, not until some information can "serve as the input to a thinking, concept-applying, and reasoning system" can a person be said to undergo

[29] As I said above, upon enjoying the sound, I may turn my head rightwards if the sound came from my right hand side. This is intentional behavior because it is based on my auditory experience of the sound. But it is non-voluntary intentional behavior because my auditory experience of the sound is a non-conceptual representation of the sound: it is not a belief.

an experience as opposed to some part of his or her brain receiving and processing the information.[30]

In terms of my revised version of the higher-order thought theory of conscious experiential states (states with sensory properties), I want to distinguish the fact that there is something it is like to undergo a sensory experience from the fact that a sensory experience is a conscious mental state. The latter, I would argue, must be the target of a higher-order thought. The former, I would call a state of consciousness, not a conscious mental state. When I say that a sensory state – a state encoding a piece of information analogically – must serve as a possible input to a concept-forming ability for it to count as a conscious experience, I mean to state a necessary condition for a state of consciousness, not for a conscious mental state in the higher-order thought theory sense of the expression. To undergo states of consciousness, the creature must have concept forming abilities. This is different from having the meta-representational ability to form higher-order thoughts about lower-order mental states. I don't claim that I have provided arguments for such a picture. Rather, I think this picture shows how informational semantics may be happily wedded to a revised version of the higher-order thought theory of conscious states.

---

[30] Suppose Nagel (1974) is right to hold that bats enjoy experiences. Then the difference between bats and mere information-processors is that bats have the capacity to digitalize information, for example, they may exploit information provided by their echo-location system to detect insects and catch them. The fact that their digitalizing abilities are genetically determined does not matter. See chapter 8.

3

Three problems for informational semantics

The intentional realist's metaphysical program, I claimed in the first chapter, is twofold: he must show how the semantic properties of an individual's propositional attitudes can arise out of non-semantic or less than fully semantic properties and relations. This is what the naturalization of intentionality is about. The intentional realist must also show how semantic properties can be causally efficacious. He must justify what I called the strong causal thesis. Discussion of the strong causal thesis, however, requires knowing more about what semantic properties of propositional attitudes are and will be deferred until the second part. In the previous chapter, we have gone some way into exploring informationally based attempts at naturalizing intentionality. In the present chapter, I want to pursue my incursion into informational semantic territory to see how far it can take us into promised land – towards an approximation of the semantic properties of beliefs.

One of the striking features of a belief content is its *uniqueness*. Beliefs may generate new beliefs in virtue of their contents. One's singular belief that *a* is *F* may generate the general belief that there are *F*s. One's belief that *P* may generate the disjunctive belief that *P* or *Q*. One's conjunctive belief that *P* and *Q* may generate either the belief that *P* or the belief that *Q*, and so on. But for all that, there being *F*s is not part of the content of the belief that *a* is *F*. Nor is the disjunction that *P* or *Q* part of the content of the belief that *P*, and so on. At the end of the previous chapter, I mentioned Dretske's notion of a signal's semantic content as the information it carries in *digital* form. Now, a signal's semantic content, unlike other pieces of information analogically carried by a signal, seems unique in being the only piece of information which the signal carries in digital form. As I will argue, from the standpoint of informational semantics, the uniqueness problem has two sides: one is what I will call the insensitivity of a belief content to its informational origins; the other one is the threat of indeterminacy which arises from what I will call the transitivity of nomic dependencies. I say that the uniqueness problem can be approached from two avenues – the insensitivity of a belief content to its informational origins and the indeterminacy arising from the transitivity of nomic dependencies. I will, however, in the sequel treat the two sides of the uniqueness problem as two distinct problems. The first problem we shall have to face, therefore, is whether semantic content can in fact capture the insensitivity of belief contents to their informational origins.

Then, our task in the present chapter will be to examine further features of the semantic properties of beliefs. Consider the proto-belief that object *a* has property *F*.[1] Call it *r*. Surely, *r* is a *representation* of the fact that *a* is *F*.[2] I can think of at least three minimal conditions of adequacy which something must satisfy for it to be a representation of the fact that *a* is *F*. In other words, I suggest that we break the representation relation (or the aboutness relation) into three features.

First of all, *r* is complex in the sense that anyone able to entertain it must also presumably be able to entertain related representations such as the representation of the fact that some other object *b* is *F* (in case he or she has a way of representing object *b*) and the representation of the fact that *a* has some other property *G* (in case he or she has a way of representing property *G*). This constraint has been called the generality constraint by Evans (1982: 100–5) and systematicity by Fodor (1987b: 147–54), about which more in chapters 5 and 6. It seems reasonable and it entails that *r* possesses a complex semantic property which combines the simpler semantic property of a representation of object *a* together with the semantic property of a representation of property *F*. Clearly, this is a combinatorial problem. I will call it the compositionality problem.

Secondly, representations are referentially *opaque* or *intensional* (with

---

[1] I call it a "proto-belief" because in actual life, the fact that *a* is *F* is not an appropriate object of an individual's belief.

[2] This is what I called the weak almost analytic content of Representationalism in chapter 1.

an *s*) in the following relevant sense.³ A representation is referentially opaque or intensional if one of its constituents is not substitutable by some other coextensional constituent without altering the truth-value of the whole. Here is how Davidson (1982: 474–75) puts the importance of intensionality or referential opacity for propositional attitudes:

> One way of telling that we are attributing a propositional attitude is by noting that the sentences we use to do the attributing may change from true to false if, in the words that pick out the object of the attitude, we substitute for some referring expression another expression that refers to the same thing . . . For it has long been recognized that semantic opacity distinguishes talk about propositional attitudes from talk of other things.

Non-substitutability of coreferential constituents *salva veritate* in referentially opaque or intensional linguistic contexts may be illustrated by replacing a constituent either in subject position or in predicate position. To illustrate the former possibility, consider (1) and (2):

(1)   "Cicero" has six letters.
(2)   Cicero = Tully.

Although (1) and (2) express truths, replacement of "Cicero" by "Tully" in (1), as licensed by (2), to form (3) does not preserve truth:

(3)   "Tully" has six letters.

The reason the quotation context in (1) is called referentially opaque is that one cannot in (1), as it were, see transparently through the name "Cicero" and reach the individual the name refers to. In (1) the name is opaque for it is not used to refer to the individual; it is mentioned: the quotation marks allow us to refer to the name itself. To illustrate the latter possibility, suppose now that all *F*s are *G*s, that *F* and *G* are coextensional properties (or that predicates "F" and "G" standing respectively for properties *F* and *G* are coreferential). Then, in spite of the coextension between properties *F* and *G*, *r* will none the less represent the fact that *a* is *F*, not the fact that *a* is *G*.⁴ I will call it the *intensionality* problem.

---

³ In chapter 2, section 2, we examined the opacity of laws.

⁴ In this latter case, the predicative constituent of *r* expressing or denoting property *F* is not replaceable *salva veritate* by a coreferential predicate expressing or denoting property *G* coextensional with property *F*. Another symptom of referential opacity or intensionality is that the rule of existential generalization does not hold. See Quine (1953b).

Thirdly, representations may be *false*. So *r* may falsely represent the fact that *a* is *F*. *r* may say that *a* is *F* in spite of the fact that *a* is not *F*. The fact that a representation can be a misrepresentation is an important property of representations. I will call this the problem of *misrepresentation*. That it is a constitutive feature of representations that they can be misrepresentations has been eloquently illustrated by Malcolm's (1972–73) famous dog – which Davidson (1982) discusses – which is chasing a cat and barking up the wrong tree: the cat managed to climb up a maple tree, but the dog erroneously thinks that the cat went up the oak tree.[5] Now, from the standpoint of informational semantics which I assume, it will turn out that one ought to distinguish two distinct problems – which I will call respectively the problem of imperfect correlation and the problem of transitivity (of correlations). As I already said above, the latter in turn, which is at bottom a problem of indeterminacy, is closely related to the problem of the uniqueness of belief contents.

In the present chapter, I will restrict myself to the following four problems: the problem of the insensitivity of belief contents to their informational origins, the intensionality problem, the problem of misrepresentation (i.e., the problem of imperfect correlation)[6] and the transitivity problem. The language of thought hypothesis – defended by Fodor – is tailor made to solve the compositionality problem. I will postpone examination of the compositionality problem until I discuss the idea of a language of thought which will not be introduced until chapter 5 in which I will deal with what I will call the computational representational theory of mind.

To be naturalistic, i.e., for it not to be loaded with what Field (1972) calls "semanticalism," a solution to the problems of intensionality and misrepresentation must be stated in non-representational, non-semantic terms. In Schiffer's (1987: 10) terms, a solution to these problems must be "statable by sentences devoid of semantic or psychological terms." Presently, I want to see how far the

---

[5] Davidson (1982) gives important arguments for why we should not, on the grounds of misrepresentation, credit the dog with the belief that the cat went up the oak tree. Whether or not we should credit the dog with beliefs, there is presumably some state within the dog which is a representation of the cat up a wrong tree. It is presumably an open empirical question what concepts if any dogs have of oak trees and cats.

[6] For reasons which will emerge in due course, the problem of imperfect correlation is also called the disjunction problem.

informational approach will take us towards an approximation of the semantic properties of beliefs. I will first argue that informational semantics can accommodate the uniqueness of belief contents. I will argue secondly that it can accommodate a good deal, though not all, of the intensional characteristics of belief contents (or representations). I will, therefore, examine non-semantic ways to supplement informational semantics in order to accommodate some of the higher-order intensional features of belief contents. I will finally argue that informational semantics must be supplemented by teleological concepts in order to solve some of the problems lumped together under the label "misrepresentation."

3.2 THE INSENSITIVITY OF BELIEF CONTENTS TO THEIR INFORMATIONAL ORIGINS

I will now deal with the first obstacle to identifying the semantic property of a belief with a signal's semantic content. There is one respect in which a signal's semantic content – defined as information digitally carried by the signal – falls short of capturing the representational content of a belief: a belief content is a unique semantic property of a belief; a signal may have more than one semantic content. The problem I have in mind is not that if a signal r carries the information that P, then, given the fact that the information that P logically entails the information that P or Q, r also carries the information that P or Q. This is a (logical) version of the disjunction problem to which I will turn later in this chapter.

Suppose the most specific information carried by signal r about s is that s is F: suppose all other information carried by r about s is nested in the information that s is F. If so, then the information that s is F is carried digitally by r. Suppose, though, that r carries the information that s is F *in virtue of* carrying some other information *not* about s: let r carry the information that s is F in virtue of carrying the information that t is L. Imagine for instance an archeologist (e.g., Champollion) discovering his first sample of ancient Egyptian hieroglyphs (or an illiterate child experiencing a sentence which he cannot read). As he perceives a particular sequence t of hieroglyphical symbols, he enters a visual perceptual state carrying the information that t is L, that it looks so-and-so, has a certain visual appearance with a particular texture, shape and color. Now, in virtue of carrying the information that t is L (that a particular sequence of hieroglyphical symbols has a certain texture, shape and color), the archeologist's perceptual experience may carry another piece of information, for example, the information about Cleopatra, s, that she was fat (as it might be), F. I am here assuming that the visual (or auditive for that matter) experience of a particular token of a linguistic symbol encodes a specific information about the physical properties of the tokened symbol. Another experience of a different token of the same type would encode information about different physical properties – the physical properties of another token of the same type. If the different tokens are tokens of the same type, they will have the same meaning. This is why the information about the physical properties of symbols (that t is L) is more specific than the information about what the symbol means (that s is F).

If so, then even though the information that s is F (the information that Cleopatra was fat) satisfies the previous definition for being r's semantic content, in virtue of being the most specific information about s, still the information that s is F is itself nested in the information that t is L. In order to retrieve the information that s is F, the archeologist of course must learn the syntax and semantics of the language to which the sequence of hieroglyphical symbols belongs. While not about s, the information that t is L is none the less carried by r and it is more specific than the information that s is F. The semantic content of a signal, then, is at risk of proliferating: r may carry digitally both pieces of information – that s is F and that t is L. In this respect, the definition of a signal's semantic content as information digitally coded by the signal is too weak for it is insufficiently discriminative.

Towards the end of the previous chapter, I referred to the difference between the way experiences and beliefs carry information. The crucial step in the strengthening of the notion of semantic content is to realize that, unlike an experience, the information contained in a belief state does not reflect (or bear witness to) its *informational origins*.

Suppose I come to believe that s is F (that it is going to rain, as it might be) as a result of a perceptual (e.g., visual) experience which carries the profuse information that t is L (that the sky above me is cloudy). Suppose my perceptual experience does carry the information that s is F *in virtue* of carrying the more specific information that t is L. According to informational semantics, the step from the perceptual experience to the belief involves the extraction of the information that *s* is *F* from the information that *t* is *L*. Now, there is a major difference between the way my belief represents the fact that *s* is *F* and the way my perceptual experience carries the same information. This in essence is the difference between sensory (or experiential) and conceptual representations. My perceptual experience bears witness to the fact that it carries the information that *s* is *F* *in virtue of* the fact that it carries the information that *t* is *L*. It is constitutive of the non-conceptual content of my experience that the information that *s* is *F* is nested or embedded into the information that *t* is *L*. It is constitutive of its non-conceptual content that my experience carries the information that *s* is *F* in virtue of carrying the information that *t* is *L*. But my belief that *s* is *F* does not bear witness to its informational origin: if I acquired this belief as a result of a perceptual experience carrying the more specific information that *t* is *L*, then the informational origin of my belief is not reflected in the semantic property of my belief.

The following adaptation of an example of Dretske's (1981: 185–9) should make this point more clearly. When I read a sentence on a page in a language I understand, I may come to believe what the sentence expresses.[7] I form my belief (that *s* is *F*, as it might be), if and when I do, as a result of visually experiencing the linguistic symbols on the page. My visual experience itself carries the information that *s* is *F* in virtue of carrying more specific information about the shapes, size, color, and other physical properties of the linguistic symbols on the page. Suppose now that the very same information that *s* is *F* is contained in a sequence of linguistic symbols which belong to a language which I do *not* understand (e.g., Chinese). And suppose that this information is the most specific information contained in the page about *s*. Although I cannot interpret the symbols, the perception of the symbols on the page causes me to have a visual experience which depends on the shapes and other physical properties of the symbols. Let us say that my visual experience carries the information that *t* is *L* about the physical properties of the

---

[7] I may or may not come to believe what the sentence I detected expresses, depending on whether or not I take the source of information to be reliable. This illustrates the fact that beliefs, unlike experiences, are not merely anchored in their informational origins. They also interact with one another. See chapter 6 in which this latter phenomenon is called "cognitive holism" and where I argue that an intentional realist informational semanticist is not bound to accept what Fodor (1987b) calls "semantic atomism".

symbols on the page. Nested in this information is the information that *s* is *F*. In this case, my visual experience still carries the information that *s* is *F*. This information, being the most specific information about *s,* is carried digitally. My experience carries it in virtue of carrying the information that *t* is *L*. In order to retrieve the information that *s* is *F*, I need to know the grammar of Chinese. I would say that the information that *s* is *F* is, therefore, grammatically nested in the information that *t* is *L*. In this case, I have a visual experience but I cannot form the belief that *s* is *F* by extracting it from the information that *t* is *L* contained in my experience.[8] Lack of knowledge of the grammar of Chinese is what prevents me from forming the belief that *s* is *F* from my experience that *t* is *L* just as lack of the concept of a doorbell would prevent, for example, a mouse from forming the belief that someone is at the door from the acoustic experience of a doorbell ringing.

The insensitivity of belief contents to their informational origins has been noted by Fodor (1983): he calls it the relative inaccessibility of representations computed by modular perceptual input systems to central conceptual systems. Fodor reports an experiment in which a subject is asked what time it is. The subject looks at his watch. He is then asked to report the shape of the numerals on the face of his watch without looking again. The subject cannot. As Fodor (1983: 57) says:

> The point is that visual information which specifies the shape of the numerals must be registered when one reads one's watch, but from the point of view of access to later report, that information doesn't take . . . There are similar phenomena in the case of language, where it is easy to show that details of syntax (or the choice of vocabulary) are lost within moments of hearing an utterance, only the gist being retained. (Which did I just say was rapidly lost? Was it the syntactic details or the details of syntax?) Yet it is inconceivable that such information is not registered somewhere in the comprehension process . . .

Assuming that what one reports is what one believes,[9] then Fodor's examples are further instantiations of the insensitivity of belief contents to their informational history.

---

[8] This is a case where I do not have the resources for digitalizing the information that *s* is *F*, although it is contained in my experiential state carrying the information that *t* is *L*.

[9] It seems to me reasonable to assume that the content of a verbal (or linguistic) report of a perceptual experience involves a conceptual representation of the experiential state one is reporting about.

As the examples suggest, the fact that my visual experience contains the information that s is F *in virtue of* carrying some more specific information about the physical properties of symbols is built into the content of my experience.[10] When, however, I have acquired the belief that s is F, the belief state carrying this information is mute about the process of belief acquisition, i.e., about the fact that I acquired the belief via entering a prior perceptual state which itself carried the information that s is F in virtue of carrying more specific information about the physical properties of symbols. Had I been supplied with the information that s is F by means of an auditory experience – by processing an utterance – the phenomenological quality of my belief (if any) would not be any different. The informational history of the belief is deleted from the belief state. The content of the belief is cut off from its informational origins. Arguably, one should distinguish the two closely related theses: one is that, as a matter of cognitive architecture, after a belief has been formed by (what Fodor 1983 calls) central thought processes, the agent does not have easy access any more to the earlier steps of belief formation. The other thesis is that the semantic property of the belief bears no (modality-specific) trace of its informational history.

In order to capture the insensitivity of a belief content to its informational origins, Dretske (1981: 185) has strengthened the notion of mere digital encoding of information into *complete* digitalization of information so that for the information that s is F to be r's semantic content, not only must r, of course, carry this information but also there cannot be any other information carried by r in which the information that s is F would be nested.

3.3 INFORMATIONAL SEMANTICS AND THE INTENSIONALITY PROBLEMS

I now turn to the important matter of the level (or degree) of intensionality appropriate to representations. I want to distinguish two levels (or degrees) of intensionality. A structure – be it linguistic or non-linguistic, i.e., mental – is *weakly* intensional if replacement of

---

[10] The reason I say that the information about the physical properties of symbols is more *specific* than the information the symbols are used to express is precisely that the same information could be expressed using symbols with different physical properties (either from the same language or from different languages).

one constituent "F" by some coextensional constituent "H" alters its informational content (or truth-value).

Let two properties F and H be coextensional. From the fact that r carries the information that s is F, it does not follow that r carries the information that s is H too. Informational semantics provides an elegant explanation of weak intensionality. As I said in the previous chapter, r's being G can only carry the information that s is F if the former *nomically* depends on the latter. Information is a matter of nomic dependency (or nomic correlation) between instantiated properties. But from the fact that properties F and H are merely coextensional, it does not follow that r's being G nomically depends on s's being H. Mere coextension between properties is weaker than nomic coextension. This is why mere coextension between properties does not preserve nomic dependency between properties. It is, on my view, precisely one of the attractions of an informational account of semantic properties (of an individual's propositional attitudes) that it offers a simple explanation of weak intensionality.[11]

This shows that mere informational content is weakly intensional. Representations and beliefs, however, have one more degree of intensionality. Suppose it's a *law* that all Fs are Hs or that properties F and H are *nomically* coextensional.[12] According to informational semantics, if r carries the information that s is water, then r depends nomically on s's being water. Given that properties F (being water) and H (being a substance composed of H_2O molecules) are nomically coextensional, r cannot fail to carry the information that s is a substance composed of H_2O molecules if it carries the information that s is water. Even so, representation r of the fact that s is F is not *ipso facto* a representation of the fact that s is H. I may believe that this glass in front of me contains water without believing that it contains a substance composed of H_2O molecules; "x believes that this glass contains water" and "x believes that this glass contains a substance composed of H_2O" may have different truth-values for any instantiation of x – even though nothing can

---

[11] In chapter 2, I argued that some of the features of conscious experiences can be understood on the basis of informational semantics. I took this to vindicate the strong claim made by Representationalism (in chapter 1). A second reason for adopting informational semantics (as a tool for the task of naturalizing intentionality) is that weak intensionality falls naturally out of informational semantics.

[12] The counterpart of this assumption for linguistic representations (or utterances) would be to suppose that two predicates "F" and "H" are necessarily coextensional.

be water without being a substance composed of H_2O molecules. I will say that a representation is *strongly* intensional if replacement of one constituent "F" by a *nomically* coextensional constituent "H" can alter its content (or truth-value).

The contents of beliefs and representations are, therefore, strongly intensional. Their intensionality is stronger than the intensionality of informational content. *r* may carry the information that *s* is *F*, not the information that *s* is *H*, even though *F* and *H* are merely coextensional. But if *F* and *H* are *nomically* coextensional, then *r* cannot carry the information that *s* is *F* unless it carries the information that *s* is *H* as well. So it seems that semantic content informationally characterized lacks the second degree or level of intensionality characteristic of representations. Is the second degree of intensionality which is characteristic of belief contents out of reach of informational semantics? I am going to argue that informational semantics should not concede defeat right away.

Whether or not informational semantics is bound to treat the property of being water and the property of being a substance composed of H_2O molecules as one and the same property on the ground that every signal which carries the information that *s* is water *ipso facto* must carry the information that *s* is a substance composed of H_2O molecules, I shall leave open.[13] What the informational semanticist, however, can argue is that the (intensional) difference between a representation that *s* is water and a representation that *s* is a substance composed of H_2O molecules reflects the non-semantic difference between two distinct *vehicles* of one and the same piece of information. This difference could be captured in terms of the difference between two *modes of presentation* of the same information: just as we can speak of different modes of presentation of one and the same property, we may speak of different modes of presentation of one and the same piece of information. Alternatively, if we make, as I think we must, a distinction between concepts and properties, we may express the relevant difference in terms of a difference between two *concepts*: just as one (or more) person can think of one and the same property

---

[13] I do not want to suggest that from the fact that every signal which carries the information that *s* is water must carry the information that *s* is composed of H_2O molecules, it follows that the property of being water ought to be identified with the property of being composed of H_2O molecules. Nor do I believe this. I merely mean to say that I do not want to take a stand on this issue here.

under different concepts, we may say that different thoughts encode one and the same piece of information under different concepts. This in effect is the line adopted by such informational semanticists as Dretske (1981: 215–18), Fodor (1989a; 1994: ch. 1–2).

Notice that talk of "concept" is both ubiquitous and often ambiguous in philosophy and psychology. In the philosophical tradition to which Frege's classical (1892) work belongs, what is usually meant by "concept" is what Frege called the *Sinn* or sense of an expression. It is, therefore, both something appropriately abstract and something expressed by an expression (or a symbol). In this sense, the same concept can be expressed by different symbols or different expressions. It ought, therefore, not to be confused with the expression (or symbol) itself. However, there is a tendency in psychology to use "concept" as standing for a mental representation, for something having content, rather than for content itself (or for a constituent of content). So when the informational semanticist recommends that we distinguish two informationally equivalent concepts – the concept of water and the concept of H_2O – by appealing to non-semantic differences in vehicles or modes or presentation, he is using "concept" ambiguously. What he is suggesting is that two information-carrying structures may carry the same information while the structures carrying the information may differ in some non-informational respect. And furthermore, he is recommending that the latter difference counts as a difference between (or among) concepts. How damaging the ambiguity is, I will examine later in chapter 5.[14]

The idea, then, is that the concept WATER differs from the concept of a SUBSTANCE COMPOSED OF H_2O MOLECULES (or H_2O for short). I shall adopt the convention of referring to concepts by means of words in capital letters. Although they have the same semantic *qua* informational value, the two concepts differ exactly as the English word "water" differs from the English noun phrase "substance composed of H_2O molecules." At this point, it will be hard to resist introducing the idea of a language of thought into the informational semanticist's account of the intensional difference between the representation of the fact that *s* is water and the representation of the fact that *s* is H_2O. The language of thought hypothesis would allow us to account for the difference between the above two concepts by

---

[14] This ambiguity has been explicitly acknowledged by Fodor (1990c: FN 12, 133).

appealing to the syntactic constituent structures of two mental symbols. But I will resist this move until the fifth chapter when I deal with the causal efficacy of the semantic properties of beliefs.

The difference, then, between the concept WATER and the concept H_2O consists in the fact that the vehicle of the latter, unlike the vehicle of the former, includes the constituents "H," "2" and "O." One can have or entertain the concept WATER, not the concept H_2O, without having the concepts HYDROGEN, OXYGEN, and NUMBER 2. So the difference between nomically coextensive thoughts must· turn on their respective combinatorial (or compositional) properties, in particular on the internal structure of their constituent concepts. The concept of a CIRCLE differs from the concept of a CLOSED FIGURE EVERY POINT OF WHICH IS EQUIDISTANT FROM ITS CENTRE even though the two concepts are analytically coextensive. The latter, not the former, includes the constituent EQUIDISTANT FROM ITS CENTRE. What the informational semanticist is committed to, at this stage, is the assumption that nomically or analytically coextensive concepts or information-carrying structures must differ in their compositional structure: if any two such informationally equivalent structures differ, then either only one of them is *primitive* or, if they are both complex, then they have different constituent structures and are built out of different constituents.

But now, a new problem arises: two belief contents may differ even though they seemingly contain mental ingredients which could be expressed by linguistic symbols which are both informationally equivalent and both putatively primitive. I may, for example, believe that someone is a lawyer without believing that he or she is an attorney. At least, I might hold true a sentence containing the word "lawyer" and false a sentence in which the word "lawyer" has been replaced by the word "attorney." Kripke (1979: 268) mentions the fact that Hebrew has two names for Germany "transliterable roughly" as "Ashkenaz" and "Germaniah." And as he puts it (*ibid.*), "plainly, a normal Hebrew speaker . . . could assent to a Hebrew sentence involving 'Ashkenaz' while dissenting from its counterpart with 'Germaniah.'"[15] So the question is: Can the informational semanticist accommodate the fact that two information-carrying structures containing two primitive informationally equivalent vehicles differ in a non-semantic way?

---

[15] Another example might involve the predicates "Greek" and "Hellenic."

Presumably, the line open to the informational semanticist, then, will be one of the following two. On the one hand, he may look for (hidden) compositional differences which are not obvious at first glance and reduce the case to the above distinction between the concept of WATER and the concept of SUBSTANCE COMPOSED OF H_2O MOLECULES. On the other hand, if this strategy fails, he may notice that two informationally equivalent primitive vehicles *are* distinct (primitive) vehicles. Given his prior appeal to compositional differences between (or among) distinct vehicles of one and the same piece of information (or informational constituent), the informational semanticist may perhaps invoke the non-compositional differences between distinct vehicles as well. He may argue that the fact that two informationally equivalent primitive vehicles are two distinct vehicles may contribute a difference to what Taschek (1995), following Putnam (1954), calls the "logical structure" of the representation.

Consider two nomically coreferential (and therefore information-ally indistinguishable) vehicles "α" and "β." We must, as pointed out by Taschek (1995), count as structurally (and, therefore, logically) dis-tinct the following two schemata: "$\Phi\alpha$" and "$\Phi\beta$." Surely, any two instantiations of these two schemata will differ in a way in which two distinct instantiations of only one of these two schemata, for example, "$\Phi\alpha$," won't. Any two instantiations of "$\Phi\alpha$" and "$\Phi\beta$" may, there-fore, unlike two instantiations of "$\Phi\alpha$," have distinct inferential potentials. For example, from two premises instantiating "$\Phi\alpha$" and "$\Psi\alpha$," we may logically infer "$(\exists x)(\Phi x \& \Psi x)$." However, we may not derive this conclusion from two premises one of which instantiates "$\Phi\alpha$" and the other of which instantiates "$\Psi\beta$" without an additional identity statement to the effect that "$\alpha = \beta$" is true. For example, from my belief that Cicero was bald and from my belief that Cicero was fat, I may derive the belief that someone was both bald and fat. From my belief that Cicero was bald and my belief that Tully was fat, I cannot, without the further premiss that Cicero was Tully, conclude that someone was both bald and fat.[16]

So the difference in belief contents expressible by two information-ally equivalent and primitive vehicles might derive from the very structural (or logical) difference which arises from the mere

---

[16] In order for the beliefs to have the appropriately strong level of intensionality, I assume with Kripke (1972) that Cicero was necessarily (or nomically) identical to Tully.

non-semantic fact that "α" differs from "β."[17] Perhaps the fact that two such informationally equivalent vehicles differing from each other as "α" differs from "β" must be stored at different addresses in a creature's cognitive architecture can explain why two informationally equivalent primitive information-carrying structures have the potential for such cognitive differences in the creature.[18]

Clearly, to accommodate the highest level of intensionality thus far considered, the system having information-carrying states must be credited with logical abilities or sensitivities: it must detect differences in logical structures or logical potentials between distinct, though informationally equivalent information-carrying structures. Furthermore, it must have the logical capacity to move from the singular thoughts that, for example, $\Phi\alpha$ and $\Psi\alpha$ to the general thought that $(\exists x)\,(\Phi x\ \&\ \Psi x)$. In other words, it must have the capacity to form quantified thoughts.[19] In the process of examining how informational semantics can account for the intensionality of belief contents, we have reached a level of intensionality which the mere informational relations between an individual's mind and his or her environment cannot account for unless they are supplemented by some logical or inferential mechanisms (or abilities). Now, as I will argue in chapter 6, it is an important feature of belief contents (as opposed to merely information-carrying states) that beliefs generate new beliefs by means of such inferential relations. This is what distinguishes genuine belief states from what Dennett (1969) has called "sub-personal" information-carrying states, what Stich (1978b) has called "sub-dox-

---

[17] Taschek (1995) first considers Putnam's (1954) notion of *local* logical structure: two sentences *S* and *S'* share the same local logical structure just in case there is no logical schemata which is instantiated by *S* and not by *S'*. He argues that, in order to accommodate counterexamples, this notion must be strengthened into the notion of *global* logical structure: two sentences *S* and *S'* share the same global logical structure just in case for all logical schemata *Z* and *Z'* and any sentence *S**, *S* and *S** are corresponding instances of *Z* and *Z'* (respectively) if and only if *S'* and *S** are corresponding instances of *Z* and *Z'* (respectively). Global logical structure, unlike local logical structure, is a relational logical notion.

[18] Perhaps the informational semanticist could further appeal to differences in chronological order with respect to which two distinct informationally equivalent vehicles have been learnt, acquired or stored at different addresses.

[19] In chapter 5, I will argue that, on the reasonable assumption that thinking requires the ability to form such quantified thoughts, the language of thought hypothesis cannot be a "mere" empirical hypothesis.

astic" states. This feature of belief, I will call cognitive holism.[20] Before moving on to consider the problem of misrepresentation, it is worth insisting on the fact that the highest level of intensionality is really typical of belief contents. Not all representational states have this level of intensionality. Only creatures capable of the relevant logical capacities have the ability to form genuine beliefs with the appropriate level of intensionality. Only such creatures have the ability to derive new beliefs out of older beliefs. As we shall see in chapter 6, such semantic features of belief contents can only be captured by inferential role semantics.

3.4 THE PROBLEM OF MISREPRESENTATION

Undoubtedly, with the problem of misrepresentation, we reach a new level of complexity. According to informational semantics, informational content is a matter of reliable nomic causal dependency or correlation between property G of signal r and property F of source s in the environment. If a signal's informational content arises out of the nomic dependency of property G of the signal upon property F of the source, then the signal cannot *mis*inform about its source. If the dilation of a metal bar r carries information about variations in temperature in virtue of the nomic dependency of the former upon the latter, then the length of the metal bar cannot misinform about temperature. If this reasoning is correct, then informational semantics simply cannot account for misrepresentation and informational semantics is seriously incomplete. Since a belief can misrepresent the fact that s is F when s is not F, informational semantics must be supplemented by some other naturalistic account.

This version of the problem of misrepresentation arises from the strong assumption that informational content requires *perfect* correlation between some property of the source and some property of the signal. The assumption of perfect correlation is, however, unnecessarily strong. Nor is it plausible. If we do not assume perfect correlation, we must still, I contend, distinguish at least two ways misrepresentation may constitute a problem for informational semantics. Both may

---

[20] In chapter 6, I will argue that accepting an informationally based semantics does not force us, contrary to recent claims of Fodor (1987b) and Fodor & Lepore (1992), to accept what they call "semantic atomism."

seem to have some claim to be called the *disjunction* problem in the sense that both seem to be problems of indeterminacy. But appearances are somewhat misleading. Only one of the two problems, I will now argue, is a genuinely disjunction problem, and has an informational solution. The other problem is not so much a disjunction problem as a conjunction problem. It is less a misrepresentation problem, I will argue, than a problem of indeterminacy. The disjunction problem arises from the imperfection of nomic correlations. I will call it the problem of imperfect correlation. What I would rather call a conjunction problem arises from the transitivity of correlation in a chain of correlations. I shall call it the transitivity problem.

Although the assumption of perfect correlation is not inevitable, the above reasoning does suggest a tension between informational or correlational semantics and the possibility of error or misrepresentation – a tension emphasized by Fodor (1990b: 90–91):

> What the disjunction problem is really about deep down is the difference between meaning and *information* . . . Information is tied to etiology in a way that meaning isn't. If the tokens of a symbol have two kinds of etiology, it follows that there are two kinds of information that tokens of that symbol carry . . . *the meaning of a symbol is one thing that all its tokens have in common, however they may happen to be caused* . . . information follows etiology and meaning doesn't, and that's why you get a disjunction problem if you identify the meaning of a symbol with the information that its tokens carry.

In the words of Antony and Levine (1991), the task facing informational semantics is to *detach* the meaning of a mental representation from its causes.

One natural thought which underlies what I will presently call *teleosemantic* approaches to the problem of misrepresentation is to solve it by appeal to *functions*. The length of a metal bar is nomically correlated with the surrounding temperature. It, therefore, carries information about temperature. Unlike a thermometer, however, it cannot misrepresent the temperature. The reason it cannot, so teleosemantics tells us, is that, unlike a thermometer, it does not have the *function* of carrying information about the surrounding temperature. The level of mercury in the glass tube of a thermometer may tell us something fallacious about the temperature because it may fail to do what it is *supposed* to do – what it is its function to do, i.e., to carry information about temperature. Since an instrument's function underwrites the difference between normal functioning and misfunctioning, norms (of proper functioning) arise from functions.

There are two reasons why such an account should look suspicious as an account of misrepresentation in general. For one thing, suppose some such account explains why a thermometer, unlike a metal bar, can misrepresent the temperature. Still, it will not solve the problem of misrepresentation for mental representation since a thermometer's function depends on a human designer's propositional attitudes. Unless mental representations – or mechanisms for producing them – could acquire "natural" functions through a process independent of an individual's propositional attitudes, the above account is simply unavailable for mental misrepresentations. As teleosemanticists have been quick to point out, such processes are available either through evolution by natural selection or through individual learning. My second reason for doubting that the above account of the misrepresentational power of a thermometer based on the instrument's function can be a general account of misrepresentation is that, as I am about to argue, unlike the transitivity problem, the problem of misrepresentation (or disjunction problem) may have an informational solution. If I am right, the problem of transitivity of correlations does require a teleological solution. On my view then, the teleosemantic approach is designed to solve not the problem of imperfect correlation, which is a problem of misrepresentation, but the transitivity problem, which is a problem of intedeterminacy, not a misrepresentation problem.

3.5 THE PROBLEM OF IMPERFECT CORRELATION

What I call the problem of imperfect correlation is what Fodor (1987b: 101–2; 1990b,c) calls the disjunction problem. Suppose that the information carried by a signal is a matter of reliable correlation between properties. No correlation between properties, however, is perfect. Sometimes – most of the times – the instantiation of property G by signal r is correlated with the instantiation of property A. Some other times, the instantiation of property G is correlated with the instantiation of property B. Most of the times my HORSE concept is correlated with horses – i.e., with particular instantiations of the property of being a horse. On other occasions, my HORSE concept is correlated with donkeys seen at a distance. Still on further occasions, my HORSE concept is correlated with cows on a dark night. So, according to Fodor, the disjunction problem arises because what the instantiation of property *G* by the tokening of signal *r* is better correlated with is the disjunctive property *A or B,* neither property *A* nor property *B.* What my HORSE concept is maximally correlated with is, not instantiations of horsehood, but instantiations of horsehood or donkeyhood seen at a distance or cowhood on a dark night.

Now, the reason why the problem of imperfect correlation is a problem of misrepresentation or a disjunction problem is clear enough. If the content of a signal is what the signal is maximally correlated with, then the content of *r*'s being *G* will be *A or B.* The content of my HORSE concept will be horse or donkey-seen-at-a-distance or cow-on-a-dark-night. But if so, then error or misrepresentation seems impossible again. When my HORSE concept is tokened in the presence of either a donkey seen at a distance or a cow on a dark night, my HORSE tokening does not count as a case of misrepresentation. But intuitively, we do want to count a tokening of my HORSE concept in the presence of a donkey or of a cow as an error.

Fodor's (1987b; 1990b,c) own solution to the problem of imperfect correlation is what he calls the "Asymmetrical Nomic Dependency Condition." The intuitive idea behind this condition is that false tokenings depend on true or veridical ones; and not vice-versa: "the possibility of saying 'that's a horse' falsely presupposes the existence of a semantic setup for saying it truly, but not vice-versa" (Fodor 1987b: 108). We want, however, a non-semantic account of this asymmetrical dependency. In Fodor's (1990c: 91) words, there being donkey-caused HORSE concept tokenings or cow-caused HORSE concept tokenings depends on there being horse-caused HORSE concept tokenings; and not the other way around. To simplify matters, suppose there are only two nomic dependencies: there is one nomic dependency between tokenings of my HORSE concept and horses; and there is one nomic dependency between tokenings of my HORSE concept and donkeys-seen-at-a-distance (donkeys for short). Then Fodor's solution is to assume the existence of a higher-order dependency between our two (first-order) nomic dependencies: the nomic dependency between HORSE tokenings and donkeys is itself asymmetrically dependent upon the nomic dependency between HORSE

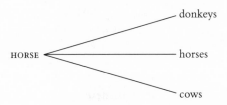

Figure 3 The problem of imperfect correlation

tokenings and horses (and not conversely). In other words, HORSE tokenings would not be correlated with donkeys if they were not correlated with horses.

Sterelny (1990: 120–1) has raised what I shall call the proximal stimulus objection which should be reminiscent of what I called in the second chapter the distality problem. Consider a particular veridical tokening of my HORSE concept: not only does it depend upon some particular horse; it also depends upon a proximal stimulus (some horsish retinal image). Furthermore, we may say that the nomic dependency of the tokening of my HORSE concept upon the particular horse depends itself upon the dependency of my HORSE concept upon the proximal stimulus (my retinal image). If so, then according to the Asymmetrical Dependency Condition, should we not say that what my HORSE concept represents is not horses (or the property of horsehood), but the proximal stimulus, i.e., my retinal image? As pointed out by Fodor (1990c: 109–10), what distinguishes my HORSE concept from my horsish retinal images which serve as links in the causal chain from the distal stimulus to my HORSE concept is the variability of the retinal images by contrast with the stability or constancy of my HORSE concept. In the second chapter, the variability of proximal events helped explain why visual experiences carry information about properties of distal, not proximal, stimuli. Whereas my HORSE concept is *nomically* correlated with horses, the correlation between horses and horsish retinal images is a correlation between horses and a *disjunction* of proximal events. Now, if the proximal events which are correlated with horses constitute an *open* disjunction, then arguably, the correlation is *not* nomic. A disjunction of properties (or predicates) is open or heterogeneous if it involves an infinite set of properties or if we do not know what is common to these properties – what makes them members of the disjunctive class. If a class is disjunctive in this sense, then presumably it is not nomic: it will not occur in nomic correlations. If the correlation between proximal events and horses were not nomic, then we could deflate the proximal stimulus objection by arguing that the nomic dependency between my HORSE concept and horses does *not* asymmetrically depend on any *nomic* dependency between horsish proximal retinal images and horses after all. Horsish retinal images, therefore, would not be candidates for being the contents of my HORSE concept.

This reply cannot, I believe, stand as it is, for it presupposes that the dependency between my horsish retinal images and horses is utterly non-nomic or that the proximal events correlated with horses form an arbitrarily open disjunction. But surely, this cannot be right: even though my HORSE concept is better correlated with (distal) horses than with horsish retinal images – even if there is more variability in my horsish retinal images than in my HORSE concept – still the dependency of my horsish retinal images on horses must be nomic. Horses may be correlated with a disjunction of horsish retinal images. But the disjunction may not be completely or arbitrarily open; the correlation cannot be utterly non-nomic (or anomalous). So the proximal stimulus objection is somewhat of a problem for Fodor's Asymmetrical Dependency Condition.

There is another problem with Fodor's solution, however: there is a sense in which it seems to beg the question or to smack of circularity. Some of Fodor's (1987b: 107–8) formulations do clearly beg the question as when he writes:

> misidentifying a cow as a horse wouldn't have led me to say "horse" *except that there was independently a semantic relation between "horse" tokenings and horses*. But for the fact that the word "horse" expresses the property of *being a horse* (i.e., but for the fact that one calls *horses* "horses"), it would not have been *that* word that taking a cow to be a horse would have caused me to utter. Whereas, by contrast, since "horse" does mean *horse*, the fact that horses cause me to say "horse" does not depend upon there being a semantic – or, indeed, any – connection between "horse" tokenings and cows.

Clearly, appeal to an independent *semantic* relation between a symbol and a property (or instantiations thereof) in a solution to the disjunction problem is ruled out by the naturalistic principle according to which conditions on semanticity must be stated in non-semantic terms. In fact, this objection is not fatal for Fodor can avoid using semantic terms: he can state his Asymmetrical Dependency Condition, as I did above, purely in terms of a higher-order dependency between nomic dependencies.

But the question, then, as noticed by Godfrey-Smith (1989: 539), is whether switching from talk of a "semantic setup" between my HORSE concept and horses to talk of a nomic dependency of my HORSE concept upon horses will avoid begging the question. The problem lies in the *singling out* of the dependency of my HORSE concept upon horses from other dependencies of my HORSE concepts upon the instantiations of other properties. In actual fact, correlations being imperfect as they are, my HORSE concept is maximally correlated with horses, donkeys seen at a distance, and cows on a dark night. Singling out the dependency of my HORSE concept upon horses from the disjunctive class of things with which it is actually correlated looks very much like presupposing the very converse semantic relation between my HORSE concept and horses which we want to explain in non-semantic terms. If we did not presuppose some semantic asymmetry between the fact that my HORSE concept applies correctly to horses, not to non-horses, what reason would we have for distinguishing the converse nomic correlation between my HORSE concept and horses from the other correlations holding between my HORSE concept and either donkeys or cows?

I am not altogether sure whether the circularity which threatens Fodor's Asymmetrical Dependency Condition can be avoided. I am tempted to follow Dretske's (1981, 1993) lead into thinking that the solution to what I call the problem of imperfect correlation lies in a deeper understanding of what in the second chapter I called the problem of channel conditions, i.e., one of the two problems which arise out of the relativity of information. In other words, I think that the way to a solution to the problem of imperfect correlation which would minimize the threat of presupposing intentionality is to remind ourselves that the information carried by a signal does not nomically depend merely upon some environmental condition. Nor does the tokening of a concept merely depend upon the instantiation of a given property. It also depends on channel conditions C. Dretske's solution to the problem of the distinction between channel conditions C and source s's being F was that the obtaining of the former, unlike the obtaining of the latter, does not generate new information for it lacks relevant possible alternatives. A solution to the problem of imperfect correlation requires explaining why a token of my HORSE concept in the presence of a donkey at a distance or a different token of the same concept prompted by a cow on a dark night fail to carry the same information as a third token of the same concept occasioned by a horse in good viewing conditions. So the way to a solution to Fodor's version of the disjunction problem is to make plain why distinct pairings of source and channel conditions can all bring about tokens of the same mental type while explaining at the same time why not all such tokens carry the same information.

3.6 THE TRANSITIVITY PROBLEM

The connection between the problem of imperfect correlation and misrepresentation (or disjunction) was that, although r's being G may be maximally correlated with instantiations of the disjunctive property A *or* B, we none the less want to be able to count B-correlated tokenings of r as *false*. Consider a pair of competing properties involved in the problem of imperfect correlation: for example, the property of being a horse and the property of being a donkey. Along what Godfrey-Smith (1989) has called "the horizontal axis" – i.e., the causal chain leading to the tokening of my HORSE concept – the tokenings of such rival properties in the environment are so to speak equally distant from the mental token. Instantiation of the former is neither more remote (or distal) nor more proximal in the causal chain than instantiation of the latter.[21]

The transitivity problem, however, arises from considering properties at different "horizontal" positions in the causal chain leading to the tokening of the relevant mental representation. It is generated by the existence of chains of reliable correlations. One property will be instantiated at one step in the chain; a competing property will be instantiated at a more remote step in the chain. Signal r's being G

[21] I am using somewhat metaphorically the notion of the distance between the tokening of a property in the environment and the mental token. I do not mean that every instantiated cow which triggers a tokening of my HORSE concept must be at the same distance of my brain as every instantiated horse which also prompts a tokening of my HORSE concept. I don't since I assumed that a cow would have to be seen at a greater distance than a horse to be mistaken for a horse. So what I mean is that they occupy the same abstract position in a chain of causal or nomic dependencies.

nomically depends upon *s*'s being *F* which in turn nomically depends upon *t*'s being *H*. Presumably, then, *r*'s being *G* carries information about *s*'s being *F*. Since *s*'s being *F* nomically depends upon *t*'s being *H*, *r*'s being *G* carries information about *t*'s being *H* too. Again, we have the ingredients of a conjunction, not a disjunction problem.

To illustrate, consider a thermometer. The level of mercury in the glass tube of the thermometer is reliably correlated with the surrounding air temperature, *T*. But now suppose that the surrounding air temperature itself were reliably correlated with atmospheric pressure, *P*.[22] Then the level of mercury in the glass tube would carry not only information about the surrounding temperature *T* but also about atmospheric pressure *P*. Would the thermometer, then, carry information about temperature *T and* atmospheric pressure *P*? Would it carry information about both *T and P*? Now, the instantiation of *P* in the chain leading to a particular level of mercury in the thermometer's glass tube is a sequentially more remote factor than the instantiation of *T*. Given that the instantiation of *P* would be a more remote nomic factor than the instantiation of *T* in bringing the mercury to its level, we may say that the level of mercury in the thermometer carries information about *P* in virtue of the fact that it carries information about *T* and in virtue of the fact that the instantiation of *T* is nomically dependent upon the instantiation of *P*. Importantly, and unlike in the case of imperfect correlation, we do *not* want to consider the fact that the level of mercury carries information about atmospheric pressure if it does, as well as about temperature, as a case of misrepresentation. What happens in the case of the transitivity of nomic dependencies is that we are facing a problem of *indeterminacy*, *not* a problem of *error*.

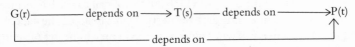

Figure 4 The transitivity problem

I will now succinctly consider the parallel problem of the marine bacteria described by Dretske (1986: 26):

Some marine bacteria have internal magnets (called magnetosomes) that function like compass needles, aligning themselves (and, as a result, the

---

[22] For the sake of simplicity, I am here assuming that the instantiation of a given temperature in a given volume of air nomically depends on air pressure.

bacteria) parallel to the earth's magnetic field. Since these magnetic lines incline downwards (towards geomagnetic north) in the northern hemisphere (upwards in the southern hemisphere), bacteria in the northern hemisphere, oriented by their internal magnesotomes, propel themselves towards geomagnetic north. The survival value of magnetotaxis (as this sensory mechanism is called) is not obvious, but it is reasonable to suppose that it functions so as to enable the bacteria to avoid surface water. Since these organisms are capable of living only in the absence of oxygen, movement towards geomagnetic north will take the bacteria away from oxygen-rich surface water and towards the comparatively oxygen-free sediment at the bottom. Southern-hemispheric bacteria have their magnetosomes reversed, allowing them to swim towards geomagnetic south with the same beneficial results. Transplant a southern bacterium in the North Atlantic and it will destroy itself – swimming upwards (towards magnetic south) into the toxic, oxygen-rich surface water.

Dretske's example of the marine bacteria clearly raises a problem of indeterminacy which I want to treat as a case of transitivity, not a problem of error. And we can see how the indeterminacy involved in a transitivity problem is linked to one side of the problem of the uniqueness of belief contents.

Right now, I merely state my solution to the problem. I will justify it and consider a rival account in the next chapter. In the northern hemisphere, the bacterium's magnetosome is nomically correlated with geomagnetic north, N. In the northern hemisphere, geomagnetic north happens to be correlated with anaerobic (oxygen-poor) water conditions, A, which are beneficial to the bacterium. So the magnetosome indicates property A in virtue of the fact that it indicates property N whose instantiation in turn indicates property A. This is why I say that it is a transitivity problem. Instantiation of property N occurs earlier in the chain of correlations in which the magnetosome is involved than instantiation of property A which is a more remote nomic factor. But evidently, we have a single chain of correlations. So now, what does the magnetosome represent, if anything? When it inclines towards geomagnetic north (N), does it represent N or anaerobic water conditions, A?

Notice that we cannot solve this indeterminacy problem by ruling out the instantiation of N (geomagnetic north) on the ground that it is a proximal event. Nor can we solve it as a problem of imperfect correlation. At the bottom of the solution to the problem of imperfect correlation was the fact that the rival properties are involved in distinct channels of information transmission. But the problem of transitivity arises from the existence of several steps along a single chain of causal or reliable correlations. As I noted above, we do have the intuition that the level of mercury on the glass tube of a thermometer has a job: its job is to detect or carry information about temperature, not atmospheric pressure. This job, however, is the function a human designer with propositional attitudes assigned to the thermometer. My claim is that the transitivity problem of Dretske's marine bacteria cannot receive a purely informational solution. It requires a teleological solution. Only appeal to what I will call the *etiological* function – or design – of the baterium's magnetosome can help us resolve the transitivity problem. The *etiological* function of the bacterium's magnetosome, or so I presently claim, is to covary with, or to carry information about, the whereabouts of the geomagnetic north pole, not the whereabouts of anaerobic water conditions. This is what Dretske (1988) calls an indicator function – an information-carrying function, and, I will argue, it is what the magnetosome was selected for in the course of evolution. Arguing for this claim, however, will have to be postponed until the fourth chapter. Furthermore, I will argue that we should also look at the way the magnetosome contributes to the fitness of the bacterium of which it is a part. This is, as we shall see, the way Millikan (1989b; 1990a,b) looks at the matter. This involves another, though perfectly legitimate, notion of function – which I will call *analytic* function. From the point of view of the magnetosome's analytic indicator function, indicating anaerobic conditions (in virtue of indicating geomagnetic north) becomes relevant. I will argue that the magnetosome can only have its analytic indicator function, though, in virtue of having its etiological indicator function.

In this chapter, I have argued that the problem of imperfect correlation should be distinguished from the problem of transitivity of correlations. Both problems arise from my informational assumptions. For someone who, like Millikan, does not assume that information is a genuine ingredient of representation, the problem of transitivity simply does not arise. Nor should, according to her assumptions, the problem of misrepresentation or the disjunction problem be conceptualized as a problem of imperfect correlation. Now, from an informational standpoint, each problem raises a different challenge. As I said above, unlike the problem of imperfect correlation, the transitivity problem is a problem of indeterminacy. I will try in the next chapter to offer a solution to the transitivity problem based on the notion of indicator function. However, sup-pose we were to con-clude that what is represented by the direction of the northern marine baterium's magnetosome is indeterminate, it would be wrong to con-clude that *ipso facto* the contents (or semantic properties) of a human being's propositional attitudes would thereby be indeterminate too. As I have already mentioned in relation with the intensionality problem, a creature with beliefs must, unlike a bacterium (marine or not), be credited with logical or inferential abilities. A bacterium may detect information. Perhaps its information-carrying states may be credited with representational content (or semantic property). However, to say that the direction of a bacterium's magnetosome may represent geomagnetic north is not to say that the direction of the bac-terium's magnetosome is the content of one of the bacterium's belief states. As we shall see in chapters 5 and 6, the interactions between an individual's propositional attitudes might well exert pressure on their representational contents and thereby contribute to minimizing inde-terminacy.

4

Information and teleology

4.1 TELEOLOGY, ANALYTIC FUNCTIONS, AND ETIOLOGICAL FUNCTIONS

In the last chapter, we examined informationally-based solutions to three problems raised by the semantic properties of beliefs: the insensitivity of belief contents to their informational origins; the intensionality of belief contents; and the problem of misrepresentation. I claimed that the first problem has an informational solution. Informational semantics – or so I argued – elegantly accounts for weak intensionality. It can accommodate strong intensionality so long as the difference between two information-carrying structures can be traced to differences in their compositional features. If we want to distinguish two information-carrying structures of a device containing two primitive constituents, then, I argued, the device must be credited with some logical power not derivable from informational relations between it and the environment. I then went on to distinguish two further problems: one was the problem of misrepresentation (or the disjunction problem) which arises from the imperfection of nomic correlations; the other one was the problem of indeterminacy – a conjunction problem – which arises from the transitivity of correlations. I argued that, on my informational assumptions, only the former, not the latter, can receive a purely informational solution. The latter, I claimed, requires a teleological solution, i.e., an appeal to functions.

Arguing for this claim amounts to a defense of a mixed approach to the transitivity problem: an informationally based teleological theory. I have discussed informational semantics at length in the second and third chapter. But I have said next to nothing about teleological approaches. I must, therefore, present the basis of the teleological approach which I want to endorse and which I want to combine with

105

the informational approach to provide a solution to what I call the problem of transitivity.

I will first succinctly express my endorsement of a teleological framework based on a very elegant view of functions and function-ascriptions – the *etiological* view – due to the philosopher Larry Wright (cf. Wright 1973, 1976), and which has been much discussed and refined in recent years by a number of philosophers of biology and philosophers of mind (such as Millikan, Neander, Godfrey-Smith, and others). I will then argue in favor of a "modest" or "minimalist" stimulus-based teleosemantic solution to the transitivity problem of Dretske's marine bacteria. This stimulus-based teleosemantic approach steers a middle course between Fodor's (1990a,b) anti-teleological stance and Millikan's benefit-based teleosemantics. In the process, I will contrast it with Millikan's rival benefit- or consumer-based teleo-semantic approach. I will thirdly defend the informationally based teleosemantic account from an alleged conflict with adaptationist constraints. I will finally defend the informationally based teleological account against the misdirected criticisms of Fodor (1990b).

Following Millikan (1989) and Godfrey-Smith (1993), I will assume that the concept of a function can be at the service of two different, though possibly complementary explanatory projects, one of which could be called the project of "functional analysis" and the other of which could be called the "etiological" project. I will argue that both projects are relevant to teleosemantics: they complement each other the way a top-down approach to an item's function relates to a bottom-up approach.

On Cummins' (1975) view, as more generally in the functionalist literature in the philosophy of mind, providing a functional analysis consists in showing how a complex system manages to perform a complex task by analyzing (decomposing) the complex task of the complex system into simpler tasks which can be accomplished by simpler (ultimately primitive) sub-systems. Cummins (1975) has linked an item's having a function to the role of the item in accounting for the capacity of the whole system of which the item is a component to perform a complex task. On this view, the job of a functional or, as he calls it, an "analytic" explanation[1] is to explain the contribution made by a component of a system to some complex capacity exhibited

---

[1] Cummins (1983) draws a contrast between the Hempelian D-N (or I-S) model of explanation as subsumption under law and his notion of analytic explanation.

by the system. As emphasized by Millikan (1989a), this view makes an element's function depend on its *current* dispositions, not on its historical properties. By reference to Cummins' clarification of the notion of an analytic explanation, I will call *analytic* the function of an item as it contributes to a complex task performed by the complex system to which it belongs. Obviously, in order to determine an item's analytic function, one has to know something of the complex task of the encompassing system to which the item belongs. I will argue that the analytic function of an information-carrying state is relevant to Millikan's benefit-based teleosemantic approach.[2]

On the etiological view, the function of a device is, in Wright's (1973) words, something the device does which can "account for its being there." Wright (1976: 81) has offered the following illuminatingly simple definition of function:

The function of X is Z iff:

   (i) Z is a consequence (result) of X's being there,

   (ii) X is there because it does (results in) Z.[3]

In other words, a device X has function Z iff Z is some effect produced by X which helps explain why X is present or why X persists. The very fact that X does Z explains why X exists or persists, where device X can be an artefact or a biological organ as well.

A device X can generally produce several different effects. Only one of them, however, is the device's etiological function.[4] To borrow

---

[2] I am going to call the notion of function appropriate for functional analysis the "analytic" notion of function. This view of functional analysis fits in with functionalism and the notion of a functional property in the philosophy of mind. See chapters 6–7. One motivation for adopting Cummins' view of functional analysis in the philosophy of mind is the hope that functional analysis so construed will allow us to explain the performance of complex cognitive tasks without relying on intelligent homunculi.

[3] I am going to call the etiological notion of function "etiological" function. Since I assume a metaphysical realist picture of causal relations and nomic dependencies, I assume that the seemingly intentional notions in Wright's definition (expressed by locutions such as "is a consequence of" or "because") can be explained away naturalistically.

[4] Admittedly, it is a simplification to claim that a device has only one etiological function. As will emerge in section 3, one and the same biological device may have several functions hierarchically organized: something may do X by (or in virtue of) doing Y, and so on.

examples from Wright (1973: 349), a telephone facilitates communication among humans; it also takes up space on one's desk; it absorbs and reflects light; it wakes one up at night. The etiological function of a telephone, however, is to facilitate human communication, not to take up space, not to absorb and reflect light, nor to wake one up at night. A heart pumps blood; it produces a thumping noise; it makes wiggly lines on electrocardiograms. The etiological function of a heart, however, is to pump blood, not to make a thumping noise, nor to make wiggly lines on electrocardiograms. According to the etiological account, hearts pump blood and the fact that this is something they do explains why hearts (still) exist or why creatures having a heart have survived and proliferated. On the etiological theory, an item's (etiological) function depends on *historical* properties of the item. In the following, I will simply assume with Millikan (1989a) and Godfrey-Smith (1993) that there is explanatory room for both – Cummins' analytic style and Wright's etiological style – notions of a function. In fact, I am going to argue that we need both and that an appropriate teleological account of the indeterminacy raised by the transitivity of correlations must appeal to both notions of function.

Both the etiological function of an artefact and the etiological function of a biological organ (or trait) can be seen as the result of some *selection* process. In the case of an artefact, the selection will generally result from an intentional process involving a (human) designer with propositional attitudes. In the case of an animal's or a plant's biological trait (or organ), however, the selection process results from the action of natural selection at work on the biological evolution of the species to which the plant or the animal belongs. Given our interest in information-carrying structures and representations, however, nothing precludes extending the etiological account of function to representations acquired through a process of individual learning. Innate information-carrying structures and representations present in a plant or an animal will result from the process of natural selection at work in the evolution of the species. Acquired representations will be selected via an individual process of learning.[5]

Arguably, as noticed by Godfrey-Smith (1989: 542–3), what results

---

[5] For discussion of the causal role of innate and acquired representations in the production of intentional behavior, see chapter 8.

from the action of natural selection are not particular representational states of a plant or an animal (such as beliefs in a human being). What natural selection shapes are an individual's mechanisms (e.g., belief-forming mechanisms) responsible for the production of particular representational states (such as particular beliefs). What is produced by natural selection is an individual's belief-forming capacity, not an individual's particular beliefs. What is presumably adaptive, for an organism, is to have, for example, a visual system, not to enjoy any particular visual experience. On this view, no particular sensory experience nor any particular belief in an animal can result directly from natural selection. Only an animal's sensory mechanism (his visual, auditory, or olfactory system) can arise out of natural selection. This is what Millikan (1984) calls *direct proper* function. However, following Millikan (1984) and Dretske (1995), one may, I take it, assume that particular (experiential or belief) states can derive their function from the function of their producing mechanism. As Millikan (1986: 56–57) puts it:

> Not only body organs and systems but also various states and activities of these organs and systems have proper functions. Consider a chameleon. Its skin contains a system whose job is to arrange pigmented matter in such a way that the chameleon will match whatever it is sitting on at the moment. Obvious further proper functions of this system are to arrange that the chameleon will be invisible to predators and hence will avoid being eaten. If we look at any particular color pattern that characterizes any particular chameleon at a particular time, we can say what the proper functions of this pattern are, even though it is possible (though unlikely) that no chameleon has ever displayed just this particular kind of pattern before. The proper functions of the pattern are to make the chameleon invisible and to prevent it from being eaten – functions that it derives from the proper functions of the mechanisms that produced it.[6]

On this view, then, producing mechanisms have a primary proper function; states may have derived (or adapted) proper functions.

Etiological function attributions refer to what a device is *supposed* to do: what the device has been selected for doing. A device's

---

[6] Notice that in order to ascribe to a particular colored pattern of the chameleon's skin a derived proper function, Millikan must appeal to something like the notion of analytic function, i.e., the contribution of a particular state of the chameleon's skin to the survival of the whole chameleon. This point will be relevant later.

etiological function is something it is the device's job to do. This normative dimension of functions has been abundantly emphasized by Millikan, who has drawn a contrast between what a device is supposed to do and what it is statistically normal for a device to do. In the case of an artifact's function, the job of the artifact is usually, though not always, something which has been assigned by a human designer with propositional attitudes. I say an artifact's function is not always assigned by a human designer for two reasons. On the one hand, a person who uses an artifact and who is not the artifact's designer may assign a function different from the function originally assigned by the designer. On the other hand, some artifacts (e.g., dams and nests) are produced by creatures (e.g., beavers and birds) of which it is controversial to say that they possess propositional attitudes. Consider a biological organ or a cognitive trait present in an organism. Its job is something which corresponding traits or organs present in ancestors of the organism did in the past and which contributed to the survival and proliferation of the ancestors. The important point is that an organ or trait may have an etiological function and yet not be able to perform it properly – if, for example, it is malformed. A person's heart may be malformed. A malformed heart may not be able to pump blood properly even though pumping blood is its etiological function. Pumping blood is its etiological function because ancestors of the person whose heart it is had hearts which pumped blood and their doing so in the past explains why the ancestors who had hearts in the past survived and proliferated.

As I just said, etiological function attributions have a normative dimension. As Millikan (1986) has pointed out, unlike biological organs and biological systems, there is nothing like failing to perform its job at the level of basic physics and chemistry. An electron cannot fail to gravitate around the nucleus of a hydrogen atom. Nor can a molecule (organic or inorganic) fail to preserve the bonds between its constitutive atoms. If and when it does, it turns into a new molecule. Unlike an electron, an atom or a molecule, an individual's visual system, his or her auditory system, his or her cardio-vascular system, or his or her kidney may well fail to do what they are supposed to do. This is what it means to talk of biological norms.

Note that such biological norms, if they exist, differ from other (ethical or esthetical) norms. For example, as reported by Dawkins

(1995), some female digger wasps lay their eggs in a caterpillar. Before doing so, they carefully insert their sting into each ganglion of their prey's central nervous system so as to paralyze it without killing it. "This way, the meat stays fresh for the growing larva." "It is not known," says Dawkins (1995: 80), "whether the paralysis acts as a general anesthestic or if it is like curare in just freezing the victim's ability to move. If the latter, the prey might be aware of being eaten alive from inside but unable to move a muscle to do anything about it." This is, from a biological point of view, normal parasitic behavior on the part of the digger wasp. However, whether or not the paralysis acts as a general anesthetic, it is not what we might call a good thing, let alone a good thing for the caterpillar. From the fact that something *x* is biologically normal, it does not follow that *x* is good.

4.2 FUNCTIONS AND INTENTIONALITY

Some philosophers – Dennett (1987c) and notably Searle (1992) – have expressed variously radical doubts towards the teleosemantic approach according to which some of the features of the semantic properties of an individual's propositional attitudes are to be derived from what I shall call etiological indicator functions of the individual's information-carrying states. If etiological functions are "in the eye of the beholder" (with propositional attitudes), then the project of deriving some of the semantic properties of an individual's propositional attitudes from etiological indicator functions could not satisfy naturalistic constraints. Searle's critique seems more radical than Dennett's. I will argue, however, that properly construed, their views are closer than it may seem at first glance and that they do not constitute a significant threat for the naturalistic teleosemantic project.

Dennett's (1987b) real target is the distinction between derived and underived (or original) intentionality, i.e., the view that semanticity has, as it were, a rock bottom from which all other semantic properties can be said to flow – an assumption central to Searle. Evolutionary biology deals with the attribution of etiological functions to living organisms and their organs. According to Dennett (1983), what he calls "adaptationism" in evolutionary biology relies on optimality assumptions. Furthermore, optimality assumptions are to evolutionary biology what rationality assumptions are to psychology. Rationality assumptions in the interpretation and ascription of propositional attitudes are involved in justifying the intentional stance in psychology. Dennett's (1983) view, then, is that "adaptationism" in evolutionary biology is just the adoption of the intentional stance in biology. If so, then etiological function ascriptions in biology may depend on adopting the intentional stance.

In chapter 1, I distinguished two components in the intentional stance as it applies to the attribution of semantic properties to an individual's propositional attitudes: one component, which I labelled "non-factualism," conflicted – or so I claimed – with intentional realism; the other component, which I labelled "patternalism," could be reconciled – or so I claimed – with a meta-representational view of the mind, which I assumed to be consistent with intentional realism. According to patternalism, only from a certain stance – the intentional stance – can patterns relating propositional attitudes and intentional behavior be discerned. Similarly, we may distinguish two ingredients in Dennett's view of etiological function ascriptions. On the one hand, if Dennett were to argue for a non-factualist interpretation of etiological function ascriptions in biology, then this view would conflict with the realist assumption that predicates used in the ascription of etiological functions may express genuine objective properties of organs. On the other hand, the counterpart to "patternalism" in biology can, it seems to me, be reconciled with a realist view of the possession of etiological functions. The view that only from a certain stance – only by making certain optimality assumptions – can one discern etiological functions does not force anyone to embrace the puzzling view that it is only a matter of stance whether, for example, a heart's etiological function is to pump blood or not.

Searle (1992) claims that "the hard, brute, blind, physical facts" make it true that the heart pumps blood, makes a thumping noise, and exerts gravitational attraction on the moon. But no such fact, according to him, can make it true that the function of the heart is to pump blood. Claims of biological function are, on his (1992: 52) view, "always made relative to an observer who assigns a normative value to the causal processes." "In addition to its various causal relations, the heart does not have any function. When we speak of its functions, we are talking about those of its causal relations to which we attach some *normative* importance" (*ibid.*: 238).

First, it is worth noticing that there is an asymmetry between

Searle's attitude (or stance) towards causal relations and his attitude (or stance) towards etiological functions. On his view, metaphysical realism is an appropriate standpoint vis-à-vis causal relations, not vis-à-vis etiological functions. This asymmetry, it seems to me, presupposes that the etiological theory of functions cannot be correct, since according to the etiological theory of functions, the relation between, for example, a heart and its etiological function (i.e., pumping blood) is nothing but a causal relation which has been singled out from among many other causal relations involving the heart and many other of its effects. So it is incumbent upon Searle to argue that it is wrong to assume – as does the etiological theorist of functions – that a subset of the set of causal relations in which a heart is involved can be singled out and promoted to the role of function by a non-intentional process, such as the process of natural selection.

Second, as I mentioned in chapter 2, Searle (1992) assumes the priority of consciousness over intentionality. He further assumes the priority of intentionality over (etiological) function. Now, there are, it seems to me, two ways one can understand the claim that etiological function-ascriptions are always intentionality-relative or relative to a conscious agent with propositional attitudes. One radical construal of this view would be the claim that it is quite wrong to assume that Harvey *discovered* that the function of the heart is to pump blood. On this view, then, what we ought to say is that Harvey's contribution was to "attach normative importance" to the fact that the heart pumps blood, as opposed to the fact that it makes a thumping noise. This quite unreasonable interpretation is presumably one which Searle would not accept. A weaker (and more plausible) construal of the claim that etiological function ascriptions are relative to a conscious agent with propositional attitudes is the view that Harvey's discovery that the heart's etiological function is to pump blood was made against the background of a set of shared biological norms according to which normative importance has been assigned to, for example, life and survival. The weaker claim would be that ascriptions of etiological functions – unlike statements of causal relations – possess truth-conditions only relative to a set of biological norms which in turn presuppose conscious agents with propositional attitudes.

My own view is that biological norms of functioning and misfunctiong are not presupposed by ascriptions of etiological functions. Rather, biological norms arise from etiological functions. On the

113

etiological view of functions, a biological organ (e.g., a heart) gets its function (e.g., pumping blood) from a process of selection which promotes or singles out the causal relation between heart beats and pumping blood from among other causal relations involving heart beats. If biological norms arise from etiological functions, and if etiological functions do arise from a non-intentional process of selection, then biological norms may differ from other non-biological norms – such as ethical and esthetical norms – in that the former, unlike the latter, do not presuppose conscious agents with propositional attitudes. As Neander (1995a) has argued, the claim that a normal heart ought to pump blood is not the same as the claim that pumping blood is a good thing – even though it is both true that a well functioning heart ought to pump blood and that pumping blood is a good thing.[7] Now, if we drop the assumption that biological norms presuppose conscious agents with propositional attitudes, then the weaker construal of Searle's view seems to reduce to the counterpart of Dennett's patternalism for biology: only from a certain stance can etiological functions be discerned. And this, I claim, is an insight which can be reconciled with a realist view of biological functions.

4.3 TRANSITIVITY, MISREPRESENTATION, STIMULUS, AND BENEFIT

Let us reexamine Dretske's magnetosome example from the end of the third chapter. Some marine bacteria in the northern hemisphere have magnetosomes (little magnets) which work like compass needles and nomically covary with the direction of geomagnetic north. As it happens, in the northern hemisphere, moving towards geomagnetic north is moving away from oxygen-rich surface water to anaerobic (oxygen-free) water areas. In the southern hemisphere, anaerobic conditions coincide with geomagnetic south and southern hemispheric bacteria have their magnetosomes reversed. Does the alignment of the magnetosome in a northern bacterium – if it represents anything – represent geomagnetic north, N? Or does it represent anaerobic conditions, A? I will argue that this innocent looking question is actually ambiguous and that, depending on one's prior assump-

---

[7] As Dawkins' (1995) example of the digger wasp behavior shows, not all biologically normal behavior is a good thing, at least not for every creature.

tions, it can be used to raise two distinct problems: a transitivity problem and a problem of misrepresentation. As I said at the end of chapter 3, the two problems are distinct problems because they have distinct logical structure: whereas a misrepresentation problem is a disjunction problem, a transitivity problem is a conjunction problem. And conjunction problems are best construed as indeterminacy problems, not as problems of error. My main goal in the present section will be to argue that this being so, a purported solution to the problem of misrepresentation could not prevail as a solution to the transitivity problem; nor could the former supplant the latter.

From the informational semantic assumptions made in chapters 2 and 3, it follows first that the alignment of the magnetosome of a northern bacterium nomically depends upon N, the direction of geomagnetic north; and it follows secondly that, in the northern hemisphere, the direction of geomagnetic north N covaries with A, anaerobic water conditions. It, therefore, follows that, in the northern hemisphere, N, the direction of geomagnetic north, carries information about (or indicates) A, the direction of anaerobic conditions. Information (or indication) being a transitive relation, it follows from informational semantic assumptions that the alignment of the magnetosome of a northern bacterium carries information about (or indicates) both N and A. Now, we might want to order the informational relation and say that the alignment of the magnetosome indicates N more strongly than A since it indicates N directly and A indirectly: it carries information about A in virtue of carrying information about N, and not vice-versa. Ordering the informational relation would allow us, therefore, to distinguish between weaker and stronger indication relations between the alignment of a northern bacterium's magnetosome and instantiations of respectively N and A. Although there is an insight in this ordering relation, it is, I think, insufficient to solve the transitivity problem: the alignment of the magnetosome still carries information about both N and A.

At the heart of the informationally based teleosemantic approach to the transitivity problem which I would like to recommend is the distinction made by Neander (1995a) between the *stimulus* and the *benefit*. I presently want to argue that acceptance of informational constraints on representation and the etiological view of functions converge in favor of an informationally based teleosemantic solution to the transitivity problem which has affinities with a teleosemantic approach which Cummins (1989: 72–75) has labelled "conservative," which Dretske (1986) calls "modest" (as opposed to "inflated"), and which could be called a stimulus-based, as opposed to a benefit-based, teleosemantic approach.

In the case of the northern marine bacterium, the stimulus of the magnetosome is N, the direction of geomagnetic north; the benefit is A, the direction of anaerobic conditions. According to the etiological theory of functions, the etiological function of a device is something which the device *does*, a fortiori something the device *can* do. Now, if we combine this view of etiological functions with informational constraints, then, as Dretske (1986: 32) has put it, it follows that the magnetosome is "after all, a *magneto*tactic, not a *chemo*tactic, sensor": what the magnetosome of a northern bacterium can detect – what it nomically covaries with – are instantiations of N, not of A. Magnetotactic detection of property N, not chemotactic detection of property A, is something magnetosomes in ancestor marine bacteria in the northern hemisphere could do and did in the past which explains why ancestor marine bacteria with a magnetosome did better than marine bacteria without a magnetosome and for which oxygen-rich water conditions too were lethal. In other words, instantiations of N, not instantiations of A, can serve as (distal) stimuli for the magnetosome of a northern bacterium. If we, furthermore, assume that what the alignment of the magnetosome represents is what it is its etiological function to indicate (or carry information about), then the modest stimulus-(informationally)-based teleosemantic solution to the northern bacterium's transitivity problem is that the alignment of the magnetosome represents N. Although the alignment of the magnetosome carries information about both N and A, it represents N, not A. This, I want to argue, remains true once we recognize that what is beneficial to a northern bacterium is to detect A, anaerobic conditions.

On this view, then, what the northern bacterium benefits from is A, not N. But what the alignment of the magnetosome of a northern bacterium has the etiological function to indicate – and therefore, what it represents – is N, not A. To assume that the etiological indicator function of the magnetosome is to carry information about A, the whereabouts of anaerobic conditions, would be, as Dretske (1986) puts it, to "inflate" its etiological function. Dretske's (1986; 1988) general informationally based framework should, I think, incline him towards accepting the above "modest" or stimulus-based teleo-semantic approach to the transitivity problem. In response to queries of Stich's (1990b), Dretske (1990a: 826) has in effect endorsed the "modest" stimulus-informationally-based teleosemantic approach as a general solution to transitivity problems:

> ... when an indicator, C, indicates both F and G, and its indication of G is via its indication of F ..., then despite the fact that it is the existence of G that is most directly relevant to explaining C's recruitment as a cause of M (F is relevant only in so far as it indicates that G exists), C acquires the function of indicating that F. It is F – the (as it were) maximally indicated state – that C comes to *represent*.

What further militates in favor of this stimulus-informationally-based teleosemantic approach to the problem of transitivity is what could be called the principle of *shared responsibility*: as Dretske (1986: 30) has put it, "getting things right ... is often a shared responsibility." It is not the function of a gas gauge to see to it that the liquid in the gas tank is gasoline; it is our responsibility. When one reads one's watch to know what time it is, it is not one's eye's responsibility to keep the clock from running slow. Similarly, it could be said, even though the bacterium benefits from anaerobic conditions, A, it is not the responsibility of the magnetosome to see to it that the direction of geomagnetic north N coincides with A.

Still, Dretske has expressed his fear that, if we adopt this stimulus-informationally-based solution to the transitivity problem, then we run the risk of depriving ourselves of the possibility of ever describing what the bacterium does as a case of misrepresentation. Dretske (1986: 32) puts his worry this way (where the predicate "mean_n" stands for Grice's notion of natural meaning or indication):

> A northern bacterium (transplanted in the southern hemisphere) will not be misrepresenting anything when, under the guidance of its magne-totactic sensor, it moves upwards (towards geomagnetic north) into the lethal surface water. The alignment of its magnetosomes will mean_n what it has always meant_n, what it is its function to mean_n: namely that *that* is the direction of magnetic north. The disaster can be blamed on the abnormal surroundings. Nor can we salvage some residual misrepresentational capacity by supposing that the bacterium, under the influence of a bar magnet, at least misrepresents the direction of geomagnetic

north. For, once again, the same problem emerges: why suppose it is the function of this mechanism to indicate the direction of geomagnetic north rather than simply, the direction of the surrounding magnetic field?

In this passage, Dretske advances two reasons why adopting the "modest" stimulus-based solution to the transitivity problem might deprive us of ever being able to describe what the bacterium does as a case of misrepresentation. One is that, although a northern bacterium transplanted in the southern hemisphere would die from moving into oxygen-rich surface water, we should say that its magnetosome was not misrepresenting the direction of geomagnetic north. I do not think it absurd to say that the magnetosome of a northern bacterium transplanted in the southern hemisphere is doing its job when it is indicating the direction of geomagnetic north and "blame" the environment. After all, the magnetosome derived its etiological indicator function in the northern hemisphere where the direction of geomagnetic north coincided with anaerobic water conditions – a coincidence which no longer obtains in the southern hemisphere.

Dretske's second reason may look more problematic. If we say that the etiological function of the magnetosome of a northern bacterium is to indicate the direction of geomagnetic north, we are saying that northern ancestors of the bacterium which had such an information-carrying magnetosome in the past did better at surviving than competing northern bacteria which did not have such an information-carrying device. It does not follow that the *etiological function* of such magnetosomes is to indicate whatever magnetic field happens to be produced by a nearby bar magnet. But even so, suppose that the "modest" stimulus-based solution to the transitivity problem did force us to concede that, were it to indicate the presence of a bar magnet, the magnetosome would not be misrepresenting anything. I do not think it would even follow that misrepresentation would be impossible. The magnetosome, after all, could wear out; it could misfunction, out of age and deterioration, and then fail to indicate the presence of a bar magnet.

Although Dretske clearly recognizes that, on his informational assumptions, the magnetosome example is primarily a transitivity problem, this passage is misleading because it contributes to blurring the distinction between the two problems: the transitivity problem –

which is both a conjunction problem and a problem of indeterminacy – and the problem of misrepresentation – which is a disjunction problem. First of all, as I just said, I do not think that a stimulus-informationally-based solution to the northern bacterium's transitivity problem precludes the possibility of describing what a northern bacterium transplanted in the southern hemisphere would do as a case of misrepresentation. Secondly, it would be a mistake to expect that a solution to the transitivity problem ought to be a solution to the problem of misrepresentation.

Conversely, it would, on my view, be a mistake to expect a solution to, or perhaps a dissolution of, the northern bacterium's transitivity problem from a solution to the problem of misrepresentation. Let me now argue for this latter claim. Consider Millikan's *consumerist* theory – a theory, by the way, which repudiates any informational basis (or component). Millikan (1989b: 92) sees it as a virtue of her consumer- or as I shall say *benefit*-oriented teleosemantic approach that it "cleanly bypasse[s] the whole genre of causal-informational accounts of mental contents." On her (*ibid.*: 93) view:

> What the magnetosome represents is only what its *consumers* require that it correspond to in order to perform *their* tasks. Ignore, then, how the representation . . . is normally produced. Concentrate instead on how the systems that react to the representation work, on what these systems need in order to do their job. What they need is only that the pull be in the direction of oxygen-free water at the time. For example, they care not at all how it came about that the pull is in that direction . . . What the magnetosome represents, then, is univocal; it represents only the direction of oxygen-free water. For that is the only thing that corresponds . . . to it, the absence of which would matter, the absence of which would disrupt the function of those mechanisms that rely on the magnetosome for guidance.

Millikan's purely teleological approach has been called "liberal" by Cummins (1989: 72–75); it can legitimately be called a *consumer* or *benefit* teleosemantic approach for it is based on a clear-cut division between two sub-systems: a representation-producer and a representation-consumer. In the case of the northern marine bacterium, the producer is the magnetosome. But what the (rest of the) bacterium needs to know for the bacterium to survive – what contributes to maximizing the bacterium's overall inclusive fitness – is the whereabouts of anaerobic conditions. The teleosemantic principle that the organism's benefit – what the consumers of the representation need to know to perform their tasks – dictates function, and, therefore, representational content, neatly avoids any indeterminacy: the alignment of the magnetosome represents anaerobic conditions. Not only does it avoid any indeterminacy, but it simultaneously accounts for the problem of misrepresentation. Consider again a northern marine bacterium transplanted in the southern hemisphere. The alignment of the magnetosome with geomagnetic north will fatally orient the bacterium towards toxic surface water rich in oxygen. On this consumer-based (or benefit-based) teleosemantic account, the northern bacterium will then be credited with the power to misrepresent its environment: it was the job of the magnetosome to represent the direction of anaerobic conditions. The magnetosome of a northern bacterium transplanted in the southern hemisphere, then, misrepresents oxygen-rich surface water as anaerobic conditions. The consumer-based (or benefit-based) teleosemantic approach seems at once to avoid indeterminacy and to solve the problem of misrepresentation.

The first thing to notice, I think, is that the consumer- or benefit-based teleosemantic approach is a top-down approach to the magnetosome's function: it relies on what I called above the *analytic* notion of function. It is the analytic function of the magnetosome to contribute to the complex task performed by the whole bacterium, i.e., maximizing its overall fitness or survival, which involves finding anaerobic conditions. It is my contention that the magnetosome does have both the above analytic function of contributing to maximizing the inclusive fitness of the nothern marine bacterium and it has the etiological function of indicating the direction of geomagnetic north. The magnetosome contributes to maximizing the inclusive fitness of the northern marine bacterium in virtue of the fact that it has the analytic function of indicating the direction of anaerobic conditions. It has the latter analytic indicator function in virtue of the fact that it has the etiological function to indicate the direction of geomagnetic north. As Neander (1995a) has argued, biological functions may have several descriptions which are linked by a "by" relation (or a "in virtue of" relation). As the following example from Neander (*ibid.*) will illustrate, functions may form hierarchical structures: a trait in an antelope population may have altered the structure of the hemoglobin, causing thereby higher oxygen uptake in the antelope, which allowed the antelope to survive at higher ground which had adaptive value for the antelope or contributed to its inclusive fitness. One and the same trait in the antelope may have

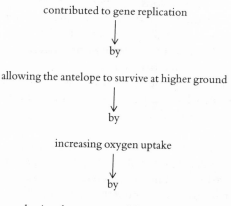

contributed to gene replication

↓

by

allowing the antelope to survive at higher ground

↓

by

increasing oxygen uptake

↓

by

altering the structure of the hemoglobin

Figure 5   From Neander (1995a: 115)

Assuming, then, that the magnetosome's etiological indicator function is to carry information about *N*, the direction of geomagnetic north, its analytic indicator function is to represent *A*, the direction of anaerobic conditions. Notice that it is the magnetosome's analytic function, not its etiological function, to indicate *A*. But the magnetosome in a northern bacterium derives its analytic function to indicate *A* from three facts: (i) from the fact that it has the etiological function to indicate *N*; (ii) from the fact that, in the northern hemisphere, *N* covaries with *A*; and (iii) from the fact that indicating *A* contributes to maximizing the northern bacterium's inclusive fitness (or replication of its genes).

The second thing to notice is that it would be a mistake to conclude from the benefit-oriented purely teleosemantic solution to the problem of misrepresentation that the transitivity problem is a pseudo-problem or that it ought to be dissolved (rather than solved). The benefit-oriented purely teleosemantic approach is an alternative to the informational approach to the problem of misrepresentation (what I labelled earlier the problem of imperfect correlation). On the benefit-based purely teleosemantic approach to misrepresentation, the transitivity problem simply does not arise since it only arises from the assumptions that the bacterium's magnetosome carries information about N and that the latter covaries with A. Since Millikan does not accept these assumptions, no transitivity problem arises on her approach. But it would be wrong, I think, to argue from the benefit-based purely teleosemantic approach to the problem of misrepresentation that the transitivity problem has thereby been dissolved. Given that we may agree that representing A is the magnetosome's analytic function, the question is: should we sacrifice informational semantics? To see why not, I want to consider reasons why a purely teleosemantic approach devoid of any informational basis might be puzzling.

First of all, following Millikan's recommendation, suppose we were to "ignore how the representation is normally produced," then we will simply bypass the difference between the way a magnetosome works in a northern bacterium and the way it works in a southern bacterium. Remember: in a northern bacterium, the magnetosome aligns the bacterium with the direction of geomagnetic north, whereas in a southern bacterium, the magnetosome aligns the bacterium with the direction of geomagnetic south. Why should this difference be left out, given the fact that a southern bacterium transplanted in the northern hemisphere will destroy itself and vice-versa?

Secondly, the benefit- or consumer-based teleosemantic account leaves us, I think, with a homunculus puzzle: the theory puts the burden of determining content on the interpretive power of the consumer sub-system. The view is that we can disregard the mechanisms which produce the state with representational property. We can, therefore, disregard the fact that the magnetosome is a magnetotactic, not a chemotactic device. What confers onto a state its function and representational power is what the consumer sub-system needs to know to perform its own task. How could a sub-system, which is going to use a representation, endow it retroactively so to speak with its own "knowledge"? Ironically perhaps, the consumer- or benefit-oriented teleosemantic view has affinities with an interpretivist projectivist view of content: the semantic property is projected onto a state by a consumer sub-system which "knows" things which the producer sub-system does not, no matter what the causal powers of the producing mechanism are. This, it seems to me, reinstates some of the mystery of teleology which the etiological theory had elegantly dissipated.

Millikan (1990b) considers the case of hoverflies. Female hoverflies cruise at a standard velocity; male hoverflies "spend much of the day hovering in one spot . . . ready to dart instantly after any passing female that they sight." The male hoverfly, however, responds quite indiscriminately to distal objects other than female hoverflies (including pebbles, distant birds, and even jet planes). On Millikan's (1990b: 222) benefit-based teleosemantic view, none the less, the male hoverfly obeys the "distal hoverfly rule": "If you see a female, catch it." Her reason is that "it was only when ancestor hoverflies conformed to the distal hoverfly rule that they *became* ancestors" (*ibid.*: 223). It is true that, only catching a female hoverfly, not catching distant birds and jet planes, contributed to the proliferation of ancestor hoverflies. But the problem, as Neander (1995a: 126–27) points out, is: "Why stop there?"

> It had to be a female hoverfly, certainly not a bird or a jet-plane . . . It was only the female hoverflies which were caught and fertile and survived long enough to lay eggs, which in turn hatched into viable offspring, which were also fertile, and so on, that were actually causally efficacious. In other words, taken as is, the standard [benefit-based] teleological approach implies that our lusty hoverfly misrepresents if he chases an infertile female or one who is soon to be the dinner of some passing bat.

What is puzzling on Millikan's benefit-based purely teleological approach is that the male hoverfly should not presumably be credited with the *perceptual* ability to detect whether its prospective mate "is about to be gobbled up" or whether it "carries nasty diseases or is infertile." But on her approach, there seems to be no reason why the male hoverfly should not be credited with such abilities. But then, if the male hoverfly does have such perceptual abilities, it becomes a mystery why it ever chases distant birds, let alone jet planes. In terms of our principle of shared responsibility, it is no more the responsibility of a northern bacterium's magnetosome to make sure that the direction of geomagnetic north coincides with the direction of anaerobic conditions than it is the responsibility of the hoverfly perceptual system to make sure that what it detects is a catchable fertile female hoverfly not about to be gobbled up. As Millikan (1990a: 127) puts it, on the etiological theory of function, the function of a representation producer must be something the producer can do or *effect*. However, it is no objection to the stimulus-informationally-based teleosemantic account that "the magnetotactic system does not help to effect that the tug of the magnet coincides with the presence of the surround of water." It is no objection, because, according to the principle of shared responsibility, it is not the magnetosome's job to make sure that there is water in the direction of geomagnetic north. Nor is it the magnetosome's job to make sure that the direction of geomagnetic north indicates in turn (or coincides with) the presence of anaerobic conditions.

In the next section, I will examine arguments purporting to show that informational constraints on teleosemantics might be counteradaptive. And as I will argue at the end of the next section (again at the end of chapter 8), taking seriously this modest or stimulus-informationally-based teleosemantic solution implies an amendment to what Dretske (1988: 96) has called "the Design Problem." In the last section, turning to Fodor's critique of teleology, I will try and defend a claim I made earlier that, unlike the informational relation, the etiological indicator function of a device is not transitive.[8]

4.4 IS INFORMATIONALLY BASED TELEOSEMANTICS COUNTERADAPTIVE?

In arguing for the above modest stimulus-based teleosemantic solution to the bacterium's transitivity problem, I have embraced a broadly evolutionary framework. For my solution to the bacterium's transitivity problem to be consistent with this broadly evolutionary framework, it must be shown that it is adaptive for the bacterium to have evolved a magnetotactic device whose function it is to carry information about geomagnetic north. When I talk of biological adaptation, I mean to be talking of some biological change in an individual organism or in a species which results from a selective process. The selective process may be natural selection as it works upon the phylogenetic evolution of a species or the ontogenetic development of an individual organism. What an adaptive change results in is some improvement in the overall fit between the organism and its environment. An adaptation, in this sense, may, therefore, improve the cogni-

---

[8] A claim which is central to my purported solution to the transitivity problem.

tive architecture or equipment of an organism. As Godfrey-Smith (1992: 296) points out, adaptation so conceived does not imply that "every character of every organism is an *optimal* [my emphasis] solution to a particular problem posed by the environment." Adaptationism, therefore, does not presuppose that, given some problem, there exists a uniquely best cognitive architecture or solution better than all other possible cognitive architectures or solutions.

Millikan (1989b: 85; 1990a: 127–29), who advocates the benefit-consumer alternative teleosemantic view, has claimed that informationally based solutions are not compatible with an adaptationist point of view. Millikan's strategy against informationally based teleo-semantic views is reminiscent of some of Stich's (1990a) criticisms directed at reliabilism in epistemology – which is not surprising given the roots of informational semantics in reliabilism in epistemology. Stich (1990a) argued that natural selection might favor less reliable over more reliable belief-forming mechanisms on the ground that the reliability of a belief-forming mechanism is only one ingredient in the inclusive fitness of a cognitive system. On the one hand, Millikan argues that indicators ("natural signs") might well arise as "an accidental side effect of normal operation of many systems." On the other, she claims that "nature knows that it is better to err on the side of caution, and many of these signs [of danger] occur more often in the absence than in the presence of any real danger" (Millikan 1989a: 85). Godfrey-Smith (1992) has elaborated upon Millikan's strategy.

Godfrey-Smith's (1992) first argument consists of a twin-earth thought experiment. Imagine two physically indistinguishable predators in two distinct environments. In one environment, one predator has evolved a reliable indicator of preys. In the other environment, its twin has evolved a unreliable prey detector. According to Godfrey-Smith, it is counterintuitive to count the difference in reliability as a difference in representational content. We may suppose that both predators detect preys (instantiations of property F) indirectly by means of a G-detector: they have a detector correlated with instantiations of property G. However, in one environment, instantiations of property G are well correlated with instantiations of property F. In the other environment, instantiations of G are poorly correlated with instantiations of F. In these circumstances, I think it is no more counterintuitive to count differences in reliability as differences in representational content than in Putnam's (1974) famous thought experiment. In Putnam's thought experiment too, my experience of water on earth and my twin's experience of *t*water on twin earth may be indistinguishable. One, however, is a reliable indicator of water, the other of *t*water. So, it seems to me, the informational semanticist could reply to Godfrey-Smith's thought experiment along standard externalist lines.

Consider the adaptive task of either a predator or a prey. The task is to coordinate one of its internal state, r, with physical motions, m. The predator wants to coordinate its prey detector r_1 with its capture movements, m_1. The prey wants to coordinate its predator detector r_2 with its escape movements, m_2. The recruitment of either the prey detector or the predator detector are part – only part – of the larger adaptive task of the coordination between a detector state and some physical motion. Prima facie, a more reliable prey detector in a predator will be favored over a less reliable one. Conversely, a more reliable predator detector in a prey will be favored over a less reliable one. But reliability might have a cost. So the issue now is really about the adaptiveness of reliability of signal detection.

The complexity of the adaptive role of the reliability of signal detection can, I think, be usefully illustrated by one example among many that can be drawn from the fast growing biological literature on animal behavior. I will borrow the following example of the tactile detection system in the cockroach from Alcock (1975: 97–103). The cockroach is apparently a delightful meal for small birds and small insectivorous mammals such as shrews and mice. At the tip of its abdomen, the cockroach has two thin projections, called the cerci, each covered with a host of tiny hairs, called sensilla and inside of which there is a single receptor neuron. The sensilla move when deflected by the movement of air molecules (displaced by, for example, a predator) and each such motion can trigger the electrical discharge of the cercal sensory neuron. Messages from the cercal neurons then reach a critical so-called "giant" interneuron, which acts as a relay between sensory cercal neurons and motor neurons which send instructions for motion. According to Alcock, the following pattern was found by Roeder: if one or only a few cercal neurons fire, then the giant interneuron does not respond. If many cercal neurons fire, then the giant interneuron does react. This is the so-called "spatial summation" effect. If a number of sensory circal neurons are stimulated sequentially one after the other, the giant interneuron also responds. This is the so-called "temporal summation" effect. If, however, many input neurons are stimulated over and over again, then, after an initial burst of activity, the giant interneuron quickly stops responding. So the question is why this pattern of neural activity? Let me quote Alcock's (1975: 102) speculation in full:

> Why has natural selection favored cockroaches that had this kind of nervous system? Because the giant fiber is effective only if it is discriminating, only if it fires in response to biologically significant events for the cockroach and if it remains silent at other times. The cell relays information only about very large changes in sensory input and only for a short period of time. If a few sensilla are stimulated and a few receptors fire, the odds are that the stimulus responsible is a draft in the kitchen and not a predator rushing up for the kill. If a cockroach were to dash madly off each time a few tactile sensilla were stimulated, it would be spending most of its active hours sprinting for cover, often in response to completely innocuous stimuli. The synapse [of the giant interneuron], by acting as a barrier to low-level input, prevents wasting time and energy in unnecessary escape behavior and permits productive feeding and mating activities without interruption. However, if the change in the level of tactile stimulation is very great, it is to the cockroach's advantage to respond, for this might be associated with a predator. The relay neuron fires and sends a number of action potentials to decision-making centers in the insect's thorax. Should high-level sensory stimulation continue, the axon does not continue to forward this information to the decoder neurons because for the cockroach this really does not constitute "information." It does not increase the probability of a correct decision. The cockroach escape reaction is an either-or, yes-go, no-stay, response. Once receiving the signal to go, additional input that also signals "go" is redundant and valueless.[9]

Not only is the giant interneuron a relatively fast relayer of information since it is capable of transmitting a neural signal to the metathoracic ganglion controlling motor action in about 3 milliseconds, but in a sense, it is highly reliable. It sacrifices detailed

---

[9] Interestingly, the sand-scorpion discussed by Brownell (1984) has a very similar kind of tactile sensory *prey* detector, whose reliability raises very much the same issues as the reliability of the cockroach's predator detection system. The sand scorpion has tarsal hairs and basitarsal slit sensilla at the end of its legs whose sensory neurons detect prey vibrations in the sand.

information transmitted by each and every sensory cercal neuron. It acts as a filter of information. But the information it relays to the thoracic control centers is highly relevant information – relevant to the cockroach – and, therefore, highly reliable information: it disregards irrelevant information either produced by too low level activity in the sensory neurons or produced by redundant activity. So in a way, the activity of the giant interneuron in the cockroach illustrates a kind of reliability trade-off: relevant information is acquired at the expense of very detailed or very finegrained information.

Now, on the one hand, the detector's recruitment itself has a cost. A more reliable detector may cost more energetic resources than a less reliable one. On the other hand, there might exist trade-offs between the reliability of the detector state and the speed of the relevantly coordinated physical motion. Neither does the predator merely want to contemplate its prey with the highest degree of possible accuracy, nor conversely does the prey merely want to contemplate its predator with the highest degree of possible accuracy. The adaptive value of the coordination between r and m, therefore, is a function, not only of the reliability of r, but also of the speed and efficacy of m. This suggests quite simply that reliability might be a component of adaptation; but it cannot be a sufficient condition.

Godfrey-Smith (1992) has, however, further argued that reliability might not even be a necessary ingredient of adaptation. Speed in decision-making matters to adaptation. Suppose with Godfrey-Smith that a predator has a choice between two prey detectors: r_1 and $r_1\star$. Both r_1 and $r_1\star$ can be hooked onto the same physical motions m_1. r_1 is more reliable than $r_1\star$ in the sense that $r_1\star$ triggers more false positives: it causes more motions m_1 in the absence of a prey than r_1 does. The same motions m_1, however, when prompted by $r_1\star$ are faster and more efficient than when prompted by r_1. Let r_1 be 80% reliable. Suppose 10% only of motions m_1, when prompted by r_1, reach their target. The success rate, then, of the coordination r_1-m_1 would be 8%. Let $r_1\star$ be 20% reliable. And suppose that no motion m_1, when triggered by $r_1\star$, misses its target. Then, obviously, given the adaptive advantage of the $r_1\star$-m_1 coordination, it would be counteradaptive to prefer the more reliable prey-detector. Besides speed, the harmfulness of the consequences of false positives also matters to adaptation. It would be, for example, worse for a predator to meet its own predator than to catch something inedible. So taking into account differences in harmful consequences of false positives might cast into doubt the value of higher reliability: more, but less fatal, false positives, are preferable to less, but fatal false ones.

As Godfrey-Smith revealingly notices, the above reasoning suggests that the adaptive value of reliability might be a function of the following cost-benefit feature: reliability has greater adaptive value for organisms for which false positives are worse than false negatives. This fits in with Dretske's head-world reliability idea of information, since the latter (as I remarked in chapter 2) is compatible with false negatives. Now, faced with this reasoning, the informationally based teleosemanticist might do two things. First, he might still hold that, everything else being equal, reliability is adaptive. If it were not for the difference in speed and harmfulness of false positives, the more reliable r_1 would be better than the less reliable $r_1\star$. Second, and more importantly, he will appeal to the principle of shared responsibility in order to minimize the number and frequency of false positives. Appealing to the principle of shared responsibility amounts to observing Neander's distinction between the benefit and the stimulus over again. What an organism's indicator is correlated with is not the benefit F, but the stimulus G. What the indicator is correlated with is demoted from the benefit to the stimulus. Discussing what he calls "the Design Problem," Dretske (1988: 97, 103–4) has well described this "deflationary" ("modest" or minimalist) strategy and supplied a number of telling examples:

If there is no F indicator to convert into a cause of [movement] M, there are less optimal solutions. A G indicator will be enlisted if G exhibits enough correlation with F to make it a useful switch for M. How much is "enough" depends on the energy required to produce M and the consequences of producing M when F does not exist.

If you want chickens to hide from hawks . . ., you have to give them an internal hawk indicator, or at least an indicator of something (e.g., a certain silhouette in the sky) that is sufficiently well correlated with the approach of a hawk to make concealment a beneficial response when there is a positive indication.

. . . [stickleback] exploit rather crude indicators (a bright red underside, for instance) to recognize one another. Males use the bright red underside to recognize male intruders, and females use it to identify interested males. The fish react similarly to a variety of objects of similar coloration: painted pieces of wood elicit aggressive behavior in the males and sexual interest in the females. But in the fish's natural habitat, the correlation is good enough . . .

Now I want to do two things: first, in light of a potential counter-example, I want to offer an assessment of the trade-off between reliability and adaptiveness; second, I want to propose an amendment to Dretske's version of what he calls "the Design Problem."

First, reconsider Godfrey-Smith's example of a fatal false positive designed to show the counteradaptiveness of reliability. A less reliable prey detector is preferable to a more reliable prey detector if the latter leads a predator to its own predator and the former is triggered by an inedible animal. This seems to be a case where a false positive turns out to be worse than a false negative. Is it not a counterexample to the claim that reliability has more adaptive value when false positives are worse than false negatives? Not really, I think. For we can reanalyze the case as resulting from the combination of two mistakes: in this case, the predator is also a prey. On the one hand, its prey detector r_1 has misfired. On the other hand, its predator detector r_2 too has misfired. From the point of view of r_1 (the prey detector), the mistake is a false positive. From the point of view of r_2 (the predator detector), however, the mistake is a false *negative*. Higher reliability of r_2, there-fore, would have been indeed adaptive. So there still is room for reli-ability.

Secondly, consider Dretske's (1988: 96) fully general formulation of "the Design Problem": "We want a system that will do m, when, but only when, conditions F exist." What is meant here by "m" is some physical motion and by "F" is some condition or state of affairs (such as the fact that s is F). Dretske's (1988: 98) solution to the Design Problem is that an indicator of F be "harnessed" to "effector mecha-nisms" so that the system successfully produces m when and only when F obtains. Suppose now that F (or the fact that s is F) is the ben-eficial condition: what enhances the organism's overall fitness. Then on the one hand, it might be adaptive to weaken the requirement that m be successful when and only when F obtains so as to take into account the above cost-benefit feature. On the other hand, I suggest that provision be made for a divergence between what the indicator indicates (or covaries with) and the condition under which it is bene-ficial to successfully produce movements m.

4.5 FODOR'S CRITICISMS AGAINST TELEOSEMANTICS

The above "modest" informationally based teleosemantic account of the transitivity problem must confront two kinds of objections. It must face criticisms from above so to speak, i.e., the criticisms derived from Millikan's consumer-teleosemantic approach based on a rejection of the informational basis. And it must face criticisms from below so to speak, i.e., Fodor's objections to teleology. In the previous two sections, I have dealt with the former. I must now deal with the latter.

With Fodor (1990b), consider the much discussed case of the frog's prey detector. The frog responds behaviorally to any small dark moving dot which happens to pass its retina, whether it is a fly or not. I will assume that Millikan (1986: 75) is right when she tells us that a toad will swallow "lead pellets as fast as you toss them at him." In the words of Neander (1995a), "the distal stimulus, in the environment in which the frog evolved, was usually (or often enough) a fly, but these frogs will respond indiscriminately to other small, dark, moving things which are not flies, such as bee-bees (small pellets)." What does the frog's eye, then, tell the frog's brain? Does its visual system detect (respond to) small black moving dots or flies?

Here again, I want to distinguish two distinct problems: a disjunction (or misrepresentation) problem and a conjunction (or transitivity) problem. If the correlation between instantiations of the property of being a small dark moving dot and instantiations of the property of being a fly is broken or imperfect, then we get a disjunction problem, i.e., a problem of misrepresentation. In the case of imperfect correlation, then, does the frog's visual system misrepresent small dark moving dots as flies? Or are small dark moving dots represented as what they are, i.e., as small dark moving dots? This is the frog's disjunction problem. Again, we may compare a purely teleosemantic consumer-based solution and an informational solution to this problem.

But what I want to do now is examine a stimulus-informationally-based solution to the other problem: the problem of transitivity. In cases where the correlation between the property of being a small dark moving dot and the property of being a fly does hold, then we have a transitivity problem: when the correlation holds, then, on informational assumptions, the frog's visual system carries information − let us suppose − about the property of being a small dark moving dot; given that the correlation holds, then, the instantiation of the property of being a small dark moving dot in turn nomically covaries with the property of being a fly. And by our informational assumption, the instantiation of the property of being a small dark moving dot is a reliable indicator of the property of being a fly. It follows by transitivity that the frog's visual system indicates both the presence of small dark moving dots and the presence of flies: it carries the latter information by virtue of carrying the former. But as we saw in the third section of this chapter, this ordering of the informational relation will not suffice to solve the transitivity problem. What of a stimulus-informationally-based solution to the frog's transitivity problem? The question, therefore, is this: given that the informational relation is transitive, can a device's etiological function to carry information be non-transitive?[10]

Here is where we have to face Fodor's criticism of teleology. Fodor (1990b) claims that teleosemantics does *not* have the resources to solve the frog's transitivity problem. In his (1990b: 70) colorful words, "it is most unlikely . . . that Darwin is going to pull Brentano's chestnuts out of the fire." Let me quote Fodor (1990b: 72–73):

> Notice that, just as there is a teleological explanation of why frogs should have fly detectors . . . so too there is a teleological explanation of why frogs should have little-ambient-black-thing detectors . . . The explanation is that in the environment in which the mechanism Normally operates all (or most, or anyhow enough) of the little ambient black dots are flies. So, in this environment, what ambient-black-dot detectors Normally detect (de re, as it were) is just what fly detectors Normally detect (de dicto, as it were); viz., flies.
>
> It bears emphasis that *Darwin doesn't care which of these ways you tell the teleological story.* You can have it that the neural mechanism Normally mediates fly snaps. Or you can have it that the mechanism Normally mediates black dot snaps that are . . . "situated" in an environment in which black dots are Normally flies.
>
> . . . All that matters to selection is how many flies the frog manages to ingest in consequence of its snapping, and this number comes exactly the same whether one describes the function of the snap-guidance mechanisms with respect to a world that is populated by flies that are, de facto,

---

[10] Although he might not be convinced by my attempted solution, I am grateful to Gabriele Usberti for pressing me to address this question explicitly.

ambient black dots, or with respect to a world that is populated by
ambient black dots that are, de facto, flies . . . *Darwin cares how many flies
you eat, not what descriptions you eat them under.*

One of Fodor's reasons for thinking that a teleosemantic account
cannot solve the frog's transitivity problem does not seem to me very
convincing: he claims that a teleological account is only entitled to
appeal to facts about the *history* of the selection mechanisms, *not* to
counterfactuals. Merely historical facts, as opposed to counterfactual
possibilities, are too weak to support the intensionality required to
solve the transitivity problem (in a world where flies are reliably small
black moving dots). "When intensionality is the issue, the counterfactuals do all the work and Darwin goes out the window" says Fodor
(1991: 295). But I fail to see why counterfactuals are irrelevant to
evolutionary theorizing.

Assuming that the properties of being a small dark moving dot, G,
and being a fly, F, are nomically coextensive, then the frog's inclusive
fitness will be equally maximized whether we describe what it swal-
lows as instantiating the former property or as instantiating the latter.
If swallowing the latter enhances a frog's inclusive fitness, then so will
swallowing the former. As Fodor (1990b: 75) ironically put it: "use-
fulness is useless . . . After all, it *is* useful, in fact it's simply *super* (for a
frog) to eat flies or bee-bees in any world in which the flies or bee-bees
are reliably flies." And as Fodor points out, if two properties F and G
are (nomically) coextensive and if doing something in the presence of
the former enhances inclusive fitness, then so must doing the same
thing in the presence of the latter. If so, then Fodor's reasoning might
seem damaging only to a benefit- or consumer-based teleosemantic
approach (such as Millikan's). Such a view assumes that the content of
the frog's visual representation is what benefits the frog (or what
enhances its inclusive fitness). It would, then, be tempting to argue
that an informationally based account of the frog's transitivity
problem based on the distinction between the stimulus and the
benefit is immune from Fodor's critique. The tempting thought
would be to claim that Fodor's criticism works against a benefit-based
purely teleosemantic approach, not against a stimulus-informationally-based approach.

The thought would be that the content of the frog's perceptual
representation is part of the frog's complex snapping behavior. The

frog's snapping behavior involves the coordination of the frog's prey detector with a series of physical motions of the frog's legs and tongue. What increases the frog's inclusive fitness is swallowing flies. But given that the frog indiscriminately responds to flies and bee-bees, it is plausible that what the frog's visual system responds to is instantiations of small dark moving dots. Again the informational basis constrains the stimulus-based teleosemantic solution to the frog's perceptual transitivity problem: the frog's visual system can discriminate small dark moving dots, not flies. Notice that, on this view, the frog's visual system can still misrepresent some not small or not dark or not moving dot as a small dark moving dot. On the stimulus-based teleosemantic account, the fact that the frog's visual system responds to small dark moving dots contributes to helping the frog to catch flies which in turn contributes to enhancing the frog's inclusive fitness. Flies have one property which is causally efficacious in the process of frog feeding (e.g., their being composed of proteins). They have another property which is causally efficacious in the process whereby frogs perceptually detect food (their being small dark moving dots).

This might be a tempting thought for an advocate of the stimulus-informationally-based teleosemantic solution to the frog's transitivity problem. But it simply begs the question against Fodor's central point, which is that the teleological notion of function does not have the level of intensionality appropriate for solving the frog's transitivity problem. Given that there is a nomic dependency between the frog's prey detector and the property of being a small dark moving dot and a nomic dependency between the latter and the property of being a fly, then it must still be shown that the frog's prey-detector may have the etiological function to indicate small dark moving dots without thereby having the etiological function to indicate flies. Fodor's claim, then, is that the notion of indicator function does not have the required level of intensionality to be non-transitive.[11] Given that the informational relation is transitive, can a device's etiological indicator function be non-transitive? To this very question, Dretske (1988: 75–76) has provided a positive answer:

> Representational contents exhibit this peculiar fine-grainedness because even when properties *F* and *G* are so intimately related that nothing can indicate that something is *F* without indicating that it (or some related

[11] Usberti made Fodor's point in conversation.

item) is *G*, it can be the device's *function* to indicate one without its being its function to indicate the other.

And again, referring to the gas laws, Dretske (1995: 31) asserts that even though "an instrument cannot help delivering information about temperature [of a gas] . . . in delivering information about pressure . . . it can, none the less, *represent* the one without representing the other. An instrument can have a pressure-indicating function without having a temperature-indicating function even when it cannot deliver information about pressure without delivering information about temperature." So the question is: can indicator functions discriminate two distinct properties even when the two properties are nomically related to each other?

Consider Sober's (1984: 99) famous selection toy in which balls of different colors and different diameters are selected *for* their size, not for their color. All the balls of a given diameter have the same color. Now, as Fodor (1991: *ibid.*) recognizes, in response to Millikan (1991), one property of the balls is causally efficacious in Sober's selection process: diameter is; color is not. This difference is revealed in counterfactuals such as: had this red ball with a given size been green, it would still have been selected.[12] This example, however, is no response to Fodor's challenge for, in Sober's example, the color property of the balls and their diameter property are *merely* coextensional; they are not *nomically* coextensional. However, in a transitivity problem, two such competing properties must be nomically coextensional.

The relevant notion of indicator function here is the etiological notion: the function which results from a selection process. Two lines of thought might be exploited to argue for the view that a device's indicator function, unlike the informational relation, might be appropriately non-transitive.

The first line of thought is that the non-transitivity of a device's indicator function depends on the possibility of divorcing (or discriminating) instantiations of one of a pair of competing properties

---

[12] Sober's example is analogous to an example of Dretske's (1988: 76): dolphins are said to be able to recognize cylinders from a distance of 50 feet. From the fact that the cylinders are red, it does not follow that dolphins are thereby able to recognize red objects from this distance. However, in this case, the properties of having a cylindrical shape and of being red are merely coextensional; they are not nomically coextensional.

from instantiations of the other in the chain of nomic dependency, in counterfactual situations. The more we may separate instantiations of one property from instantiations of the other in counterfactual situations, the likelier it is that a device's indicator function will turn out to be non-transitive. The most favorable case, then, is obviously mere coextensionality of properties. But again, this case is not really relevant since mere coextensionality is not enough to support nomic dependency between properties, and, therefore, to support the informational relation. The least favorable cases, then, would be analytic (logical, mathematical or conceptual) relations between properties. So consider, for example, a device which detects trilateral objects. According to the first line of thought, it is very hard – indeed impossible – to divorce the property of trilaterality from the property of triangularity. If an object instantiates the former property, then *ipso facto* it instantiates the latter. We cannot suppose a possible world in which the object instantiates the former without instantiating the latter. According to this line of thought, chances are that if a device has the function to indicate trilateral objects, it will have the function to indicate triangular objects. According to this line of thought, then, the idea is that mere nomic dependency between properties is weaker than the dependency between conceptually or analytically related properties (e.g., triangularity and trilaterality). Even though a device whose function is to detect trilateral objects might *ipso facto* have the function to detect triangular objects, still the thought would be that nomically related (or nomically coextensional) properties may be divorced in counterfactual situations so that a device may have the function to indicate one, without having the function to indicate the other.

According to the second line of thought – which is what Dretske (1988: 76) seems to have in mind – we want to block the transitivity of a device's indicator function by appeal to the cognitive architecture (or history) of the device. The hope is that, even though two properties are nomically coextensional, instantiations of one, not instantiations of the other, were causally efficacious in the selection process whereby the device acquired its indicator function. This strategy, if it can be put to work, would apply even to properties which are analytically (logically, mathematically or conceptually) related to each other. So consider again a device which detects trilateral objects. Even though there is no possible world in which an object instantiates trilaterality without instantiating triangularity, still we may imagine that the device scans the number of sides of objects with which it is presented without surveying the number of its angles. The device is so to speak blind to the *n*-angularity of the object. It has, so to speak, built in the concept of side without having the concept of angle. Cognitive architecture, then, would help secure the non-transitivity of a device's indicator function.

If we can imagine an artefact whose cognitive architecture would block the transitivity of nomic dependencies, then why not assume that evolution by natural selection too could endow an organism with processes for producing states whose indicator function would be non-transitive? If so, then a biological device might have a non-transitive indicator function even though the information carried by its information-carrying states is transitive. Its indicator function would not inherit the transitivity of the informational relation. At this point, Fodor might retort that this is exactly what is at issue: true, in the case of an artefact, appeal to the intentions and propositional attitudes of a designer might explain why the state of a device has the function to indicate *F* without having the function to indicate *G* even though as a matter of nomic or analytical necessity nothing can indicate *F* without indicating *G*. I cannot, however, simply invoke this possibility to conclude that natural selection too could discriminate between the function to indicate *F* and the function to indicate *G*. In the end, the question is the following: even though properties *F* and *G* are nomically or analytically correlated, could the fact that a biological device *S* did covary with *F* be causally efficacious in the non-intentional selection process whereby *S* acquired the function to indicate *F*, while the fact that *S* covaried with *G* was not so causally efficacious? Should the fact that *S* covaried with *F*, unlike the fact that it covaried with *G*, be causally efficacious only if the selection process was an intentional process involving a designer's propositional attitudes? Without, I hope, begging the question, I would argue that this distinction between the causal efficacy of two nomically or analytically correlated properties makes sense in a non-intentional selection process as much as it does in an intentional selection process.

In this chapter, my goal has been to argue for an informationally based teleosemantic solution to the problem of the transitivity of dependencies. I have first argued against Millikan's pure teleosemantic approach. I have then tried to face Fodor's criticisms of teleology. My defense of the claim that a device's indicator-function might be non-transitive completes my argument in favor of an informationally based teleosemantic approach to semanticity. It also concludes the first part of my project. In the second part which starts with the next chapter, I turn to the causal explanatory role of the semantic properties of an individual's propositional attitudes.

Part II: The causal role of intentionality

5

The computational representational theory of mind (CRTM)

Let us take stock. In chapter 1, I referred to what I called the dilemma of the intentional realist. On the one hand, the intentional realist is a physicalist: a mind must be nothing but a complex physical system among many. So one horn of the dilemma is that the intentional realist is a reductionist about the mind. On the other hand, the intentional realist is a realist about the mind. So – and this is the other horn of the dilemma – the intentional realist is anti-reductionist about the mind: minds must be unique (or uniquely organized) physical systems.

Because he is gripped by the naturalistic perplexity, the intentional realist wants to bridge the gap between the mental or the semantic and the non-semantic. Even if he is a token physicalist, he would be deeply unhappy if "the semantic" were to "prove permanently recalcitrant to integration in the natural order." He cannot tolerate what Field (1972) labelled semanticalism on the model of vitalism, i.e., he cannot tolerate that semantic facts be primitive facts. So in this sense, he is after some kind of a reduction of the mental to the non-mental. Because he is a reductionist about the mental, the intentional realist must, in Fodor's (1987a) words, show that "intentionality is not a fundamental feature of the world . . . or . . . [show] how an entirely *physical* system could nevertheless exhibit intentional states." This is the program of naturalizing intentionality and it is the reason why in chapters 2 to 4, I have tried to provide some reason to believe that semantic properties of an individual's propositional attitudes can arise out of non-semantic or less than fully semantic properties and relations of the individual's mind.

Doing this, I claimed in chapter 3, involves supplying a solution to four problems: the compositionality problem, the intensionality

141

problem, the problem of misrepresentation (or disjunction problem) and the problem of transitivity. In chapter 3, I discussed the latter three problems: I first argued that information-carrying structures can approximate the intensionality of the semantic properties of beliefs. I then distinguished two problems – the problem of imperfect correlation and the problem of transitivity – one of which (i.e., the former), I argued, can be identified with the problem of misrepresentation (or disjunction problem). In chapter 3, I argued that informational semantics can solve the problem of imperfect correlation. In chapter 4, I argued for a mixed informationally based teleological solution to the problem of transitivity.

On the other hand, the intentional realist is a realist about minds. According to his anti-reductionist stance about the mind, he assumes that minds are unique physical systems. He, consequently, is bound to show at least that having a mind – entering states with semantic properties – makes a causal difference; at best that an individual with a mind can do things which a creature without cannot do. In other words, he must justify what, in chapter 1, I called the causal thesis, which, I claimed can be given a weak and a strong reading. According to the former, propositional attitudes are causes; they have an executive role. According to the latter, the semantic properties of an individual's propositional attitudes are causally efficacious properties.

In this chapter, I want to discuss one influential view, which (following current practice) I will call the computational representational theory of the mind (CRTM for short). Its most eloquent advocate over the years has been Fodor. Unlike other non-computational versions of representationalist views of the mind, the computational representational theory of mind makes a rather strong assumption about mental (or cognitive) processes: mental processes are *computational* processes, i.e., formal operations defined over symbols. As I see it, the goal of the computational representational theory is twofold: on the one hand, it purports to offer a solution to the problem raised by the compositionality of propositional attitudes. On the other hand, it purports to vindicate the strong reading of the intentional realist causal thesis according to which not only are propositional attitudes causes,[1] but the semantic properties of propositional attitudes are causally efficacious.

---

[1] As mentioned in chapter 1, the weak causal thesis can be accommodated by token physicalism.

The computational representational theory is consequently based on (or committed to) two fundamental assumptions, the first of which is the language of thought hypothesis (LOTH), and the second of which is the view that psychological explanation is both intentional and nomological, i.e., it involves lawlike generalizations which refer to, or quantify over, the contents (the semantic properties) of propositional attitudes.[2] I will call the latter the nomic intentional character of mental causation (NICMC for short).

As I said two paragraphs back, naturalizing intentionality involves discussing four problems; however, in chapters 3 and 4, I discussed only intensionality, misrepresentation and the problem of transitivity, not compositionality.[3] I now want to discuss compositionality. Consider my belief r that object a has property F. Following earlier assumptions, r is a representation of the fact that object a is F. The semantic property of r in virtue of which it represents the fact that a is F is complex since it is compounded of the semantic property of a representation of object a together with the semantic property of a representation of property F. The semantic properties of an individual's propositional attitudes, just like the semantic properties of linguistic symbols, it seems, are compositional in just this sense: the semantic properties of complex mental states (or linguistic expressions) depend on the semantic properties of their parts (or constituents) and principles of combination. Now, according to the first thesis I ascribed to intentional realism (in chapter 1),[4] the semantic properties of an individual's propositional attitudes have priority over the semantic properties of any other things having semantic properties (in particular, public linguistic symbols).[5] So the

---

[2] I purposely keep it open whether intentional psychological laws refer to, or quantify over, the semantic properties of individuals' propositional attitudes. I will try and resolve this indeterminacy in chapter 6.

[3] In chapters 3 and 4, I distinguished two problems: a disjunction problem (which, in an informational framework, arises as a problem of imperfect correlation) and a conjunction problem (which, in an informational framework, arises as a problem of transitivity of nomic dependencies).

[4] And which, as I emphasized in chapter 1, is central to the Gricean program.

[5] A public linguistic symbol is a symbol from a natural human language with phonological properties. The addition of "public" is meant to allow for the possibility that the semantic properties of symbols from the language of thought – a "private" language – have priority over the semantic properties of an individual's propositional attitudes. Symbols from a language of thought have no phonological properties.

compositionality of the semantic properties of an individual's propositional attitudes cannot depend upon the compositionality of the semantic properties of linguistic symbols. If the computational representational theory provides a solution to the compositionality of propositional attitudes, then it makes a contribution to the naturalization of intentionality.

Concurrently, the goal of the computational representational theory of mind (CRTM) is to contribute to the second task of intentional realism, by offering a vindication of the strong causal thesis. Remember: in chapter 1, I argued that the weak causal thesis can be accommodated by token physicalism. So after discussing CRTM's solution to compositionality based upon the language of thought hypothesis, I want to probe CRTM's vindication of the strong causal thesis.

What makes the computational representational theory of mind attractive is that, by making the strong assumption that mental processes are computational processes (via the language of thought hypothesis), it promises to throw light simultaneously upon the following three interconnected issues: how complex propositional attitudes can have complex semantic properties on the basis of the simpler semantic properties of their constituents; how propositional attitudes can generate other propositional attitudes; and how propositional attitudes can be involved in the production of intentional behavior. If you think of an individual's language of thought on the model of a digital computer's machine-language, then the computer model of the mind promises to explain the alignment of the semantic properties and the causal properties of propositional attitudes. In the words of Fodor (1987b: 19):

> Computers are a solution to the problem of mediating between the causal properties of symbols and their semantic properties. So if the mind is a sort of computer, we begin to see how you could have a theory of mental processes that succeeds . . . a theory which explains how there could be nonarbitrary content relations among causally related thoughts . . . In computer design, causal role is brought into phase with content by exploiting parallelisms between the syntax of a symbol and its semantics. But that idea won't do the theory of *mind* any good unless there are *mental* symbols.

I now turn to the issue of compositionality.

5.2 THE LANGUAGE OF THOUGHT HYPOTHESIS AND COMPOSITIONALITY

One of the best reasons for accepting the language of thought hypothesis (LOTH) is precisely that it provides a reasonable explanation of the compositionality of the semantic properties of an individual's propositional attitudes consistent with the assumptions of intentional realism. Now, the language of thought hypothesis has two ingredients: a semantic reductionist ingredient and a syntactic (or computational) ingredient. On the semantic side, one can see LOTH as a further purported *reduction* of the semantic properties of an individual's propositional attitudes to the semantic properties of mental symbols – symbols of a (hypothetical) *lingua mentis* or mentalese. On the intentional realist proposal, semantic properties of symbols of natural languages (and other entities having semantic properties) reduce to the semantic properties of an individual's propositional attitudes. Now, according to the language of thought hypothesis, the latter reduce in turn to the semantic properties of symbols in a language of thought. This is what Fodor (1975: 75; 1987b: 17) calls RTM (the Representational Theory of Mind):

> For any organism O, and any attitude A toward the proposition P, there is a ("computational"/"functional") relation R and a mental representation MP such that
> MP means that P, and
> O has A iff O bears R to MP.

According to the language of thought hypothesis, for an individual to have a propositional attitude is for him or her to stand in a certain (computational) relation to a mental symbol. According to the view which combines intentional realism with LOTH, then, the semantic property of an individual's propositional attitude derives from the semantic property of a mental symbol (in the individual's brain). Accordingly, on this view, the naturalization of intentionality (the informational and teleological account which was the topic of chapters 2–4) is really about the semantic properties of mental symbols (from which all other semantic properties derive).

LOTH gives rise to two questions, one of which I already raised in chapter 3, and which is that it seems to give respectability to an ambiguous usage of the notion of a concept via the notion of a mental symbol. The second question is whether LOTH is consistent with intentional realism.

According to LOTH, tokens of brain tissue in human beings – assemblies of neurons – constitute tokens of mental symbols having both semantic properties and syntactic properties. So concepts are to be identified with such mental symbols. Now, as I already said in chapter 3, psychologists often refer to concepts as mental representations. From their point of view, a concept is a vehicle: it may have physical and syntactic properties and enter causal relations. In the philosophical tradition deriving from Frege (1892), a concept is not a vehicle; it is something appropriately abstract – and, therefore, devoid of causal properties – which is expressed by a vehicle. If we think of an English symbol (or word) – for example, "dog" – then a concept is what Frege called the *Sinn* or the sense of the word – for example, what the word "dog" expresses, something instantiated by all and only individual dogs. Perhaps, a philosopher unsympathetic to the language of thought hypothesis might argue that, given that according to LOTH, mental symbols have original (underived) semantic properties – semanticity in the first instance[6] – what we ought to say is not that mental symbols have meanings (or semantic properties), but rather that they *are* meanings. I think, however, that we should not identify mental symbols with meanings. If mental symbols were (as opposed to having) meanings, then it would be completely mysterious how they could have physical properties too. Although by referring to mental symbols, LOTH is committed to the ambiguity between the vehicle of content and the content expressed by the vehicle, this ambiguity is, on my view, as innocuous as the ambiguity to which the notion of a book can give rise: when we refer to a book, we may refer to a physical object with causal properties – a vehicle – and we may refer to the content (or story) expressed by the vehicle.[7] A story told in a book is to the book what the semantic property of a mental symbol is to the mental symbol. We can no more determine the content of the story told in a book by doing a chemical analysis of the ink in which the story is printed in the book than we can determine the semantic property of a mental symbol by examining its elec-

[6] See chapter 1, section 4, for justification of the distinction between original or primitive and derived intentionality.

[7] One reason why the ambiguity is innocuous is that the LOTH theorist might use two distinct terms for the vehicle and the content – as I just did.

trical and chemical properties. The book as a vehicle, however, does have the property of being composed of letters which are printed with a certain ink which can be so analyzed chemically. So we should not think of a mental symbol as being a meaning.

Given the intentional realist thesis of the priority of the semantic properties of an individual's propositional attitudes over the semantic properties of linguistic symbols, the question naturally arises whether LOTH does not surreptitiously reintroduce the priority of the semantic properties of linguistic symbols over the semantic properties of propositional attitudes. In other words, the following question arises: is the second purported reduction step – the reduction of the semantic properties of an individual's propositional attitudes to the semantic properties of mental symbols – consistent with intentional realism? Although this is a difficult metaphysical issue, the following, I think, can be said on behalf of the consistency between intentional realism and LOTH. First, if we avail ourselves of a distinction between natural (or "public") languages (which are used for the purpose of verbal communication) and the language of thought (or mentalese), then intentional realism involves the thesis of the primacy of the semantic properties of propositional attitudes over the semantic properties of symbols belonging to a natural or public language (used for the purpose of verbal communication). The above entertained intentional realist reduction is, therefore, mute about the potential semantic properties of symbols of a hypothetical language of thought (or mentalese) and their relations to the semantic properties of propositional attitudes. Secondly, it seems to me, it is not inconsistent for an intentional realist to try and conceive of thoughts, thinking and thought processes on the model of speech. It is not incoherent for an intentional realist to think of thinking on the model of silent speech.

Not only are formulae of the language of thought supposed to have semantic properties, they also have syntactic properties or constituent structure. As several philosophers and linguists (such as Chomsky and Davidson, not to mention Frege) have noticed, natural languages have the property which Fodor calls *productivity*, namely the property of being composed of an open-ended (potentially infinite) number of sentences, each of which is a grammatical sequence of words belonging to a lexicon (or dictionary). Although a lexicon is made up of finitely many words and morphemes, thanks to its recursive syntactic (or grammatical) rules, a language contains indefinitely many well-formed sentences. The compositionality of a natural language, then, would explain its productivity: the meanings of complex expressions depend on the meanings of their parts and the rules of syntax. Now, according to intentional realism, an individual's propositional attitudes too must be productive: at any given point in his or her lifetime, an individual has entertained only a subset of the set of propositional attitudes he or she might have entertained. But, by the first thesis of intentional realism, the productivity of an individual's propositional attitudes cannot be derived from the compositionality of the natural language he or she speaks. So now the issue arises: how to account for the productivity of an individual's propositional attitudes?

Before I try to answer this question, I want to consider a closely related property of natural languages: the property Fodor (1987b) and Fodor & Lepore (1992) call *systematicity*, i.e., the property that if a language contains a sentence S expressing a complex proposition P, then it must contain other sentences expressing structurally (or syntactically) related propositions. If, for example, a language contains a sentence S expressing the proposition that Rab, then it must contain a sentence expressing the proposition that Rba.[8] Just like productivity, the systematicity of a language can be explained by the compositional structure of the language: the fact that the meanings of some complex expressions depend on the meanings of their parts and on the syntactic rules of combination (and recombination). Now, again – according to intentional realism – a person's propositional attitudes too must be systematic, or as Evans (1982: 75; 100–5) put it, they must obey what he called the *generality* constraint. They must have the parallel property that, if a person can think the thought that Fa, then he or she must be able to think structurally related thoughts, such as the thought that Fb (in case he or she has a representation of object b) or the thought that Ga (in case he or she has a representation of property G).[9] But, according to the first thesis of intentional realism, the systematicity of an individual's propositional attitudes cannot be derived from the compositional structure of the natural (or public) language he or she speaks. So two closely connected questions arise: how are we to

[8] For a discussion of whether the systematicity of thoughts is consistent with what Fodor (1987b) calls semantic atomism, see the next chapter.

[9] For the time being, I do not distinguish Fodor's notion of systematicity from Evans' generality constraint. I will examine shortly an important difference.

account for the productivity and the systematicity of thoughts (or propositional attitudes)?[10]

Now, consider my *conjunctive* belief (or thought) that *p and q*. Since I cannot have this complex belief without having the simpler belief that *p* and the simpler belief that *q*, arguably, the two latter beliefs can be held to be constituents of the complex conjunctive belief that *p and q*. So far, the productivity of beliefs would be explained by the idea that beliefs have constituent structure: complex beliefs have simpler beliefs as constituents. But now, with Fodor (1981: 29–30, 1985: 18–19), consider my *disjunctive* belief that *p or q* or my conditional belief that *if p then q*. My believing that *p or q* does not require me either to believe that *p* or to believe that *q*. Neither does my believing that *if p then q*. I might believe that *p or q* just on the basis of believing that *p* (or just on the basis of believing that *q*). So the belief that *p* and the belief that *q* need not be constituents of the complex disjunctive belief that *p or q*. Although, unlike the conjunctive belief that *p and q*, the disjunctive belief that *p or q* cannot have the belief that *p* and the belief that *q* as constituents, it would be odd to conclude that the conjunctive belief is, but the disjunctive belief is not, a complex belief with a constituent structure. We may, however, preserve the claim that the disjunctive belief has constituent structure by assuming that the tokening of the disjunctive belief involves a (computational) relation to a mental symbol token which in turn has constituent structure, i.e., a mental symbol meaning that *p or q*. Now, the meaning of this complex mental symbol may depend on the meanings of its parts (a symbol meaning that *p* and a symbol meaning that *q*) together with the syntactic rule governing the formation of a disjunctive symbol. So we account for the productivity and/or systematicity of propositional attitudes by appealing to the constituent structure of mental symbols. This, I take it, is a convincing reason for accepting the language of thought hypothesis, at least in the absence of a better account of the compositionality of propositional attitudes.

---

[10] Fodor (1987b: 148) argues that systematicity arguments for LOTH are immune from a feature which may conceivably weaken productivity arguments: the latter, unlike the former, assume that the set of an individual's possible thoughts (or propositional attitudes) is an infinite set (or is open-ended). Similarly, assuming that an individual's linguistic capacities are productive involves the assumption that he or she can understand infinitely long sentences. One way of rejecting a productivity argument for LOTH might be to reject the idealization involved.

At this stage, there are two problems to be examined. One is whether there is an alternative account of the compositionality of disjunctive beliefs which does not appeal to a computational relation to a disjunctive mental symbol meaning that *p or q*. The other problem is Fodor's (1987b: 152) view that systematicity is "a contingent feature" – not a constitutive property – of thoughts (or minds capable of entertaining thoughts). And here it seems as if Fodor's view of systematicity departs from Evans' view of what he called the generality constraint. Notice that Fodor's argument for the language of thought is an argument based on the complexity of disjunctive beliefs, i.e., on the complexity of propositional attitudes provided by a propositional connective. It does not appeal to the complexity involved in the internal structure of quantified (or general) thoughts. The difference between mere propositional thinking and (first-order) quantification might affect the view one takes on the second problem, i.e., whether systematicity is contingent or a constitutive feature of thoughts (or minds).

Künne (1995) supplies an alternative account of the compositionality of disjunctive beliefs not based on the compositional properties of disjunctive symbols in the language of thought. Propositional attitudes such as beliefs have so to speak two degrees of freedom (or dimensions) one of which is their attitude dimension (or commitment) and the other of which is their propositional content. We can as it were subtract the attitude dimension or the commitment specific to each attitude and ask the question: isn't there a mental state relating to a given propositional content and devoid of all the specific commitments associated with the different propositional attitudes? Künne's (1995) suggestion is that there is such a state, which he calls having the capacity to *entertain* a thought with a given propositional content.[11] As will appear in chapter 6, the very distinction between believing that *p* and entertaining the thought that *p* is indeed available to Fodor. *Entertaining* a thought obeys the following principles (i)–(v): (i) Whoever entertains the thought that *not-p*, must entertain the

---

11 Actually Künne makes a distinction between entertaining a thought and having the capacity to entertain a thought because he assumes a distinction between mental episodes such as judging and mental states such as believing. He suggests that having the capacity to entertain the thought that *p* is to believing that *p* what entertaining the thought that *p* is to judging that *p*. Since I disregard the distinction between episodes and states, I merely consider the state of entertaining the thought that *p*.

thought that *p*. (ii) Whoever entertains the thought that *p and q* must entertain the thought that *p* and entertain the thought that *q*. (iii) Whoever entertains the thought that *p or q* must entertain the thought that *p*. (iv) Whoever believes that *not-p* entertains (or must be able to entertain) the thought that *p*. (v) Whoever believes that *p or q* entertains (or must be able to entertain) the thought that *p*.[12] If so, then we may entertain the following alternative account of disjunctive belief: a necessary condition for having the disjunctive belief that *p or q* is that one have the capacity to entertain the thought that *p* or the capacity to entertain the thought that *q*.

Now, if this account of the compositionality of disjunctive belief is accepted as a general account of the compositionality of complex beliefs, then it has implications for the status of systematicity. As I said above, Fodor takes systematicity to be a contingent – not a constitutive – property of actual human thoughts (or minds). If systematicity is contingent, then there might be minds with non-systematic thoughts (whose thoughts would have no systematic correlates). If this were true, then there could be minds capable of thinking the thought that *Rab* without the capacity to think the thought that *Rba*. Actually, Fodor (1987b) calls such possible minds *punctate* minds.[13] Unlike Fodor, Evans (1982: 75) suggested that his generality constraint be interpreted as a constitutive property of thoughts:

> . . . we *cannot avoid thinking* [my emphasis] of a thought about an individual object *x*, to the effect that it is *F*, as the exercise of two separable capacities; one being the capacity to think of *x*, which could be equally exercised in thoughts about *x* to the effect that it is *G* or *H*; and the other being a conception of what it is to be *F*, which could be equally exercised in thoughts about other individuals, to the effect that they are *F*.

Suppose we accept the above account of the compositionality of disjunctive beliefs in terms of the complex structure of the capacity to entertain thoughts as an instance of a general account of the compositionality of any complex belief in terms of the complex structure of the capacity to entertain relevant thoughts. Then, it seems, as Künne (1995) argues, we have an argument in favor of the constitutive character (and correlatively, against the contingency) of systematicity. It is

[12] Alternatively, whoever believes that *p or q* entertains (or must be able to entertain) the thought that *q*.

[13] I shall reexamine the possibility of punctate minds in chapter 6.

presumably a logical (conceptual or constitutive) property of beliefs that if someone believes that the Eiffel Tower is higher than the World Trade Center, then he or she must believe that it is not the case that the World Trade Center is higher than the Eiffel Tower. But according to the above principle (iv), linking the belief that *not p* to the capacity to entertain the thought that *p*, anybody who believes that it is not the case that the World Trade Center is higher than the Eiffel Tower must have the capacity to entertain the thought that the World Trade Center is higher than the Eiffel Tower. It, therefore, follows that if someone believes that the Eiffel Tower is higher than the World Trade Center, then he or she must have the capacity to entertain the thought that the World Trade Center is higher than the Eiffel Tower. If so, then a person would not count as believing that the Eiffel Tower is higher than the World Trade Center unless he or she could entertain the thought that the World Trade Center is higher than the Eiffel Tower. Systematicity would, therefore, be a constitutive feature of thoughts (or minds); non-systematicity would not be an empirical option which human minds were spared.

The question of course is whether we should accept the above account of the compositionality of disjunctive beliefs in terms of the compositionality of the capacity to entertain thoughts. The advocate of the language of thought hypothesis may, I think, make at least three objections to the above account of the compositionality of disjunctive beliefs.

First of all, the advocate of the above account owes us an account of what it is to entertain or have the capacity to entertain a thought which does not amount to standing in a computational relation to a mental symbol.

Secondly, it is not clear that Künne's principle (iii) for entertaining the thought that *p or q* is a real alternative to the language of thought hypothesis. From a semantic point of view, the content of the thought that *p or q* is truth-conditionally equivalent to the thought that [*not both not p and not q*]. Both thoughts will be true and false in the same circumstances, as their truth tables reveal. Of course, their logical form (or syntactic structure) differ. Now, the question arises: can one entertain the thought that *p or q* by entertaining the thought that [*not both not p and not q*]? If one cannot, then presumably one can only entertain the thought that *p or q* in that very format. If so, then entertaining the thought that *p or q* seems to require something like standing in a relation to mental symbols. Then, Künne's account looks suspiciously indistinguishable from the language of thought hypothesis. If one can entertain the former thought by entertaining the latter, then the question arises whether principle (iii) is true of entertaining the thought that *p or q* when it is entertained as the thought that [*not both not p and not q*]. In other words, principle (iii) might be a condition restricted to the entertainment of the thought that *p or q* as such. Even though principle (iii) might not enable us to account for the complexity of the thought that [*not both not p and not q*], we might nevertheless account for it by appealing to principle (i) according to which a necessary condition for entertaining the thought that *not p* is the ability to entertain the thought that *p*. If so, then the truth-conditional equivalence between the thoughts that *p or q* and that [*not both not p and not q*] is not a fatal objection to Künne's account.

Thirdly, the argument for the constitutive (non-contingent) nature of systematicity was based on a generalization of Künne's account of the complexity of disjunctive beliefs in terms of the complex structure of the capacity to entertain relevant thoughts. But now the generalization itself seems unsuitably restricted to thoughts involving concepts of asymmetrical properties like *being higher than*. One can grant Künne that it is a logical (or conceptual) property of beliefs that if someone believes that the Eiffel Tower is higher than the World Trade Center, then he or she must have the capacity to entertain the thought that the World Trade Center is higher than the Eiffel Tower. But what of concepts of non-symmetrical relations? What of the belief that, for example, John loves Mary? To say that the thought that John loves Mary is systematic is to say that if someone believes it, then he or she must be able to entertain the thought that Mary loves John. If, however, someone believes that John loves Mary, there is simply nothing that he or she must believe as to whether Mary does or does not love John. So the ability to entertain the thought that Mary loves John is not a logical (or conceptual) feature of the belief that John loves Mary. So the above argument for the constitutive nature of systematicity seems overly restricted to do the job.

Where does this leave us with respect to the controversy over the contingency of the systematicity of thoughts? Although I do not think that the above argument for the non-contingency of systematicity ultimately succeeds for lack of generality, I am not, however, prepared to accept wholesale the view that the language of thought hypothesis is merely contingent.

First, following Peacocke (1992: 48–51), I am tempted to say that it is empirical and contingent whether a creature recognizes a pair of objects as instantiating (or falling under) a pair of concepts and whether it can conceptualize the relation holding between them. But given that it does make the conceptual discriminations appropriate to categorize a situation as an instance of a "Rab" situation, then it is *not* merely contingent whether the creature has the ability to respond to an "Rba" type of situation. Of course, if systematicity is not merely contingent, then the language of thought hypothesis is not merely an empirical hypothesis either.

Secondly, suppose we concede to Fodor that the systematicity of thoughts involving, for example, non-symmetrical relations is a contingent property of such thoughts, still there is a fundamental feature of thinking which, if accepted, seems best captured by the view that the language of thought hypothesis is not an empirical hypothesis. The feature of thinking which I have in mind is one I already mentioned in chapter 3 (in connection with super-strong intensionality), i.e., the capacity for moving from singular to general thoughts, for example, from the thought that Fa to the thought that $(\exists x)\, Fx$. Notice that, if thinking does require the ability to form general thoughts, then a creature might have mental symbols standing in informational relations to properties instantiated in her environment and not think, if she did not have the logical power to move from singular mental formulae to general mental formulae, i.e., if she could not form general thoughts. One might resist the claim that thinking is constituted by the ability to form general (or quantified) thoughts by claiming that this is too strong a condition upon thinking and by retreating to the weaker condition that for thinking, one must merely have the ability to form complex logically unstructured or unanalyzed thoughts by combining simpler ones via propositional connectives. In other words, having the capacity for propositional calculus would be sufficient for a creature to think. If, however, it is assumed that the capacity for the transitions from singular to logically general structures is constitutive of what it takes to think and if it is assumed that the logical and syntactic structure of thoughts is what allows such transitions, then we come close to recognizing, I think, that a creature capable of thinking in this sense must have a language of thought (or something close to it). And this view, which fits well with the solution (endorsed in chapter 3) to the problem of super-strong intensionality, makes the language of thought conceptually necessary for thinking.

5.3 IS THE COMPUTATIONAL REPRESENTATIONAL THEORY OF MIND A CONSISTENT POSITION?

I now turn to the computational representational theory of mind's (CRTM's) second ingredient, namely the assumption that psychological explanation involves intentional psychological laws. All versions of RTM start from the observation that, as Fodor (1981: 24) put it, what makes "cognitive psychology special among the sciences . . . [is its] (apparently ineliminable) adversion to etiologies in which objects that have propositional content figure as causal agents." Whether the purported *explanandum* is a person's intentional behavior or some change in a person's propositional attitudes, a psychological explanation is bound to give a causal explanatory role to the semantic properties of propositional attitudes. This is what makes RTM incompatible with STM (the syntactic view of the mind) defended by Stich (1983). A thesis which might be said to be intermediary between both versions of intentional realism's causal thesis – the weak and the strong causal thesis – is the following parallelism thesis according to which the semantic relations between the semantic properties (or contents) of attitudes mirror (or are parallel to) the causal relations between attitudes. According to CRTM's second ingredient, we can account for this parallelism between the semantic relations among the contents of the attitudes and the causal relations among the attitudes, by positing NICMC (the nomological intentional character of mental causation), i.e., by assuming the existence of intentional psychological laws.

So, for example, suppose I acquire the belief that "$(\exists x)$ Fx" is true on the basis of my previously formed belief that "Fa" is true. On the one hand, the singular proposition *Fa* implies the general proposition $(\exists x)$ *Fx*. On the other hand, a reasonable causal explanation might well refer to my belief that the singular proposition is true as a cause of my acquiring the belief in the truth of the general proposition. Alternatively, I may well acquire the belief that "q" is true on the basis of my non-conditional belief that "p" is true and my conditional belief that "*if p then q*" is true. The causal pattern between my beliefs would then parallel the inferential pattern which makes the proposition that *q* the conclusion of a correct (deductive) inference whose premises are propositions *p* and *if p then q*. According to the nomological intentional character of mental causation (NICMC), such folk or belief/desire psychological generalizations as "If a person *X* believes that *p* and *if p then q*, then *ceteris paribus X* will acquire the belief that *q*" or "If a person *X* desires that *q* and *X* believes that not *q* unless *p*, then *ceteris paribus X* will act so as to bring it about that *p*" express *ceteris paribus* causal generalizations.[14] This is how Fodor (1981: 25–26) expresses what I call NICMC:

> *All* generalizations about mental states . . . apply to propositional attitudes in virtue of the content of the propositional attitudes . . . our attempts at a serious cognitive psychology are founded in the hope that *this kind* of generalization can be systematized and made rigorous . . . YOU CAN'T SAVE THESE GENERALIZATIONS WITHOUT APPEALING TO THE NOTION OF THE CONTENT OF A MENTAL STATE.

If we combine NICMC (CRTM's reliance upon intentional psychological laws) with the semantic reductionism involved in the language of thought hypothesis, the picture is that causal psychological explanation appeals to intentional laws which refer to (or quantify over) the semantic properties of propositional attitudes which in turn reduce to the semantic properties of mental symbols. So on the one hand, psychological laws are held to be ineliminably semantic. On the other hand, the version of the representational theory of mind (RTM) we are presently discussing is *computational*: mental processes are computational processes. According to what Fodor (1980: 223–31) calls the Formality condition, if mental processes are computational, then they are formal: "If mental processes are formal, then they have access only to the formal properties of [mental] representations." In other words, they detect or depend only on *non*-semantic properties of mental symbols. Consonant with the assumption that mental processes are computational, the Formality condition exploits the language of thought hypothesis. According to LOTH, not only do mental symbols have semantic properties (to which the semantic

---

[14] As I shall make clear below, a lawlike generalization is said to be *ceteris paribus* or nonstrict if it has exceptions and if neither the propositions stating the exceptions nor the propositions revealing the underlying mechanisms responsible for the law can be stated in the vocabulary of the special science to which the law belongs.

properties of propositional attitudes reduce), but they have constituent structure or syntactic properties as well. LOTH and the Formality condition are, therefore, made for each other: being computational, mental processes detect the syntactic, not the semantic, properties of mental symbols.

Is the full picture of the computational representational theory of mind consistent? How could one and the same view jointly rely on contentful psychological laws *and* subscribe to the Formality condition? Stich (1983: 188) has criticized Fodor for wanting to have his cake and eat it:

> How is it possible for Fodor to have it both ways, for him to urge *both* that cognitive generalizations apply to mental states in virtue of their content and that "only *non*-semantic properties of mental representations can figure in determining which mental operations apply to them"?

This puzzle dissolves, I think, once we recognize the distinction between psychological *laws* and mental *processes* or *mechanisms* whereby psychological laws are implemented. On Fodor's (1987b, 1989) view, it is a general feature of the "special sciences" that causal nomological generalizations belonging to a science of level *n* (e.g., geology or Mendelian genetics) are implemented by mechanisms revealed by a science of level *n* − 1 (e.g., hydrodynamic or biochemical mechanisms). Similarly, in the case of psychology, intentional psychological laws are implemented by non-semantic computational or syntactic mechanisms.

Whether the above puzzle dissolves or not, none the less the computational representational theory of mind (CRTM) raises two separate issues: assuming the existence of causal intentional psychological laws, does CRTM vindicate the strong intentional realist causal thesis? Are intentional psychological generalizations causal psychological laws?

5.4 DOES CRTM VINDICATE THE STRONG CAUSAL THESIS?

I now turn to the first of the latter two questions. According to the strong causal thesis, semantic properties of propositional attitudes are causally efficacious. If they are not, then they are epiphenomenal. Does the computational theory of mind (CRTM) vindicate the strong causal thesis? This is a delicate question. If CRTM is correct, then there are two parts to the response to this question. On the one hand, semantic properties are involved in intentional psychological laws. This is what makes CRTM a species of RTM (what makes it a representational theory of mind) and what makes it incompatible with Stich's (1983) STM (the syntactic theory of the mind). On the other hand, if CRTM is correct, then semantic properties do not appear in the (causal) mechanisms responsible for the implementation of intentional psychological laws; only syntactic (computational), formal or non-semantic properties of mental symbols do. Fodor (1987b: 139–40) is quite emphatic about the lack of causal efficacy of semantic properties at the level of such mechanisms:

> I don't believe that there are intentional mechanisms. That is, I don't believe that contents per se determine causal roles. In consequence, it's got to be possible to tell the whole story about mental causation (the whole story about the implementation of the generalizations that belief/desire psychologies articulate) without referring to the intentional properties of the mental states that such generalizations subsume . . . while I'm prepared to sign on for counterfactual-supporting intentional generalizations, I balk at intentional causation.

With Fodor (1987b: 140), consider the following analogy: intentional psychological lawlike generalizations are supposed to be implemented by formal, syntactic, non-semantic mechanisms just in the way Mendel's laws of the transmission of hereditary features are supposed to be implemented by biochemical mechanisms pertaining to the genetic code. Let us assume that the genetic causal explanation of the transmission of the phenotypic property T of being tall by a parent, A, to his or her offspring, B, is a reasonable model of mental causation. On the genetic model of explanation, A has a genotypical property G which plays a role in two distinct processes: first, it played a role in A's ontogenetic acquisition of the phenotypical property T. Second, it contributes to conferring upon B (via genetic transmission) a genotype which in turn plays a role in B's ontogenetic acquisition of the phenotypical property T. In neither of the two processes does A's phenotypical property T play a causal role. Something like the picture shown in figure 6 would be true.

If it is assumed that intentional psychological laws which apply to the semantic properties of mental symbols are being implemented by mental processes which detect the syntactic form of mental symbols,

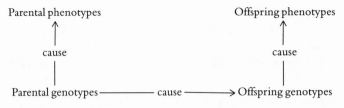

Figure 6 From Segal & Sober (1991: 5)

and if semantic or (intentional) properties are like phenotypical property *T* (of being tall), then semantic properties *per se*, unlike syntactic properties, should be denied any direct causal role. Semantic properties, on this view, seem pretty epiphenomenal after all.

We may choose to emphasize the role of semantic properties in intentional psychological laws or we may choose to emphasize their irrelevance to underlying mechanisms. One thing, however, is clear: CRTM is committed to the following asymmetry: semantic properties of mental symbols are relevant to intentional psychological laws; and, unlike syntactic properties of mental symbols, semantic properties are causally inert in the underlying mechanisms responsible for the implementation of psychological intentional laws.

According to the Formality condition, mental processes can only detect the *formal,* non-semantic properties of mental symbols. Arguably, and as noticed by Devitt (1989), the notion of the *formal* property of a symbol might be thought to be an ambiguous notion. By referring to the form of a symbol, one can refer either to its *shape* or to its *syntactic* property. And these are different properties of a symbol. Consider three distinct symbols with distinct shapes, such as "&," "." and "∧." These three different symbols with distinct shapes are given the same syntactic properties (and semantic truth-functional role) in Propositional Calculus. Or consider such syntactic properties as being a predicate or being a noun phrase. They are distinct from the shape of the symbols which are predicates or noun phrases. It is true, therefore, that the syntactic property of a symbol is not identical to its shape. If one thinks of the shape of a symbol as a (basic) physical property of the symbol, then one may think of its syntactic property as one of its higher-order physical properties. In a word, a symbol's syntactic property can be thought of as one of the symbol's *functional* properties. In Fodor's (1987b: 18) words, the key to solving the mystery of mental causation is

159

[to] connect the causal properties of a symbol with its semantic properties *via its syntax* . . . It's easy . . . to imagine symbol tokens interacting
causally *in virtue of* their syntactic structures. The syntax of a symbol
might determine the causes and effects of its tokenings in much the way
that the geometry of a key determines which locks it will open.

To sum up: the computational theory of mind (CRTM) assumes an
asymmetry between the causal efficacy respectively of the syntactic
and the semantic properties of symbols. In a sense, unlike syntactic
properties of symbols, semantic properties have only causal efficacy by
proxy. In another sense, semantic properties are not epiphenomenal
since they occur in psychological intentional laws. Be that as it may,
syntactic properties are *not* basic physical properties of a symbol: a
symbol's syntactic property is not identical to the symbol's shape.
Furthermore, the syntactic properties of symbols are those formal
properties suitable for the statement of the symbol's semantic properties. Isn't it, therefore, puzzling to deny direct causal efficacy to
semantic properties and grant it to syntactic properties of symbols? I
think there is justice in the assumed asymmetry between syntax and
semantics. The key to this puzzle, I suggest and will argue in chapter 7,
lies in the fact that syntactic properties, unlike semantic properties of
symbols, *are* functional properties which can be defined as higher-
order properties of basic physical properties (e.g., the shape) of
symbols. According to functional role semantics, as we will see, a
symbol's semantic property too is a functional property of the symbol.
But, as I shall argue, only if it is expected to supervene on the symbol's
physical property, can a higher-order property − be it syntactic or
semantic − be thought of as one of the symbol's functional properties.
This is one reason why most advocates of functional role semantics
recognize a distinction between a symbol's *narrow* semantic property
and its *broad* semantic property. Only the former is taken to be one of
the symbol's functional properties.[15] Although I think that the asymmetry between syntactic and semantic properties is justified, there is,
I think, room for doubting that the computational theory of mind
does indeed vindicate the strong causal thesis, as I will argue in the last
chapter.

---

[15] See chapters 6 and 7 for further discussion of content-dualism.

5.5 ARE INTENTIONAL PSYCHOLOGICAL GENERALIZATIONS
CAUSAL LAWS?

I now turn to the problem raised by CRTM's commitment to the existence of psychological intentional laws which involve the semantic properties of mental symbols. This is the assumption I have labelled the nomological and intentional character of mental causation (NICMC). Well, are there such laws? Do folk or belief/desire psychological generalizations such as "If X believes that p and if p then q, then *ceteris paribus* X will acquire the belief that q" and "If X desires that q and he or she also believes that not q unless p, then *ceteris paribus* he or she will act so as to bring it about that p" express genuine causal laws? In discussing this issue, I find it useful to bring out the large measure of agreement between CRTM, as developed by Fodor, and another influential view of psychological explanation: Davidson's anomalous monism (AM).

As first expounded by Davidson (1970), AM results from three premisses. Firstly, Davidson, unlike Dennett, accepts the weak causal thesis: propositional attitudes enter individual (or singular) causal relations (or interactions); they can be causes and effects of physical and other mental events. Davidson's acceptance of the weak causal thesis is his major disagreement with Dennett (1981b; 1982a), who emphasizes that propositional attitudes are better thought of as what (following Reichenbach) he calls *abstracta*, rather than *illata*. Both kinds of entities are unobservable theoretical entities; but *abstracta* (such as centers of gravity), unlike *illata* (such as electrons), are supposed to be devoid of causal powers (or causal properties).[16] Secondly, Davidson assumes the principle of the strict nomological character of causation (SNCC): every singular causal relation implies the existence of a strict physical law. In other words, individual causal interactions hold in virtue of some strict physical law. Thirdly, Davidson assumes the principle of mental anomalism (MA) according to which there can be neither strict psychophysical nor strict psychological laws. From the conjunction of the weak causal thesis, SNCC and MA, Davidson infers AM (anomalous monism), the twofold view that (i) all events are physical or that every mental event must be identical to

---

[16] So *illata* and *abstracta* are unobservable for different reasons: *illata* (such as quarks) may be unobservable for lack of powerful enough optical instruments. To try and observe *abstracta* (such as centers of gravity) would be making a category mistake.

some physical event, and (ii) that not all events can be given a purely physical explanation or that "mental concepts are not reducible by definition or natural law to physical concepts."[17]

On the one hand, the first ingredient of AM puts it clearly in the camp of monist physicalism. If a mental event, having a mental description, enters some causal relation, then (by SNCC) it must have a physical description under which it falls under some strict physical law. If an event has a physical description, then it is a physical event. As Davidson (1970: 214) puts it with his tongue in his cheek, "anomalous monism shows an ontological bias [towards materialism or physicalism] only in that it allows the possibility that not all events are mental, while insisting that all events are physical." On the other hand, the second ingredient of AM is clearly anti-reductionist: mental concepts are not reducible to physical concepts. The burden of the anti-reductionist strand of AM lies squarely on the shoulder of the second premiss, MA (mental anomalism). Davidson (1970: *ibid.*) resolves whatever tension might arise from holding both mental anomalism and physicalism by assuming that "mental characteristics are in some sense dependent, or supervenient, on physical characteristics." Clearly, from the standpoint of the present chapter, the distinctive assumptions of AM are MA (mental anomalism) and SNCC (the strict nomological character of causation).

As I said in chapter 2, the topic of lawlikeness is an exceedingly difficult topic in the philosophy of science. Now, in embracing an informationally based approach to the naturalization of intentionality, I have assumed that the fact that internal state r (of some physical device S) has property G carries information about the fact that (some condition or instantiated property in the environment) s is F iff the fact that r is G depends nomically on the fact that s is F. So I am committed to the assumption that such nomic correlations or dependencies between properties one of which is informational, the other of which is not, do exist. In the kind of nomic correlations needed for informational semantics, informational properties occur only in consequents of lawlike generalizations. Isn't Davidson's assumption (MA) that there cannot be strict psychophysical laws incompatible with informational semantics? Not really, I think, and this for three independent reasons.

---

[17] As Davidson (1993: 3) puts it. See also Davidson (1970: 214).

First of all, as pointed out by Cummins (1983), in many scientific areas other than psychological explanation, not all lawlike generalizations are causal: that a signal cannot travel at a speed greater than the speed of light is not a causal law. Nor is the identity expressible by such a sentence as "Water is H_2O." Part (though by no means all) of what MA asserts may well be that some psychophysical correlations between mental and physical events and/or properties are best interpreted as identity theses, not as causal generalizations. However, this is not really relevant since the nomic correlations between properties required by informational semantics purport to be causal dependencies, not statements of identity between properties (let alone between events).

Secondly, informational semantics does require a distinction between mere accidental generalizations and nomic dependencies involving informational properties in the consequent. It does not, however, require the nomic dependency to be strict. I shall shortly come back to the Fodorian contrast between strict (or basic) and non-strict (or non-basic) laws. As I hinted in chapter 2, I do not want to commit myself to the assumption, which both Davidson and Fodor endorse, that there are strict physical laws. As I pointed out in chapter 2, what distinguishes genuine laws from universal accidental generalizations is that the former, unlike the latter, are referentially opaque (or intensional). Whether a law may have exceptions may depend on whether we want to include within the law the statement of all the conditions which have to hold for the consequent of the law to come true if the antecedent is true. If a law has exceptions, then it is not a strict law. In fact, there are reasons to be skeptical about the existence of strict laws. To see why, imagine a situation in which the fact that event c has property F causally explains the fact that event e has property G. Suppose there is a nomic dependency between instantiations of property F and instantiations of property G. For this nomic dependency to be a strict law, it has to be the case that the instantiation of property F is a sufficient condition for the instantiation of property G. So if the law is strict, then c's being F should guarantee the instantiation of G by e. However, presumably, c possesses many properties other than F. So for the nomic dependency between properties F and G to be strict, it must be the case that no other properties of c will prevent e from being G. If you think that this is unlikely, then you must conclude that it is unlikely that there are strict laws or strict nomic dependencies between properties.

Thirdly, Davidson has offered two complementary kinds of reasons in favor of the acceptance of MA (mental anomalism). On the one hand, Davidson (1970) has drawn a famous contrast between what he calls respectively *homonomic* and *heterononomic* generalizations: "All emeralds are green" expresses a homonomic generalization; Goodman's "All emeralds are grue" expresses a heteronomic generalization in that the predicates "is an emerald" and "is grue" are "not suited to one another." On the other hand, Davidson (1970) has emphasized the "disparate commitments of the mental and physical schemes" between which "there cannot be tight connections . . . if each is to retain its allegiance to its proper source of evidence." Now, the features of the mental on which Davidson bases his claim of disparity between the mental and the physical realms are the holism and normativity which are, according to him, constitutive of genuine intentionality.[18] Davidson (1984) has offered many arguments in favor of the holistic character of intentionality. For example, for me to believe that a cloud is passing before the sun, I must believe that there is a sun, that clouds are made of water vapor, that water can exist in liquid or gaseous form (Davidson 1977: 200).[19] Not only is holism, according to Davidson, a unique trait of intentionality not shared by the physical, but rationality too involves a normative element not to be found in the physical realm. In Davidson's (1970: 223) own terms, "nomological slack between the mental and the physical is essential as long as we conceive of man as a rational animal."[20]

The fact that holism and rationality are both constitutive of, and unique to, the mental is, therefore, at the root of Davidson's mental anomalism (MA), i.e., "the nomological irreducibility of the mental" to the physical. However, the goal of informational semantics is to reduce intentionality to non-semantic or less than fully semantic properties and relations. As I was at pains to argue in chapters 2-4, not all characteristic features of full intentionality are possessed by

---

[18] Interestingly, although, unlike Davidson, she is not interested in holism at all, Millikan (1986) too seems to take the normativity of intentionality as grounds for denying the existence of intentional psychological lawlike generalizations.

[19] In the next chapter, I will distinguish various forms of holism such as cognitive holism, meaning holism and belief holism (which I do not distinguish right now).

[20] As Davidson (1974a: 239) puts it, "the limit . . . placed on the social sciences is set not by nature, but by us when we decide to view men as rational agents with goals and purposes, and as subject to moral evaluation."

informational properties. So granting Davidson the disparity between the physical realm and the realm of full intentionality does not force us to give up the assumption that the correlations between pairs of properties, one of which is informational, are nomic. So on the one hand, it is not clear that informational semantics is incompatible with Davidson's views on the relation between the physical realm and full-blown intentionality. On the other hand, whether full intentionality is both inherently holistic and normative is a deep and difficult problem. I will return to holism in the next chapter. Here, I will merely note that it is not obvious that intentionality is intrinsically normative.

Consider the simple assertion that the word "chat" in French means cats. Of course, the word "chat" possesses merely derived (or derivative), not primitive (or original), intentionality. However, this is irrelevant to whether meaning (or intentionality) is intrinsically normative. The very same question would arise with a thought about, or mental symbol meaning, cats. Clearly, if the word "chat" means cats, then normative consequences follow: there are circumstances in which it is appropriate or correct to use the word "chat" and there are other circumstances in which it is not appropriate or it is incorrect to use the word "chat." If a thing is a cat, then it can truly be called "chat"; if a thing is not a cat, then it cannot truly be called "chat"; and so on. Similarly, from the fact that a thought constituent is about cats, there are circumstances in which it is, and there are circumstances in which it is not, appropriate or correct to token such a thought constituent. But from the fact that such a meaning statement has these normative implications, does it follow straightforwardly that the meaning statement itself is normative? Does it follow that meaning (or intentionality) is normative? Not necessarily. One possible view is that what is responsible for the normative implications of the meaning statement is that meaning is intrinsically normative. But an alternative view would be that the normative implications follow from the combination of the meaning assertion together with independent normative considerations pertaining to the appropriate conditions of use of words.[21] This alternative view would undermine one of

---

[21] The latter line of thought according to which meaning is not intrinsically normative has been brilliantly defended by Paul Horwich in a series of lectures at the Institut d'histoire et de philosophie des sciences et des techniques, in Paris, in the Fall 1994.

Davidson's grounds for the nomological irreducibility of the mental to the physical.

Let us now consider folk or belief/desire intentional generalizations containing genuinely semantic properties in the antecedent and/or in the consequent. A feature of all such generalizations emphasized by mental anomalism (MA) (which, according to Davidson, distinguishes them from physical laws) is that they are not, and cannot be, strict. A strict law is presumably such that if the property mentioned in its antecedent is instantiated, then the property mentioned in its consequent cannot fail to be instantiated. Strict physical laws, are, on Davidson's view, homonomic. Unlike psychophysical correlations, however, intentional psychological generalizations containing mental predicates (as Davidson would say)[22] or involving reference to semantic properties (as I say) in both antecedent and consequent positions may be homonomic too. If so, then being homonomic is obviously not sufficient for being strict. As Davidson (1973: 250) has put it, unlike laws of basic physics, intentional psychological generalizations "cannot be sharpened without limit," [they] "cannot be turned into the strict laws of a science within its area of application." Unlike intentional psychological generalizations, physical laws, drawing as they do "[their] concepts from a comprehensive closed theory . . . may be sharpened indefinitely by drawing upon further physical concepts" (Davidson 1970: 219).[23]

Given Davidson's assumption about there being strict laws of basic physics, what, on his view, is unique about them is that they are perfectible (or refinable) within basic physics itself. Not so with intentional psychological generalizations. Now this very contrast seems to demarcate strict laws of basic physics from the generalizations of any higher-level special science. Unlike strict laws of basic physics, causal generalizations in the special sciences have exceptions. Furthermore, the propositions stating the exceptions of a causal generalization – the idealizations necessary for applying the law – cannot be expressed in

---

[22] Davidson's framework is nominalistic in the sense that for him, events satisfy descriptions; they do not instantiate properties.

[23] Perhaps when we think of Davidson's contrast between homonomic and heteronomic laws, we should distinguish two questions: one is whether the conditions which must be filled for a (strict) law not to have exceptions could be part of the law itself; the other is whether the conditions of application of a law can be stated in the same vocabulary as the law.

the vocabulary of the special science to which the causal generalization belongs. Suppose with Fodor (1987b: 4–5) that it is a geological
law that meandering rivers erode their outside bank. This is not a law
of basic physics for it has exceptions such as that a river may freeze;
or it may dry up; or humans may build a dam. The statements of the
exceptions cannot be expressed in the vocabulary of geology proper.
This is one feature which makes non-basic laws non-strict: they are
"hedged"; their application depends on "escape clauses," idealizations
or *ceteris paribus* (auxiliary) propositions where the latter are not
expressible in the same vocabulary as the law.[24]

So far, it seems, intentional psychological laws are in the same boat
as all non-basic special science laws. On Fodor's interpretation of
NICMC (the nomological intentional character of mental causation),
however, hedged *ceteris paribus* special science laws have a second
feature: not only do they have exceptions, but they hold in virtue of
more basic *mechanisms*; they are implemented by underlying mechanisms. Again, such underlying mechanisms cannot be described in the
vocabulary of the special science law. Mendel's laws of inheritance
depend on biochemical mechanisms; geological laws depend on
chemical and hydrodynamic mechanisms; intentional psychological
laws depend on syntactic mechanisms. In Fodor's (1989b: 144) words:

> . . . a metaphysically interesting difference between basic and nonbasic
> laws is that, in the case of the latter but not the former, there always has to
> be a mechanism in virtue of which the satisfaction of its antecedent
> brings about the satisfaction of its consequent. If "Fs cause Gs" is basic,
> then there is no answer to the question how do Fs cause Gs; they just do,
> and that they do is among the not-to-be-further-explained facts about
> the way the world is put together. Whereas, if "Fs cause Gs" is non-
> basic, then there is always a story about what goes on when – and in
> virtue of which – Fs cause Gs.

Here, we reach a significant difference of emphasis between
NICMC (as developed by Fodor) and Davidson's combination of MA
(mental anomalism) and SNCC (the strict nomological character of
causation). According to Fodor's NICMC, non-basic (non-strict)
intentional psychological generalizations are causal generalizations

---

[24] This twofold characterization of *ceteris paribus* (or hedged) special science laws might
contribute to bridging the gap between Fodor's commitment to NICMC and
Millikan's (1986) denial that there are intentional psychological laws.

which can subsume or cover singular causal relations involving propositional attitudes. One condition why such generalizations are causal is that they hold in virtue of underlying computational mechanisms. For someone like Davidson, who does not seem at all to be attracted to this picture, there are two basic options: either intentional psychological generalizations are basically accidental generalizations or they are conceptual connexions. If the former, then, as argued by Antony (1991), it becomes difficult to distinguish intentional psychological generalizations from mere coincidences. If the latter, which seems in fact to be Davidson's preferred route, then, as I will argue, it seems difficult to maintain, as Davidson (1963) has famously done, that reason explanations are causal explanations.

Following the lead of Davidson (1974: 233), who called them "truisms," several philosophers (e.g., Pettit 1986: 27; Schiffer 1987: 148) have emphasized the quasi-analytic or conceptual nature of such intentional psychological generalizations as the practical syllogism and reasoning according to *modus ponens*. Does not the practical syllogism state purely conceptual relations between beliefs and desires which are constitutive of what it is to have beliefs and desires? Is not the generalization about reasoning according to *modus ponens* a constitutive principle about what it is to have beliefs? We do not, it seems, need inductive evidence to know the truth of such principles. Are not such generalizations knowable *a priori*? In response, Fodor (1990a: 184) has taken a hard Quinean line and responded that analyticity here, as with any profound scientific principle, is just an illusion fostered by "centrality misperceived": belief/desire generalizations are so central to our conceptual scheme that we do not know how to give them up. But so are fundamental laws of physics. This does not make them analytic or knowable *a priori*.

Given the highly controversial nature of the analytic/synthetic distinction, I cannot hope to do justice to this issue in the rest of this chapter. However, I will first try to indicate what I take to be non-analytic in psychological intentional generalizations. Then, I will say why it might be puzzling, given Davidson's endorsement of the weak causal thesis, to take a strong position against the possibility that intentional psychological generalizations be causal lawlike *ceteris paribus* (non-strict) generalizations.

First, suppose I pick up cup c_1 in front of me because I believe that it contains coffee and I want a sip of coffee. What explains my intentional behavior is some belief/desire psychological principle to the effect that if I want a cup of coffee and if I believe that cup c_1 in front of me contains coffee, then *ceteris paribus* I will grab c_1. Isn't this generalization analytic? Well, what makes it seem analytic, I suggest, is that, given my desire, the connection between the content of my belief and my action seems purely conceptual. Given that I believe that cup c_1 contains coffee and, given my desire for coffee, how could I fail to pick up c_1? Well, I could. The connection between my belief/desire pair and my action may seem to be purely conceptual; but it is not. What happens is that we take it for granted, as part of our background assumptions that particular cups of coffee do not instantaneously disappear; they do not miraculously come and go. So if I form the perceptual belief that cup c_1 contains coffee, then, given my desire for coffee, chances are that I will grab c_1. However, unbeknownst to me, c_1 might be replaced by indistinguishable cup c_2. So, given my desire, I might well believe that c_1 contains coffee and seize c_2 while believing that I am seizing c_1. What this shows is that it is not analytic that if I want some coffee, and if I believe that cup c_1 contains coffee, then I will pick up c_1. What might seem to be analytic, then, is that if I want some coffee, and I believe that cup c_1 contains coffee, then I *intend*, or will *try*, to pick up c_1. Arguably, however, not even the conditional relating my belief/desire pair to my intending or trying to pick up c_1 is analytic. I might, after all, have a stroke after I have the belief/desire pair and before I form the intention or before I try to pick up the cup.

Secondly and lastly, not only does Davidson, as I said, accept the weak causal thesis: propositional attitudes enter individual causal relations. But Davidson (1963) is also famous for having argued that reason explanations are causal explanations. Now, I want to argue that the view that reason explanations are causal explanations should incline him to accept the view that intentional psychological generalizations are causal laws.

First, I will try and defuse the worry that acceptance of the strict nomological character of causation (SNCC) might entail that the mental (or semantic) property of a mental event be screened off by its physical property. By SNCC, any individual causal relation requires the existence of a strict physical law. By mental anomalism (MA), intentional psychological laws cannot be strict (physical) laws. So the worry is that anomalous monism (AM) makes semantic (or mental) properties epiphenomenal. This worry has been typically expressed by Sosa (1984: 277–78):

> I extend my hand because of a certain neurological event. That event is my sudden desire to quench my thirst. Thus, if my grasping is caused by that neurological event, it's my sudden desire that caused my grasping ... Assuming the anomalism of the mental, though my extending my hand is, in a certain sense, caused by my sudden desire to quench my thirst, it is not caused by my desire qua desire but only by my desire *qua neurological* event of a certain sort ... The being a desire of my desire has no causal relevance to my extending my hand (if the mental is indeed anomalous): if the event that is in fact my desire had not been my desire but had remained a neurological event of a certain sort, then it would have caused my extending my hand just the same.

Clearly, Sosa's reasoning is that, from MA and SNCC, it follows that only a mental state's physical property, not its mental (or semantic) property, can be causally efficacious in producing behavior. As Lepore & Loewer (1987: 638) have put it, "c's being a certain neural state, Nc, screens off c's being a desire to quench thirst, Mc, from e's being an extending of the hand Be. More generally, ... neural properties screen off intentional properties."[25] Two responses seem to cast doubt on Sosa's counterfactual conditional "if c were N but not M, then e would still be B."[26]

First, with Lepore & Loewer (1987), we might turn the *multiple realizability* of the mental (or semantic) properties of a mental event by physical properties against Sosa's counterfactual. The assumption of the multiple realizability of the mental by the physical is equivalent to the assumption that the former supervenes on the latter.[27] From the assumption of the multiple realizability of the mental by the physical, we might argue that if c were not N, c's being M would then be realized by some other neural property $N^\star$ of c. In which case, if c were M but not N, then e would still be B. The mental would then screen off the physical. Lepore & Loewer (1987) take this last consequence to be a *reductio* of Sosa's counterfactual "if c were N but not M, then e would

[25] Call c my desire, N its neural property, M its mental (or semantic) property; call e c's behavioral effect, and B, e's behavioral property.

[26] This relation between c's being M and e's being B has been nicknamed "quausation" by Horgan (1989). I will return to quausation in chapter 7.

[27] See chapter 1, section 5, for the definition of supervenience.

still be *B*." Lepore & Loewer's (1987) idea is that even if there were a strict law connecting *c*'s being *N* and *e*'s being *B*, then multiple realizability would entail that *c*'s being *N* could be screened off by *c*'s being *M*. On their view, Sosa (1984) has assumed a sufficient condition for a property to be causally irrelevant (or to lack causal efficacy) in a causal process which is too strong. He has assumed a condition of the type: *c*'s being *F* is causally irrelevant to *e*'s being *G*, if there is a property *F*★ of *c* such that if *c* were *F*★ and not *F*, then *e* would still be *G*. Lepore & Loewer's (1987) point is that this condition should be blamed, not anomalous monism (in particular, not mental anomalism, MA). To see why, consider their example of a hurricane striking the coast and causing the streets to be flooded. The causation involved is obviously not mental. Let us suppose that the event of the hurricane was a certain molecular event with physical property *P*: so the event had the property of being a hurricane and it had property *P*. Now, suppose that the hurricane had consisted of a slightly different molecular event having property *P'*, not property *P*. The hurricane would then have been a slightly different molecular event with property *P'*. It could still have flooded the streets all the same. But by Sosa's sufficient condition for causal irrelevance, then the property of the event of being a hurricane would be screened off from (or causally irrelevant to) the flooding of the streets. Intuitively, however, we do want to count the property of the event of being a hurricane, not merely its property of being a molecular event with some microphysical property *P*, to be causally efficacious in flooding the streets. What this example shows is that Sosa's reasoning relies on too strong a screening condition in general, having nothing in particular to do with mental anomalism (MA).

Secondly, the question arises whether anomalous monism (AM) entails that *only* strict physical laws can cover particular causal relations. From mental anomalism (MA) and the strict nomological character of causation (SNCC), what follows is the existential claim to the effect that if *c* causes *e*, then there must exist a strict physical law which subsumes the causal transaction between *c* and *e*. Now, as noticed by McLaughlin (1989), to say that individual causal relations require strict physical laws is not to say that *only* strict physical laws can ground individual causal relations. The former does not entail the latter, unless one assumes some further principle of explanatory *exclusion* (or *preemption*) to the effect that individual causal relations hold *only* in virtue of strict physical laws or that the very existence of a strict physical law makes any other non-strict law explanatorily superfluous.[28] So, strictly speaking, anomalous monism (AM) is not committed to the view that individual causal relations involving propositional attitudes cannot be multiply grounded by strict physical laws and by psychological intentional generalizations as well.

However, the view that the latter are analytic truisms would interfere with such multiple groundings. Now, I take it, given one's acceptance of the weak causal thesis, one motivation for accepting the view that reason explanations are causal explanations is that we do not want to assume that individual causal relations involving propositional attitudes are either mere coincidences or brute metaphysical facts. But this desideratum, I suggest, is better served by some version of the nomological intentional character of mental causation (NICMC) than by the view that intentional psychological generalizations are analytic truisms. It is better served, on my view, by making two assumptions: by assuming that at least some intentional psychological generalizations are nomic intermediaries between individual causal relations involving propositional attitudes and strict physical laws; and by assuming that such nomic intentional psychological generalizations hold in virtue of some underlying mechanisms.

On the one hand, it would be puzzling if individual causal relations involving propositional attitudes were left dangling (or hanging) with no support but strict physical laws. This would raise an epistemological puzzle: how could we ever recognize the fact that propositional attitudes can enter singular causal relations if this depended only on strict physical laws – which we may never know – not on any intentional psychological causal generalization? It would be similarly puzzling if singular causal relations involving chemical or biological events depended merely on strict physical laws, not on any intermediary chemical or biological generalizations. On the other hand, if reason explanations are causal explanations – if reasons are causes – then we must be able to capture within our explanatory net (or practice) both the fact that propositional attitudes are reasons for action and the fact that they are causes. The puzzle, then, would be that only by being in a (brain) state with some basic physical property would several individuals share a nomic property sufficient for the causal

[28] I will return to the issue of explanatory exclusion (or preemption) in chapter 7.

172

explanation of something they might all be inclined to do. Being in a (brain) state with a common mental (or semantic) property would never contribute to causally explain why different individuals might do the same thing. If intentional generalizations involve nomic dependencies between properties at least one of which (or both) may be mental (or semantic), then this would help us capture this dual aspect of propositional attitudes: their being reasons and their being causes. What, however, remains to be seen in the next chapters is whether a view such as the nomological intentional character of mental causation (NICMC) does vindicate what I call "the strong causal thesis."

6

Must an intentional realist be a meaning atomist?

Beliefs (and propositional attitudes generally) have three complementary features, two of which correspond to the two tasks I have
ascribed to the program of intentional realism. They have been well
captured by Ramsey's (1931) and Armstrong's (1973) slogan according
to which an individual's beliefs are internal maps by means of which
he or she steers.

On the one hand, on the informationally based teleosemantic
account which I defended earlier, the semantic properties of an individual's propositional attitudes arise primarily out of two factors.
They arise out of the nomic dependencies between an individual's
states of mind and states of the world around him or her. And they
arise out of the selective processes at work both on the phylogenetic
evolution of the species to which the individual belongs and in the
individual's ontogenetic history. So, on the above account, a belief
derives its semantic property from its informational and selectional
pedigree (or heritage). In this sense, beliefs are backward-looking
structures.

On the other hand, beliefs are forward-looking structures. Unlike
an individual's conscious experiences, an individual's beliefs have
executive responsibilities. As I said in chapter 2, a conscious experience supplies an individual with analogically coded information
which is then submitted to a process of digitalization or abstraction
and exploited by higher cognitive states. As I then suggested, the
acoustic experience of a particular sound produced on a particular
piano differs from one's belief that the sound produced is a C of the
third octave. The experience can provide a profuse informational

manifold out of which a selected piece will be extracted for cognitive use. The enjoyment of an acoustic experience may well leave one linguistically (or conceptually) baffled about the identity of the note perceived. Not until the selected piece of information has been turned into an object of belief can it serve as a basis for identification and action (e.g., linguistic behavior). An individual's beliefs, therefore, have, as we might say, a hand on the steering wheel: whereas an individual's conscious experiences can be causes of his or her intentional non-voluntary behavior, an individual's propositional attitudes guide his or her intentional voluntary behavior.[1]

An individual's propositional attitudes, however, have a third feature: they interact a lot with one another. Old beliefs give rise to new ones: some old beliefs are deleted from an individual's belief-set; new beliefs are added; some old beliefs are refined; others are weakened; still others are strengthened. Such interactions are a rich source of enlargement of an individual's cognitive structure. Perception, memory, communication, and inference are four major sources from which a human being builds his or her representation of his or her environment. The interactive or interdependent feature of propositional attitudes has already been mentioned in chapter 3 in relation to the highest degree of intensionality. There, I argued that two informationally equivalent primitive information-carrying structures can be distinguished by their logical potentials. An individual's propositional attitudes have such logical features. A creature with such states must therefore have inferential abilities.

Beliefs interact with other propositional attitudes and they can, in Evans' (1981) words, be "at the service of many distinct projects." The link between the executive role (forward-looking) and the interactive (or interdependent) feature of genuine beliefs has been well illustrated by Wright (1986: 33–34) who developed Evans' (1981) comparison between a rat's disposition to avoid foodstuff which is poisonous and the human belief that a substance is poisonous:

> Thus, my belief that a certain substance is poisonous may manifest itself in a literally indefinite variety of ways. I may, like the rat, avoid the substance. But I may also take steps to ensure my family avoid it, or take steps

[1] As I already noticed in footnote 15 of chapter 2, there is, I think nothing paradoxical in assuming that an individual's non-voluntary behavior is under the unconscious control of his or her conscious sensory experiences.

to ensure they don't! I may take small but daily increasing quantities of the stuff in the belief that I can thereby inure myself against its effects, and that background circumstances are such that it may stand to my advantage to have done so. I may take a large quantity if I wish to commit suicide, and a smaller one if I wish to incapacitate myself to avoid an obligation. My belief that the substance is poisonous is thus, as Evans puts it, at the service of indefinitely many potential projects corresponding to indefinitely many transformations in my other beliefs and desires. With the rat, in contrast, concepts like the desire for suicide, or malign intent, can get no grip.

The rat's disposition serves only one purpose: avoidance of a particular foodstuff. My belief can serve many purposes. This link between the interactive or interdependent feature of propositional attitudes and their being at the service of multipurpose action clearly derives from a functionalist perspective on propositional attitudes. I will call the interactive or interdependent feature of propositional attitudes *cognitive holism*. It clearly fits with a functionalist perspective on propositional attitudes.

According to what Block (1980a: 172) has called metaphysical functionalism, and which I will call psychofunctionalism, an individual's beliefs are brain-state tokens of the individual which are characterized by their actual or possible causal relations to sensory inputs, other propositional attitudes and behavioral outputs. What constitutes a belief-*type* – what is common to all tokens of the same type of belief – is functional. So the various causal relations which a propositional attitude S bears to other propositional attitudes are constitutive of what kind of state S is. Many philosophers of a functionalist persuasion have been drawn to the view that the semantic property of a belief depends partly or completely upon the belief's functional, conceptual or inferential role (see, for example, Block 1986, 1987; Field 1977; Fodor 1987b; Harman 1982; Loar 1982). This view could be called *semantic functionalism*. Field (1977), for example, has made the influential proposal that the inferential (functional, conceptual or causal) role of an individual's belief be cashed in terms of the conditional probability that the belief be true relative to the individual's other beliefs.

According to semantic functionalism, what confers (all or part of) its semantic property upon, for example, my belief that Anna went into the kitchen are such things as that I have seen Anna's bodily motions towards the kitchen – unless I have had some other sensory experience: I might have heard her go or she might have informed me verbally that she was going into the kitchen, and so on. Believing that Anna went into the kitchen, I am presently in a state which causes me to have other beliefs such as that someone went into the kitchen, that Anna went somewhere, that someone went somewhere, and so on and so forth. If I happen to have the previous conditional belief that if someone goes into the kitchen, then he or she should check whether there is milk left in the ice-box, then upon forming the belief that Anna went into the kitchen, I will also acquire the belief that she should check whether there is milk left in the ice-box. Believing that Anna went into the kitchen, I am also presently in a state which inclines me to utter, for example, the English sentence "Anna went into the kitchen" or – depending on who I am talking to – perhaps a French equivalent.

Here, philosophers attracted to semantic functionalism may diverge as to whether functional (inferential or conceptual) role captures all or only part of a belief's semantic property. Harman (1982) has advocated what Block (1986) calls a "long-armed" view of conceptual role which is designed to capture all of a belief's semantic property. Those who opt for the latter will argue for a *content-dualist* picture according to which one ingredient of a belief's content is *narrow* content and the other ingredient is *broad* (or wide) content. Content-dualists identify a belief's narrow content (or narrow semantic property) with the belief's inferential (functional or conceptual) role, for example, Field's (1977) conditional probability. They identify the belief's broad content with its truth-condition – what must obtain for the belief to be true.

In fact, content-dualism arose not only as a response to the challenge facing informationally based (or more generally externalist) semantic theories and consisting in accommodating the role of *internal* relations among propositional attitudes in the determination of their semantic properties. It also, as I will argue in the next chapter, arose out of the constraint that the semantic properties of an individual's propositional attitudes relevant to the causal explanation of what he or she does ought to *supervene* upon the physical properties of his or her brain.[2] Now, since presumably (as Putnam's 1974 thought experiment shows) the broad semantic properties of an individual's propositional attitudes do not supervene upon the physical properties of his or her brain, content-dualists hoped that some notion of narrow semantic property would so supervene.[3] So it was that Fodor (1981; 1987b) assumed that intentional psychological laws would refer to the narrow, not to the broad, contents of an individual's propositional attitudes.

6.2 THE ROAD FROM SEMANTIC FUNCTIONALISM TO MEANING HOLISM

I earlier called cognitive holism the interdependence of propositional attitudes. With Fodor (1987b) and Fodor & Lepore (1992), let us call meaning (or semantic) holism the view that the content (or semantic property) of an individual's belief depends upon its causal and/or inferential relations to the individual's other propositional attitudes. Meaning holism can be true of all or only the narrow part of the semantic property of an individual's belief according to whether one thinks that functional role captures all of a belief's semantic property or only (if one subscribes to content-dualism) narrow content, not broad content. Now, if all or part of the semantic property (or content) of an individual's belief depends upon its causal and/or inferential relations to the individual's other propositional attitudes, and if no two individuals have all the same propositional attitudes, then, as Fodor (1987b; 1990) and Fodor & Lepore (1992) have emphasized, the risk is that no pair of individuals will ever instantiate any one intentional psychological law.[4] If the task of human psychology is, as I assumed with Fodor in chapter 5, to subsume individuals under inten-

---

[2] As I defined *supervenience* in chapter 1, a set of properties A supervene on a set of subvening properties B iff for each instantiation of an A-property, a B-property is coinstantiated; the A-property would not be instantiated if a B-property were not coinstantiated; and given that one and the same B-property is instantiated, then one and the same A-property must be instantiated.

[3] As I will also argue in the next chapter, the hope that the appropriate notion of narrow content of an individual's belief would supervene on physical properties of his or her brain cannot be satisfied.

[4] Assuming that intentional psychological laws must refer to the contents of individuals' propositional attitudes. For detailed assessment of the risk, see below.

tional psychological laws, then it must be possible for one and the same belief-state to be instantiated by different individuals. If inferential (or functional) role semantics leads to meaning (or semantic) holism, and if semantic holism is incompatible with scientific psychology, then so might be inferential role semantics. If inferential role semantics is an outgrowth of functionalism, then functionalism too might turn out to be inconsistent with scientific psychology.

Notice that, on the assumption that intentional psychological laws must refer to the contents of individuals' mental states, the content-dualist cannot hope to evade the problem of meaning holism by arguing that, unlike narrow content, broad content can remain purely informational and, therefore, not be infected by meaning holism. The reason the content dualist cannot use this ploy is that – as a content-dualist – he assumes that intentional psychological laws must refer to semantic properties of an individual's propositional attitudes which supervene upon the physical properties of an individual's brain, i.e., to the narrow, not to the broad, semantic properties of an individual's propositional attitudes. So if the narrow semantic properties of an individual's propositional attitudes were holistic, then no intentional psychological law would subsume more than one individual at a time. For the purpose of the causal psychological explanation of an individual's behavior, a content-dualist, therefore, cannot concede holism of narrow semantic properties and stick to an atomistic view of broad content. For the time being, I merely state the Fodorian argument for the incompatibility between narrow content holism and there being intentional psychological laws subsuming different individuals in virtue of the contents of their mental states. I will shortly (in section 4) examine a way of evading the Fodorian conclusion based on the distinction between the idea that intentional psychological laws must refer to the contents of individuals' mental states and the idea that intentional psychological laws must quantify over the contents of individuals' mental states.

If meaning holism is incompatible with the possibility of intentional psychological laws, then – as argued in chapter 5 – meaning holism threatens the second part of the intentional realist program: provide an account of the causal role of semantic properties of an individual's propositional attitudes. In fact, it might be thought – and Fodor (1990e: xi; 1994: 6) has said so on several occasions – that meaning holism is incompatible with the first part of the intentional realist program as well: the naturalization of intentionality. Meaning holism might be thought to conflict with the basic assumptions of informational semantics according to which the semantic properties of a system's internal states arise out of the nomic dependencies between internal states of the system and properties from his or her environment. Assuming that the pressure for rejecting meaning holism comes from both sides of the intentional realist coin, Fodor & Lepore (1991: 330–31) have drawn a contrast between a view which they call either "New Testament Semantics" or "structuralism" – and which Fodor (1994: 4, 6, 14, 86–87) calls the "intrasymbolic" view – and a view which they call "Old Testament Semantics." According to the former, which is no other than conceptual (inferential or functional) role semantics, and which they reject, semantic properties may arise "from relations among symbols." According to the latter, which is no other than informational semantics, and which they accept, semantic properties arise from relations between thoughts and the world.

Let us pause briefly to reflect on the irony of the situation we presently find ourselves in. Functionalism was put forward in the 1960s (first by Putnam, then by Fodor, Dennett and others) as a framework for scientific computational psychology.[5]

On the one hand, Putnam (1983; 1988; 1994), who now thinks that the scope of computational psychology has narrow limits, rejects functionalism presumably for three reasons having to do with externalism, holism, and the normativity of meaning.

First, his view seems to be that functionalism is inconsistent with an externalist view of the semantic properties of an individual's propositional attitudes (about which more in the next two chapters). It is not, however, obvious that a semantic functionalist cannot subscribe to externalism, as Harman's (1982) "long-armed" version of functional role testifies. It all depends on how inputs and outputs are individuated. A semantic functionalist will individuate the semantic property of an individual's mental state M by its causal or inferential relations to inputs, outputs, and other mental states. If the individual's environment enters the individuation of inputs and outputs, i.e., if the princi-

---

5 Lewis (1966) was one of the early proponents of functionalism. Unlike Putnam, Fodor and Dennett, however, he did not care much about *computational* psychology. He was rather interested in functionalism as a framework for capturing commonsense "platitudinous" psychology.

ples of individuation of inputs and outputs, are externalist, then so will be *M*'s inferential or causal role.

Secondly, Putnam (1983: 149–54) now sharply distinguishes the goals of computational psychology from what he calls "interpretation theory" which he takes to be essentially holistic. As he puts it (*ibid.*: 150): "to have a description of how a system of representations works in functionalist terms is one thing; to have an *interpretation* of that system of representations is quite another thing." But again, it is far from clear that a semantic functionalist who subscribes to content-dualism cannot accept a holistic view of narrow content, as, for example, Block's (1986; 1987) two-factor theory shows: on this view, narrow content (which is functional, causal or inferential role) is, but broad content need not be, holistic.

Finally, Putnam (1983; 1988) assumes that interpretation theory – as opposed to computational psychology and science more generally – has some kind of interest-relativity built into it. This kind of interest-relativity, which Putnam (1988: 11–15) connects to the normativity of meaning or intentionality, does not preempt the existence of standards of correctness for interpretive schemes. In particular, it does not entail that as far as interpretation is concerned, as Feyerabend (1975) would say of scientific theorizing, "anything goes." Far from it. It does, however, demarcate interpretation (and translation) practices from the natural sciences. We might say that Putnam (1983; 1988) sees the limitations of functionalism from the top down: from a hermeneutic (or interpretative) point of view which is based on his acceptance of externalism, semantic holism, and the interest-relativity of interpretation.[6]

On the other hand, Fodor (1987b; 1990; 1994), a staunch advocate of computationalism in psychology, now sees the dangers of functionalism from the bottom up: from the standpoint of someone who (as made clear in chapter 5) takes the goal of scientific psychology to come up with species-wide universal psychological intentional laws and rejects semantic holism. In particular, Fodor (1987b) expected intentional psychological laws to refer to the narrow semantic

---

[6] Although, as I just said above, perhaps only the interest-relativity of interpretation might be a strong reason for rejecting functionalism. Putnam's views about the holistic and normative character of intentionality is related to Davidson's views discussed in chapter 5, section 5, where I suggested a way of deflating the role of the normativity of intentionality as one of Davidson's grounds for mental anomalism.

properties of an individual's propositional attitudes. The broad semantic properties of an individual's propositional attitudes might be rooted in nomic covariations between the individual's mind and his or her environment, and thus protected from semantic holism. The narrow semantic properties of his or her mental states, however, to which intentional psychological laws would refer, would be the primary victims of semantic holism.[7] This is the main reason why Fodor (1994) has given up on content-dualism and rejected all forms of intrasymbolic view of meaning, i.e., any version of semantic functionalism.

Putnam and Fodor then agree that semantic holism is destructive of a computationally based intentional scientific psychology, i.e., of a psychological approach which is simultaneously based on computational theorizing and aimed at disclosing general causal laws based on the contents of mental states. Putnam, who seems to accept semantic holism, is therefore pessimistic towards the prospects of a computationally based intentional scientific psychology. Fodor, who embraces informational semantics and assumes the existence of psychological intentional laws, accepts what he calls semantic atomism. According to semantic atomism (about which more soon), a symbol or a mental state derives its semantic property entirely from its informational relation with a property instantiated in the environment. No relation among symbols can generate any semantic property. As I will argue in this chapter, I think there is room for a third position between meaning holism and meaning atomism. If this is right, then we are not bound to accept meaning atomism in order to protect the possibility of intentional psychological laws. Nor do I think that informational semantics precludes any other view but semantic atomism.

6.3 THE VARIETIES OF HOLISM

Semantic holism is a property of contents or semantic properties. It is, therefore, a property of properties of either propositional attitudes or linguistic symbols. Now, holism was introduced into contemporary philosophy of mind via the philosophy of science. It rose to prominence in the philosophy of science when Quine (1951) resurrected

---

[7] Again, I emphasize the fact that Fodor assumes that intentional psychological laws must *refer* to the contents (or semantic properties) of individuals' mental states. I will question this assumption in section 4.

Duhem's (1906) thesis according to which scientific hypotheses face the tribunal of sense experience only as a corporate body. An experimental or observational prediction can be derived from a particular hypothesis only in conjunction with a collection of auxiliary hypotheses – including logic – some of which have been implemented in the design of the experimental (or observational) apparatus needed to gather the evidence. When a prediction fails to be confirmed by some evidence, then in principle (if not in practice) any proposition which was needed to derive the prediction could be blamed for the failure. This holistic feature of the confirmation of scientific hypotheses can be called *confirmation* holism. Quine (1951) argued from confirmation holism to the denial of the analytic/synthetic distinction and for the view that logic which is required in the confirmation of scientific hypotheses cannot be divorced from the rest of empirical science. Not only does Fodor (1983) accept confirmation holism, but he is willing to take the confirmation of scientific hypotheses as a model for the process of belief-fixation by what he calls central thought processes, by contrast with perceptual modular input systems. He, therefore, is willing to draw a sharp distinction between the holistic feature of central thought processes and what he calls the informational encapsulation of modular input systems.

Now, presumably, unless one adopts a radically nihilistic view of content (and semantic properties),[8] the very notion of confirmation holism presupposes that scientific hypotheses which are brought to a test have contents (or semantic properties) to begin with. In order to determine whether a hypothesis is true or false, one must know what its content is. So confirmation holism cannot help determine meaning or content and should, therefore, be distinguished from meaning (or semantic) holism – which is about content.

As I said at the beginning of the present chapter, beliefs have at least two kinds of properties: they have semantic properties (they are backward-looking structures) and they are beliefs (they have beliefhood, they are forward-looking structures). I called cognitive holism the interdependence of propositional attitudes. Cognitive holism, then, which I take to be an uncontroversial property of beliefs, could be a (higher-order) property of either properties of beliefs: their semantic

---

[8] For example, an eliminativist view such as I discussed in chapter 1, section 2.

properties or their beliefhood. To see the dilemma at work, consider the following subtle passage from Davidson (1975: 156–57):

> If someone is glad that, or notices that, or remembers that, or knows that, the gun is loaded, then he must believe that the gun is loaded. Even to wonder whether the gun is loaded, or to speculate on the possibility that the gun is loaded, requires the belief, for example, that the gun is a weapon, that it is a more or less enduring physical object, and so on. There are good reasons for not insisting on any particular list of beliefs that are needed if a creature is to wonder whether a gun is loaded. Nevertheless, it is necessary that there be endless interlocked beliefs . . . There is probably no definite list of things that must be believed by someone who understands the sentence "The gun is loaded", but it is necessary that there be endless interlocked beliefs.

There are at least three ideas to be distinguished in these lines: one idea could be called, following Fodor & Lepore (1992: 105–35), the *primacy of belief*; the second idea could be called *belief holism*; the third idea is *meaning holism*. According to the first thesis, beliefs have some kind of priority over other propositional attitudes. According to the second thesis, for a creature to have a given particular belief, he or she must have a set of "endless interlocked" other beliefs. According to the third thesis, for one thought to have content (to have a semantic property), there must exist a surrounding network of other thoughts with contents (or semantic properties). Framed in terms of content identity (rather than as a condition for what it takes to have a thought content), meaning holism can be put within a semantic functionalist framework as follows: the content of an individual's thought depends on (or is constituted by) its causal inferential relations to the individual's other thoughts.[9] I will not be particularly concerned with the primacy of belief. Many of the interactive features of beliefs which I called cognitive holism above might either follow from belief holism or from meaning holism. According to Fodor (1987b; 1994) and Fodor & Lepore (1992), what is destructive of the goals of intentional psychology – what is inconsistent with there being causal intentional psychological laws – is meaning holism, not belief holism.

Meaning holism, however, has not been given a completely uni-

---

[9] See section 5 of the present chapter for more on semantic functionalism or functional role semantics.

vocal construal by Fodor himself. Fodor (1987b: 56–57) called meaning holism the view that the content (or semantic property) of an individual's belief *B* is determined by the relations between *B* and *all* his or her other actual beliefs – by the totality of what Fodor called *B*'s "epistemic liaisons." I will call this version of meaning holism the *universal* or *all*-interpretation of meaning holism. It entails that no two individuals can share a belief unless they share every other actual belief.

Now, Fodor & Lepore (1992: 1–10, and see the Glossary) called a property *P anatomic* just in case if anything has it, then at least one other thing has it too. Being a sibling is such an anatomic property since if *x* is *y*'s sibling, then it follows that *y* is *x*'s sibling.[10] A property is said to be *atomic* if it is *not* anatomic. And a property is *holistic* if it is very anatomic: it is holistic just in case if anything has it, then *many* other things have it too. Fodor & Lepore (1992: 258) define meaning holism as the "metaphysical claim that properties like having content are holistic in the sense that no expression in a language can have them unless many other (nonsynonymous) expressions in that language have them too." I will call this latter version of meaning holism the *many*-interpretation of meaning holism.

Consider again Fodor & Lepore's (1992) definition according to which a semantic property is holistic just in case if anything has it, then many other things have it too. Not only is there a possible ambiguity between the many-interpretation and the all-interpretation of meaning holism, but there are two ways meaning holism might apply to semantic properties because semantic properties may give rise to two distinct questions. On the one hand, we may ask whether some physical device (or some state of a physical device) has some content (some semantic property) or other. This is the question: does the device possess what could be called *generic* semantic properties? Or, perhaps, does the device possess the right non-semantic (physical, chemical, biological, informational) properties for it to possess some semantic property or other, i.e., to possess semanticity? To have

---

[10] Notice that there is something suspicious in the fact that Fodor & Lepore (1992) are willing to draw metaphysical consequences from the difference between the properties expressed by the English predicates "brother" and "sibling." From the fact that *x* is a sibling, it follows that there is a *y* who is *x*'s sibling. From the fact that *x* is a brother, however, it does not follow that there is a *y* who is *x*'s brother since *x* might be *y*'s brother and *y* might be *x*'s sister.

semanticity is to possess generic semantic properties. The possession of generic semantic properties, then, is relevant to the program of naturalizing intentionality: in virtue of which non-semantic property or relation does a physical device possess some semantic property or other? What non-semantic property may confer upon a physical device its representational power (if any)?

Alternatively, we may wonder whether a creature may be credited, not with some content (or semantic property) or other, but with some *specific* semantic property. Can a creature be credited with – or does it possess – for example, the concept of a cat, the concept of a quark or the concept of something being to the left of something else? In dealing with the possession of specific semantic properties, we may ask: can a creature have the concept of a cat without having other concepts such as the concepts of an animal, purring, fur or paws? Or can a creature have the concept of x being to the left of y without having the concept of y being to the right of x? Equivalently, we may ask whether some particular proposition may be believed or entertained by a particular creature without some other proposition being believed or entertained by this creature. Were we to ask the question of linguistic symbols (not beliefs), we might ask whether some particular proposition may be expressed by some symbol or other of a given language without other propositions being expressed by some symbol or other of the language in question.

6.4 SOME ALLEGEDLY DREADFUL CONSEQUENCES OF MEANING HOLISM

Now, I want to argue that some of the worst consequences which Fodor (1987b) and Fodor & Lepore (1992) impute to meaning holism – particularly for intentional psychology – might follow from the all-interpretation of meaning holism, not from the many-interpretation. Ultimately, I shall suggest why meaning holism on the all-interpretation might not be destructive of intentional psychology at all. Consider the semantic property $R^\star$ which an expression δ (or a set of expressions) has just in case it refers to something or other referred to by current astronomy. Suppose a theory may conveniently be said to have $R^\star$ just in case it contains an expression which has $R^\star$. If current astronomy, say, refers to the moon and if expression δ refers to the moon, then δ is $R^\star$. Now, suppose $R^\star$ is holistic. Then depending on which definition of a holistic property one chooses, then from the fact that $R^\star$ is holistic, it might or not follow that a theory which contains δ and which does *not* refer to everything referred to by current astronomy cannot refer to anything referred to by current atronomy.

Consider the all-interpretation of meaning holism first. On this version, if a theory which has $R^\star$ does not refer to everything referred to by current astronomy, then it cannot refer to anything referred to by current astronomy. Greek astronomy for instance, which prima facie referred to the moon, has $R^\star$. But it did not refer to everything referred to by current astronomy. So if $R^\star$ is holistic, and on the all-interpretation of a holistic property, Greek astronomy did not refer to anything referred to by current astronomy, not even to stars. If the Greeks did not manage to refer to stars, then, as Fodor & Lepore (1992: 12) put it, "the Greeks did not have any views about stars." And if so, then we cannot compare what Greek astronomy and current astronomy have to say about stars. This is clearly a dreadful consequence of meaning holism. But notice that it follows – if it does – on the all-interpretation, not the many-interpretation. Does it actually follow on the all-interpretation? Arguably, it might be said that, even on the all-interpretation, the ancient Greeks and current astronomers refer to the same thing, i.e., the moon, when they use a symbol which stands for the moon. When some ancient Greek and a current astronomer think something expressible by "The moon shines," perhaps the contents of their respective thoughts are embedded in such wildly different doxastic environments that we cannot compare the contents of their thoughts. But even then it does not thereby follow that they do not both refer to the moon.

What follows from the many-interpretation? On the many-interpretation of a holistic property, and if $R^\star$ is holistic, then it is far from clear that, having $R^\star$, Greek astronomy could not refer to stars. Arguably, although it did not refer to some of the things to which current astronomy refers, still Greek astronomy did refer to many of the things which current astronomy refers to. Undoubtedly, it is the job of historians of science to draw our attention to the startling contrasts between what Greek astronomy and current astronomy predicate of what they both refer to. And it is the job of historians of science to draw our attention to the contrasts between what Greek astronomers referred to and what current astronomers refer to. But the existence of such contrasts should not, as Davidson (1974b),

Dennett (1981a: 19) and Putnam (1973b; 1981: 113–19) have insisted, blind us to the great many things referred to in common by both Greek and current astronomy. Although Greek astronomers did not refer to black holes, quarks or DNA molecules, still they presumably referred to the moon, oceans, rivers, rocks, trees, horses, birds, human beings, buildings and so on and so forth.

A similar line of reasoning applies to the possibility of intentional psychological laws. Consider the semantic property $T^\star$ which a belief has if it is a token of the same type as some belief of Smith's or perhaps a belief has $T^\star$ if it has the same content or semantic property as some belief of Smith's. Suppose now that $T^\star$ is holistic. Only on the all-interpretation does it seem to follow that, if a belief is (or has) $T^\star$, then intentional psychological laws subsuming several individuals are impossible. Only from the assumption that two individuals cannot share any belief unless they share *every* other belief would it follow that no two individuals can be said to share the same belief and be subsumed by intentional psychological laws. On the assumption that two individuals cannot share the same belief unless they share *many* other beliefs, it might well be that different individuals may indeed share beliefs and be subsumed by intentional psychological laws since arguably two distinct individuals do share many beliefs (such as that water above O° C is a liquid, gold is a metal, two is an even number, Tuesday follows Monday, grass is green, snow is white, roses are flowers, most birds are covered with feathers, and so on and so forth). *A fortiori*, will two different time slices of the same individual at different times share many beliefs.

Furthermore, it might be argued that only on one crucial additional assumption does meaning holism on the all-interpretation really threaten the possibility of intentional psychological laws: only if it is assumed that the content (or semantic property) of an individual's belief depend on all his or her *actual* beliefs. An individual's actual beliefs depend on the individual's personal biography. So it is that no two individuals (not even presumably genuine twins) can share all the same actual beliefs. None the less, it might be argued that an individual's beliefs which are relevant for species-wide intentional psychological laws are not all of an individual's actual beliefs but his or her counterfactual beliefs – the beliefs he or she would form were he or she in such or such circumstances. Such a view should appeal to a nativist like Fodor who assumes that many if not all human concepts are innate (and, therefore, common to all members of the human species).

Until now, I have accepted Fodor's assumption that intentional psychological laws must *refer* to the contents (or semantic properties) of individuals' propositional attitudes. Earlier on (in chapter 5), I have deliberately put the view as the disjunctive claim that intentional psychological laws must refer to, or quantify over, the contents of individuals' propositional attitudes. But now, following a suggestion of Evans (1980), I want to take seriously the distinction between *referring to*, and *quantifying over*, the contents of individuals' propositional attitudes. As Evans (1980: 80) puts it, the *instantiation* of an intentional psychological law may *refer* to the content of an individual's mental state. But an intentional psychological law need not: such a law may simply *quantify* over such contents. This is why we often illustrate intentional psychological laws by such schemata as: "If X believes that p and X believes that if p then q, then X is likely to acquire the belief that q"; or "if X wants q and if X believes that not q unless p, then X is likely to try to bring it about that p." In such schemata, typically, no reference is made to any particular content; particular contents are quantified over. What matters to such lawlike schemata is that what X believes and desires in the antecedent of the conditional be the same as what he believes and desires in the consequent. What matters is identity of content. Whatever it is that X believes in the first conditional schema, there is something X believes, and X's conclusion would not go through unless what q stands for is one and the same thing in the antecedent and in the conclusion. If intentional psychological laws quantify over the particular contents of individuals' propositional attitudes, then meaning holism on the all-interpretation may simply be no threat to the possibility of intentional psychological laws. In particular, contrary to the view I ascribed to Fodor (in section 2 of the present chapter), it might be possible for a content-dualist (or even for a pure internalist who rejects externalism wholesale) to assume that the narrow content of an individual's propositional attitude is holistic (on the all-interpretation) and still entertain the view that intentional psychological laws quantify over such narrow contents and apply to the attitudes of many distinct individuals.

6.5 WHY MEANING ATOMISM SHOULD BE RESISTED

From the above discussion, it follows that only the all-interpretation, not the many-interpretation, of meaning holism has the dreadful consequences which preoccupy Fodor, such as the impossibility of intentional psychological laws. Furthermore, I have argued that meaning holism would not really threaten the possibility of intentional psychological laws if the latter only require quantification over the contents of individuals' propositional attitudes. Now, not only can one, as I have just done, distinguish two interpretations of meaning holism, but one can also, I think, argue for an intermediate position between meaning holism and meaning atomism: a position which, following Fodor & Lepore (1992), we could call *meaning anatomism* or perhaps *meaning molecularism*. Before I examine Fodor & Lepore's (1992) strategy for preempting the possibility of meaning molecularism, I want to say why I do not find meaning atomism attractive.

Fodor (1987b) has explicitly argued in favor of meaning atomism or the possibility of what he has called a *punctate mind*. As I said above, meaning holism (in one version or other) may seem like a consequence of semantic functionalism (or inferential role semantics). Suppose we reject the latter. Then, as noted by Fodor (1987b: 88), it follows that "believing that *P* is compatible with believing practically anything; even *not P*." Contrary to expectations, rather than take this consequence as a refutation of his rejection of semantic functionalism (or inferential role semantics), Fodor (*ibid.*) embraces this consequence: "I accept – in fact, welcome – what amounts to the conclusion that people can believe things that are arbitrarily mad." But now, if a belief's content is divorced from any functional (or inferential) role, why should anyone bother drawing any consequences from one's beliefs? Fodor (1987b: 89) goes so far as entertaining the possibility that "the thought that three is a prime number could constitute an *entire mental life*" – the life of a punctate mind.

Presumably, a punctate mind is a device with no logical (or inferential) abilities. There are two things I would like to say about the mental life of a punctate mind. First of all, the example is, I think, rather unfortunate. If we try and make sense of a creature with a punctate mind, we would rather think of a device whose unique internal state (or mental symbol) of type r would nomologically covary with one and the same state-type s of the creature's environment. Every tokening of the creature's state type would instantiate property G, and every instantiation of property G would in turn nomically covary with the instantiation of some property F in the creature's environment. Whether we want to call thought the creature's internal state of type r carrying the information that state-type s obtains (or that property F is instantiated), I will leave open. So will I leave open the question whether we want to credit such a device with a mind. But on both issues, I strongly feel the inclination to provide a negative answer. And I do not see that doing so is in any way incompatible with intentional realism. Of course, such a denial does amount to denying the possibility of a punctate mind. But one cannot rest such a case on mere intuitions. The reason the example is unfortunate is that it is hard to make sense of the view that the content of the thought that three is a prime number could be the informational content of a creature's unique mental symbol-type whose tokenings depend upon nomic covariations with states (or instantiations of a property) of its environment. It is hard to believe that such a thought could arise out of nomic covariations between internal states of a device and states of its environment, i.e., between instantiations of property G by tokenings of the creature's internal state r and instantiations of property F in the environment.

Secondly, however, and on behalf of Fodor's line, one might argue that there is room for distinguishing between entertaining a thought (e.g., the thought that p) and having a belief (e.g., the belief that p).[11] The essence of the view, which Dennett (1988: 386) has called an "eviscerated functionalism," is to accept *psychofunctionalism* and reject *semantic functionalism* (or functional role semantics). In Fodor's (1987b: 69) words, the property of beliefhood (the property of being a belief, as opposed to being another propositional *attitude*) is "a matter of having the right connections to inputs, outputs and other mental states . . . what the philosophical motivations for Psychofunctionalism . . . do not underwrite is the much stronger claim that being the belief *that p*, being a belief that has a certain *content*, is a matter of having the right connections to inputs, outputs, and other mental states." So on this "eviscerated functionalist" view, functionalism applies to beliefhood, not to a belief's semantic

---

[11] See the preceding chapter for an attempted alternative to the account of the complexity of disjunctive beliefs in terms of the complexity of disjunctive mental symbols.

property. Unlike a belief's semantic property, a belief's beliefhood is a functional property (of a brain-state token). It follows that a punctate mind could be said to entertain a single thought, not, however, to be ascribed a single belief. Psychofunctionalism precludes belief atomism, not meaning atomism.

The view seems to be based on the acceptance of psychofunctionalism, on the rejection of semantic functionalism, and on the acceptance of meaning atomism. The question none the less arises: is meaning atomism compatible with ascribing to thoughts the property which Fodor (1987b) and Fodor & Lepore (1992) call *systematicity*? As I said in chapter 5 in relation to compositionality, systematicity is a property of both natural languages and human minds. Systematicity is the property that if a natural language contains a sentence S expressing a complex proposition P, then it must contain other sentences expressing structurally (or syntactically) related propositions. A mind is systematic in case if it can entertain a complex proposition, then it will have the capacity to entertain structurally related propositions. There seems prima facie to be a tension between meaning atomism and systematicity: the latter asserts that a mind cannot entertain a complex thought unless it can entertain another related complex thought; the former denies that the content of an individual's thought depends on the relation between the thought and any other of the individual's thoughts. I think meaning atomism is not logically incompatible with systematicity. Let me say why.

First of all, systematicity is consistent with the mere denial of meaning holism on the all-interpretation. A systematic mind with the ability to entertain a complex thought (e.g., the thought that Rab) is said to have the ability to entertain *some* other complex thoughts (e.g., the structurally related thought that Rba). The denial of meaning holism on the all-interpretation is the claim that the content of an individual's belief does not depend on its relations to all his or her other beliefs. Systematicity is thus compatible with the denial of meaning holism. Of course the denial of meaning holism (on the all-interpretation) is not meaning atomism but meaning anatomism. And it may seem that systematicity is only consistent with meaning anatomism, not with meaning atomism. But this is not strictly speaking true for the following reason.

Systematicity is a property of *complex* thoughts (or mental symbols). Or pehaps I should say that it is a property of minds with the ability to entertain complex thoughts (or mental symbols). Let us say that a complex thought (or mental symbol) will have systematic correlates in virtue of its syntactic structure. Unlike systematicity, meaning atomism presumably applies to the contents (or semantic properties) of *primitive* thoughts (or mental symbols) without a syntactic structure. It applies, for example, to constituents of complex systematic thoughts (or mental symbols). Meaning atomism and systematicity, therefore, do not apply to thoughts of the same level of complexity. It follows that meaning atomism does not formally contradict the systematicity of thoughts.[12] I do, however, think that systematicity fits better meaning anatomism than meaning atomism and I think it is a mistake to assume that an intentional realist must cling to meaning atomism.

Stich (1983), who, as I explained in chapter 5, argues in favor of STM (the syntactic theory of mind), agrees with Fodor and Putnam that meaning holism is destructive of a psychological approach based on intentional psychological laws which would involve a reference to the semantic properties of propositional attitudes. However, as I argued above, this is only true if intentional psychological laws involve a reference to content, not if they quantify over contents of individuals' propositional attitudes. Now, Stich (1983: 55–57) has designed a famous example: for many years, Mrs. T. correctly believed (as many Americans of her generation) that US President William McKinley was assassinated. Then, as she grew older, through failures of her memory, she forgot many things relating to death, assassination, and President McKinley. By then she could not confidently be ascribed the belief that President McKinley was assassinated. Stich takes his example to establish meaning holism. In Fodor & Lepore's

---

[12] Besides, it might be pointed out that Fodor himself takes systematicity to be a contingent property of complex thoughts. Given that holism might be taken to be a conceptual (constitutive or non-contingent) feature of meaning (or content), it might be argued that anatomism and atomism too are conceptual (constitutive or non-contingent) features of meaning. If so, then we would have a further contrast between meaning atomism and systematicity which would ensure their compatibility. On the one hand, however, I am not sure that it is open to Fodor to assume that meaning atomism is a non-contingent (constitutive) feature of meaning, given his stance on the analytic/synthetic distinction. On the other hand, (as I said in chapter 5), I cannot merely grant Fodor his claim that systematicity is a contingent feature of complex thoughts.

(1992) terminology, we might say that what it establishes is meaning anatomism, rather than meaning holism: what the example does seem to show is that the possession of such concepts as ASSASSINATION, DEATH, PRESIDENT, is constitutive of (or is a necessary condition for) having the belief that President McKinley was assassinated. Unless one has the above concepts, one can hardly form the belief. However, this is not at all Fodor's (1987b: 62, 92–93, 159, 161) strategy: he takes great pains to try and establish that Stich's example is compatible with meaning atomism.

Rather than examine Fodor's alternative account of Stich's example which I do not find convincing, what I want to do at this point is pause over the fact that, while he vehemently rejects any non-atomistic (or "intrasymbolic") account of belief content, he (1987b: 159) concedes that belief-*ascription* is holistic. Now I would like to argue that this asymmetry is not plausible. As I said in chapter 1, on my view, when B ascribes a belief to A, B forms a higher-order belief about A's belief. From this meta-representational perspective, it would be really odd to assume that the content of A's lower-order belief (about the fact that President McKinley was assassinated, as it might be) is atomistic and simultaneously that the content of B's higher-order belief about A's belief is holistic.

My reluctance towards semantic atomism, however, does not arise mainly from the fact that I find the above asymmetry between atomistic belief contents and the holism of belief-ascriptions unjustified. I find semantic atomism disturbing mostly because I subscribe to a version of informational semantics. As made clear (in chapters 2 and 3), according to informational semantics, for symbol r to carry information about the instantiation of property F, there must exist a nomic dependency between property G of symbol r and property F. According to semantic atomism, primitive semantic properties are never generated by relations among symbols (or things having semantic properties). In other words, primitive concepts have no internal structure: there are no inferential connections among primitive concepts. If one subscribes both to informational semantics and to semantic atomism, then for every pair of symbol and property represented, there must exist a nomic dependency between some property of the symbol and the property represented. Informational semantics must of course presuppose that some property of a signal may be under the nomic dependency of some natural kind (e.g., water). But what of properties which are obviously not natural kinds? What of artefacts? What of, for example, the property of being a shirt?[13] Assuming that my concept of a shirt has no syntactic structure and that the property of being a shirt does not enter lawlike generalizations, then, it seems to me, semantic atomism makes informational semantics needlessly difficult.

6.6 IS THE ALTERNATIVE BETWEEN MEANING HOLISM AND MEANING ATOMISM EXHAUSTIVE?

Following Fodor (1987b), the major goal of Fodor & Lepore (1992) is to preempt the possibility of meaning anatomism (or meaning molecularism) by arguing that the alternative between meaning atomism and meaning holism is exhaustive. The main weapon at their disposal is a version of what Fodor (1987b: 60) called the "Ur-Argument" and which Fodor & Lepore (1992: 23–32) call "Argument A." The conclusion of the Ur-Argument was clearly the all-interpretation of meaning holism:

[1a]   At least some epistemic liaisons of a belief determine its inten-tional content (or semantic property) (where an epistemic liaison of a belief is a proposition whose truth or falsity is rele-vant to the semantic evaluation of the belief).

[2a]   Either no epistemic liaison of a belief determines its intentional content or they all do.

[3a]   Conclusion: All the epistemic liaisons of a belief determine its intentional content.

Conclusion [3a] is a statement of meaning holism (in the all-inter-pretation). Clearly, the argument is sound. If one wants, however, to reject the conclusion, one may reject either premiss. Fodor (1987b) claims that premiss [2a] followed from the rejection of the analytic/synthetic distinction. Since he accepts Quine's criticism of the analytic/synthetic distinction, Fodor, therefore, accepts premiss [2a] and rejects premiss [1a]. Rejecting premiss [1a], of course,

---

[13] For discussion of how the property of being a shirt could be represented, see Fodor (1986; 1991) and Antony & Levine (1991). An informational semanticist who subscribes to semantic atomism will presumably claim that uninstantiated properties (e.g., being a unicorn) cannot be represented by primitive symbols with no syntactic structure.

amounts to accepting meaning atomism. I claimed earlier that there were two possible ambiguities: one was the ambiguity between the all-interpretation and the many-interpretation of meaning holism; the other was the ambiguity between the possession of generic semantic properties and the possession of specific semantic properties. As Fodor & Lepore's (1992) version of the same argument – Argument A – shows, premiss [1a], however, is ambiguous. Argument A is stated in terms of the notion of an anatomic property:

[1b] Semantic properties are anatomic.
[2b] There is no analytic/synthetic distinction.
[3b] Conclusion: semantic properties are holistic.

First of all, whereas in the Ur-Argument, premiss [2a] followed from the rejection of the analytic/synthetic distinction, in Argument A, premiss [2b] is the rejection of the analytic/synthetic distinction. Secondly, as Fodor & Lepore (1992: 27–30) recognize, given the notion of an anatomic property, the first premiss [1b] may have two readings which may be represented by a scope distinction. On the one hand, property P may be said to be *weakly* anatomic just in case in all possible worlds, for all x, if x has P, then there is a y distinct from x which has P too (with the operator for necessity "$\Box$," which can be read as "in all possible worlds," having scope over the universal quantifier, which itself has wider scope than the existential quantifier):

$$\Box \, (\forall x) \, (\exists y) \, [y \neq x \, \& \, (Px \rightarrow Py)].$$

On the other hand, property P may be said to be *strongly* anatomic just in case for all x, there is a y distinct from x such that, in all possible worlds, if x has P, then y has P too (with the quantifiers having wider scope than the operator for necessity "$\Box$"):

$$(\forall x)(\exists y) \, \Box \, [y \neq x \, \& \, (Px \rightarrow Py)].$$

Notice first that unless we specify that x and y must be distinct individuals, the weak reading is threatened to be a tautology or a logical truth: $(\forall x) \, [Px \rightarrow (\exists y) \, Py]$. Second, on the assumption that the relevant universe of discourse contains exactly two individuals, then the two notions of anatomicity will turn out to be equivalent. Obviously, the strong reading entails the weak reading. And given that there are exactly two individuals, the weak reading will be seen to entail the strong reading too.

Let P be the property of being believed by Smith. Whether property P is indeed a genuine semantic property in the required sense is something I assume provisionally and will question at the end of this chapter. Suppose P is weakly anatomic. Thus, if proposition Σ is believed by Smith, then there must be at least some other proposition which is believed by Smith too. On the weak reading, there is no unique proposition (nor is there a unique set of propositions) which Smith would be required to believe for him to believe Σ: in one possible world, Smith might be required to believe one proposition; in different possible worlds, he might be required to believe different propositions. Suppose P is strongly anatomic. Then, for all x, there is a y such that if x is a proposition believed by Smith, y is a proposition which must be believed by Smith too. On the strong reading, for any proposition that Smith believes, in every possible world, there is another unique proposition (or set of propositions) which Smith is required to believe.

In terms of the distinction I drew earlier between the possession of generic semantic properties and the possession of specific semantic properties, I want to say that weak anatomism involves the possession of generic semantic properties; strong anatomism involves the possession of specific semantic properties. Again suppose P is the property of being believed by Smith and P is weakly anatomic. Thus, if proposition Σ happens to have property P, then as a matter of Smith's cognitive design or architecture, there must be other propositions with property P: there must be some other propositions with property P whatever they are. Since the other propositions will not be the same in all possible worlds, they need not be semantically related to Σ. Weak anatomicity is a property of generic semantic properties. To say that weak anatomicity is a property of generic semantic properties is to make a claim about Smith's cognitive architecture. Weak anatomicity is a (possibly false) claim about what enables a device to have semantic properties. It claims that if a device has some semantic property, then it must have several. The claim in other words is that it would be surprising if Smith believed only one proposition. Suppose now that P, which is the property of being believed by Smith, is strongly anatomic. Then if proposition Σ has P, there must be some other specific propositions with property P: these other propositions with property P are specific in the sense that they will be the same in all possible worlds. Strong anatomicity, therefore, is a claim about specific semantic properties in the sense that it involves relations among semantically related propositions. Strong anatomicity, then, is the claim that propositions come as packages in virtue of the semantic relations holding between them.

Now, my claim is going to be that Fodor & Lepore (1992) face a dilemma: either the first premiss [1b] of Argument A is weak meaning anatomism or it is strong meaning anatomism. If the former, then, I will argue, Argument A is about the possession of generic semantic properties or about the conditions for semanticity. If so, then, I claim, premiss [2b], i.e., the rejection of the analytic/synthetic distinction ought not to be relevant. If the latter, then Argument A is about the possession of specific semantic properties. If so, however, premisses [1b] and [2b] might turn out to be inconsistent.

In their explicit statement of Argument A, Fodor & Lepore (1992: 23–24) equivocate between the possession of generic and the possession of specific semantic properties. The first premiss is stated in terms of weak generic meaning anatomism and it involves the possession of generic semantic properties: it refers to the property of being some belief-or-other-of-Smith's. The second premiss, however, is the claim that "there is no principled distinction between the propositions that Smith has to believe to believe that *p* and the propositions that Smith doesn't have to believe to believe that *p*," where "believing that *p*" expresses a specific semantic property.

Suppose the first premiss is weak meaning anatomism: suppose that being some belief-or-other-of-Smith's is weakly anatomic or that having some content (some semantic property) or other is weakly anatomic. Clearly, what is involved is the possession of generic semantic properties. From the fact that such generic semantic properties are anatomic, what might follow is generic meaning holism (on the many-interpretation): it might follow that many propositions are believed by Smith or that many things have some content (some semantic property) or other. As I said earlier, on the many-interpretation of generic meaning holism, it is not clear that any dreadful consequences follow – particularly as far as the possibility of intentional psychological laws is concerned. Furthermore, not only is weak meaning anatomism a plausible doctrine, but if the relevant generic semantic property is being some belief-or-other-of-Smith's, then weak meaning anatomism seems to be an inevitable consequence of psychofunctionalism, which precludes belief atomism, and which Fodor & Lepore (1992) accept.

Anyhow, it is hard to see why the rejection of the analytic/synthetic distinction ought to be relevant to inferring generic meaning holism from generic weak meaning anatomism. From the standpoint of intentional realism, for a physical system to have what I call generic semantic properties is metaphysically on a par with having astronomical, chemical or biological properties. Suppose geological property G is anatomic. The reason G might be holistic (on the many-interpretation), if it is anatomic, is presumably that the boundary between things which are, and things which are not, G is vague or fuzzy. Suppose that if x has G, then at least one other thing must have it too. If x has G, then presumably many things will have G too because in many cases it will be difficult to determine whether predicate "G" applies or not. The rejection of the analytic/synthetic distinction should be irrelevant. Similarly, the second premiss needed to derive generic meaning holism from weak generic meaning anatomism is the claim that generic semantic properties are vague: "having some content or other" or "being some-or-other-belief-of-Smith's" are vague predicates which express vague properties.

Consider now strong specific meaning anatomism. Perhaps specific meaning holism on the all-interpretation does have the dreadful consequence that psychological intentional laws are impossible. But it is far from obvious that those consequences follow from specific meaning holism on the many-interpretation. Nor is it obvious that specific meaning holism does follow via a sound argument from specific meaning anatomism.

Specific strong meaning anatomism is the thesis that there is at least one specific proposition y such that if Smith believes proposition Σ, then Smith must believe y. As Fodor & Lepore (1992: 24) point out, "the standard reason for holding premiss [2b] is that, on the one hand, the only principled distinction anyone can think of depends on the idea that if you can't believe p unless you believe q, then 'if p, then q' must be analytic . . . and, on the other hand, there is no principled analytic/synthetic distinction." Consider the following question: what motivates the acceptance of specific strong meaning anatomism in the first place? It seems to me rather clear that what would draw one to specific strong meaning anatomism is the prior assumption that there is some kind of analytic connection (or entailment) between propositions or propositional constituents. Such assumptions would be, for example, that Smith cannot believe that A is to the right of B unless he believes that B is to the left of A; that Smith cannot believe that A is red unless he believes that A is colored; that John left and Mary wept unless he believes that John left and he believes that Mary wept.

So, acceptance of strong meaning anatomism commits one to the analytic/synthetic distinction or at least to the existence of some analytic propositions (or analytic connections between propositions): for any proposition x, there is a proposition y such that if Smith believes the former, then he must believe the latter. If Smith cannot believe the former unless he believes the latter, then aren't they analytically related? If the second premiss denies what the first premiss requires, then one may wonder whether Argument A is sound.

Perhaps, it might be said, in favor of Argument A, that, on the strong meaning anatomist interpretation of the first premiss, there are two conceivable ways of rejecting the analytic/synthetic distinction only one of which would be inconsistent with strong meaning anatomism. One construal of the rejection of the analytic/synthetic distinction would be the claim that every proposition (or every connection between any two propositions) is synthetic. On such a way of rejecting the analytic/synthetic distinction, then there will be a tension between it and strong meaning anatomism. But, it might be said, another way of rejecting the analytic/synthetic distinction might be to claim that every connection between any two propositions is analytic. On this construal, there is no analytic/synthetic distinction because there is no synthetic proposition. On this view, it might seem that one might consistently reject the analytic/synthetic and accept the fact that strong meaning anatomism entails the existence of analytic connections between propositions. The view that all propositions are analytic, however, does not seem to me to be tenable.

To conclude this chapter, I would like to make four points. First, as I said above, I do not agree with Fodor and Lepore (1992) that either part of the intentional realist program puts any significant pressure in favor of the acceptance of meaning atomism. Meaning holism on the many-interpretation without the assumption that the content of an individual's belief depends on its relations to many of the individual's *actual* beliefs does not force one to give up on the possibility of intentional psychological laws. Actually, I think that not even meaning holism on the all-interpretation coupled with the assumption that the content of an individual's belief depends on its relations to all of the individual's actual beliefs would force one to conclude that intentional psychological laws are impossible. Since, as I argued, if what intentional psychological laws require is quantification over the contents of individuals' propositional attitudes, then contents can be holistic on the all-interpretation without preempting the possibility of intentional psychological laws. Nor do I think that an informationally based semantics must endorse meaning atomism for the semantic properties of primitive thoughts (or mental symbols) without a syntactic structure.[14] Even on an informationally based semantics, constraints from the cognitive architecture of a creature might actually prevent meaning atomism and favor meaning anatomism. Think of it this way: from an evolutionary standpoint, it might be easier to build a creature with a visual system capable of detecting several colors than just one or with an auditory system capable of detecting several notes on the musical scale than just one.

Second, consider again property P which is supposed to be a paradigmatic semantic property on which Argument A is being run. Is it a genuine semantic property? P is neither the property of being some content or other of a belief of Smith's nor is it the property of being the particular (specific) content of some belief of Smith's. Rather, it is the property of being some belief-or-other-of-Smith's. Following Fodor and Lepore (1992), P is said to be weakly anatomic just in case for all x, if x is P, then there must be at least a y, distinct from x, which is P. And it is said to be strongly anatomic if for all x, there is a y such that if x is P, then y must be P too. If, as it seems in the above definitions, x and y range over propositions, then P is the property of being believed by Smith, where Q might be the property of being desired by Smith, and R might be the property of being believed by Joanna. So P is a psychological (or functional) property, not a semantic property *stricto sensu*. It is the beliefhood property of one of Smith's beliefs, not its semantic property. But on the one hand,

---

[14] Note that Dretske (1988: 150) moves towards a two-factor theory of content and accepts the view that "a belief... will inevitably change [its] content as it becomes more tightly integrated with other states having corresponding indicator functions. A spy, working alone in the field, may have a certain information-gathering function. But as *more* spies are deployed, and their information-gathering activities start to overlap and become interdependent, the responsibilities of each may change."

as I said, acceptance or rejection of the analytic/synthetic distinction is irrelevant to the possession of generic semantic properties (to whether a system satisfies some condition for semanticity). On the other hand, Argument A for meaning holism should establish the holism of specific semantic properties, not of psychological or functional properties.

Thirdly, following an insight of Fodor & Lepore (1992), I would like to suggest that the question of the acceptance or rejection of the analytic/synthetic distinction be clearly divorced from either the linguistic question of the expressive power of a language or the psychological question of the resources of a mind to entertain a proposition. In their own (1992: 48–49) words, "from the fact that there being the proposition that p necessitates the proposition that q, it does not follow . . . that a language can't express the proposition that p unless it can also express the proposition that q . . . assumptions about necessary relations among concepts don't appear to have any psychological consequences at all." But if this is right, then, it seems to me, whether the analytic/synthetic distinction holds or not should affect neither the expressive power of a language nor the psychological capacity of a mind to entertain one of two propositions. And if this in turn is right, then, presumably, no conclusion should follow about either the expressive power of a language or the psychological capacity of a mind to entertain propositions from assumptions about the analytic/synthetic distinction.

The reason I find it important to distinguish the question of the acceptance of the analytic/synthetic distinction from either the linguistic question of the expressive power of a language or the psychological question of a mind's power to entertain propositional contents is related to my earlier distinction between the possession of generic semantic properties and the possession of specific semantic properties. Of course, if a device possesses specific semantic properties, it possesses generic semantic properties. On the one hand, I have claimed that the rejection of the analytic/synthetic distinction is hardly consistent with the rejection of strong meaning anatomicity. Strong meaning anatomicity, which concerns the possession of specific semantic properties, goes hand in hand with the acceptance of the analytic/synthetic distinction. On the other hand, I have claimed that the analytic/synthetic distinction is not relevant to the truth of weak meaning anatomicity. And weak meaning anatomicity is a thesis relative to a device's possession of generic semantic properties. By urging that we respect the distinction between the issue of the possession of specific semantic properties and the issue of the possession of generic semantic properties, I am in effect urging that we divorce the question of the acceptance of the analytic/synthetic distinction from both the linguistic question of the expressive power of a language and the psychological question of a mind's cognitive capacities to entertain conceptual or propositional contents.

Finally, given that I think that strong meaning anatomicity entails the analytic/synthetic distinction, I think that argument A is not a valid argument on the strong meaning anatomicity interpretation of premiss [1b]. Let us, therefore, consider argument A on the weak meaning anatomicity interpretation of premiss [1b]. Then, as I said above, the issue becomes a genuine cognitive or psychological issue, and I do not think that the analytic/synthetic distinction is really relevant to the transition from weak meaning anatomicity to meaning holism (on the relevant generic many-interpretation). What I am inclined to do then is: turn what Fodor (1987b) and Fodor & Lepore (1992) present as the rejection of the analytic/synthetic distinction (i.e., premisses [2a] or [2b]) into a slightly different premiss, i.e., Fodor's (1983) non-modular isotropic and Quinean view of central thought processes, which results in turn from his acceptance of two assumptions. On the one hand, he fully accepts *confirmation* holism, i.e., the Duhem–Quine view that the process of formation and confirmation of scientific hypotheses is a holistic process. On the other hand, he assumes that the process of formation and confirmation of scientific hypotheses is a good model of what he calls central thought processes. To cast doubt on Fodor's non-modular isotropic and Quinean view of central thought processes, therefore, one may keep confirmation holism for scientific hypotheses and reject the assumption that scientific hypotheses formation and confirmation is a good model of central thought processes.

To sum up: on my view, argument A is not valid on the strong meaning anatomism interpretation of its first premiss. On the weak meaning interpretation of the first premiss, I claim that the analytic/synthetic distinction is not really relevant. I propose a reformulation of the second premiss as Fodor's view that conceptual central thought processes are Quinean and isotropic, i.e., non-modular. Furthermore, since this thesis combines the assumption that scientific confirmation is holistic and that scientific confirmation is a good model for central thought processes, I propose to block argument A on the weak meaning anatomicity interpretation of the first premiss by rejecting the second conjunct of the second premiss.

If so, then what the advocate of the weak molecularist (or weak anatomist) first premiss ought to defend is perhaps not so much the analytic/synthetic distinction per se as what current psychologists call a "domain-specific" view of conceptual central thought processes. Fodor (1992: 284) himself has recently entertained the possibility that what cognitive psychologists call "theory of mind" and what he calls "intentional folk psychology" be an "innate modularized database." What psychologists call "theory of mind" is an individual's ability to ascribe propositional attitudes to other human beings. Undoubtedly, according to Fodor's (1983) distinction between modular input systems and central thought processes, an individual's ability to ascribe propositional attitudes to other human beings belongs squarely to central thought processes. Endorsing a modular view of the ability to ascribe propositional attitudes to other human beings is to move towards a modular view of central thought processes. To do so is to reject my reformulated version of the second premiss of argument A on the weak meaning anatomicity interpretation of the first premiss. And I welcome the move.

7

Functionalism and the threat of preemption

If token physicalism is true, then tokens of an individual's propositional attitudes are brain-state tokens of the individual. If so, then the weak causal thesis of intentional realism is vindicated. Tokens of an individual's propositional attitudes are secured a causal role: if tokens of propositional attitudes are brain-state tokens and if brain-state tokens are causes, then so are tokens of propositional attitudes. However, token physicalism does not *ipso facto* vindicate the strong causal thesis according to which the semantic properties of propositional attitudes are causally efficacious.

Type physicalism might have vindicated the strong causal thesis, for type physicalists entertained the possibility that the semantic property of an individual's propositional attitude be identified with a physical property of the individual's brain (or central nervous system). On the view of most type physicalists, the identity in question was supposed to be a "synthetic" (or empirical) identity – on the model of the identity between water and H_2O. The purported identity between a semantic property of an individual's propositional attitude and some physical property of his or her brain would have secured the strong causal thesis. Assuming the truth of the identity between the semantic property of an individual's propositional attitude and some physical property of his or her brain, then whatever causal efficacy the latter enjoys, the former must enjoy too. Type physicalism, however, is widely believed to have foundered on the phenomenon of *multiple realizability*. Putnam (1960) noticed that a given computer with some definite computational (or logical) property can be implemented (or realized) by a variety of physical devices with different physical properties. Subsequently, token physicalists assumed that one and the same mental state (with some given semantic property) can be realized by a variety of different brains (not to say physical devices) with different physical properties.

Now, one thing – though by no means the only one – propositional attitudes can be expected to causally explain is the production of intentional behavior.[1] Consider again my trip from my armchair to the ice-box in the kitchen: I was sitting in an armchair, got up, walked across the living room, went into the kitchen and pulled the ice-box open with my right hand. I did all of these things because I believed there was orange juice in the ice-box and I wanted a glass of orange juice. My legs and arms performed a complicated sequence of physical motions: many of my muscles and muscle fibers contracted and relaxed upon receiving specific chemical and electrical signals emitted by my brain and propagated along my nerve fibers. I was comfortably sitting in an armchair in the living room when I felt the urge for a glass of orange juice and it crossed my mind that there was orange juice in the ice-box in the kitchen. How could the semantic property of my belief contribute to the process of muscle contraction and relaxation? How could the fact that my belief was about (or represented) orange juice in the ice-box a few meters away from my armchair be causally efficacious in the propagation of electrical and chemical signals from my brain to my muscles?

The problem raised by the role of the semantic properties of an individual's propositional attitudes in the causal explanation of his or her behavior is what in chapter 1 I called the problem of mental causation. There are, it seems to me, two complementary reasons why one may doubt that the semantic property of my belief is causally efficacious in the production of my behavior. Two different features of semantic properties of an individual's propositional attitudes may threaten to make them causally inert, causally idle, impotent or epiphenomenal. The first epiphenomenalist threat I will call the *preemption* threat; the second I will call the threat of *externalism*. By distinguishing the preemption threat from the threat of externalism, I hope to move towards dissipating a little what Chomsky likes to call a "mystery" as opposed to a "problem."[2]

Assuming, as I do, the truth of token physicalism, I assume that a

---

[1] As made clear in chapters 1 and 6, propositional attitudes also generate other propositional attitudes: beliefs generate new beliefs; they generate intentions and/or desires; desires too may generate beliefs.

[2] Chomsky (1975: 138) writes for example: "when we turn to such matters as the causation of behavior, it seems to me that no progress has been made, that we are as

token of an individual's propositional attitude, being identical to a brain-state token of the individual, has several different properties. It has electrical, physical, chemical, and biological properties; and it has a semantic property. Now, semantic properties of an individual's propositional attitudes are not basic physical properties of the individual (let alone of the individual's brain). Nor by the way are a symbol's syntactic properties basic physical properties of the symbol. Just as the causal efficacy of a symbol's syntactic property runs the risk of being (in the words of Lepore & Loewer 1987) *screened off* (or preempted) by the causal efficacy of the symbol's basic physical properties, similarly the causal efficacy of the semantic property of an individual's propositional attitude runs the risk of being screened off (or preempted) by the causal efficacy of the basic physical properties of the individual's brain. On this score, i.e., in so far as it is not a basic physical property of an individual's brain, the semantic property of an individual's propositional attitude is on a par with a symbol's syntactic property.

A second important feature of semantic properties of both linguistic symbols and propositional attitudes, which, following current practice, I have already called *externalism* in the first chapter, is their relational or extrinsic character. This feature is best captured by Putnam's (1974) claim that two microphysical twins whose brain-states would be physically indistinguishable might none the less have propositional attitudes with distinct semantic properties. If so, then the semantic properties of an individual's propositional attitudes do not always supervene on the basic physical properties of his or her brain. As will appear shortly, externalism is what distinguishes semantic properties from a symbol's syntactic properties.

If, as I will assume (and as I believe it follows from the information-ally based approach to the naturalization of intentionality), external-ism is correct, then a pair of beliefs simultaneously entertained by a pair of microphysical duplicates may differ from each other as much as one member of each of the following pairs of things may differ from the other: a genuine Churchill autograph and a fake (Dennett 1981b: 44), a genuine Picasso painting and a forgery, a genuine $100 bill and a counterfeit, a photograph of Bill and a photograph of Bob, Bill's identical twin brother (Dretske 1990b: 7). Now, ask yourself: what

much in the dark as how to proceed as in the past, and that fundamental insights are lacking." One particular version of the "mystery" which Chomsky has in mind, of course, is what he calls "the creative aspect of language use."

confers upon any of the above genuine items its property of being genuine? What makes a piece of paper a genuine Churchill autograph is that it bears a special historical relation to Churchill's hand. Similarly what makes a canvas a genuine Picasso painting is that it bears a special historical relation to Picasso's brain and hand. As noted by Dretske (*ibid.*), what makes an autograph, a painting or a dollar bill genuine are "certain historical and relational facts . . . that do not supervene on the intrinsic physical properties . . . of the canvas or paper that has this value, the properties that determine the object's causal power." Unlike, then, the intrinsic physical properties of an item which determine its causal power, and like the property of being genuine or authentic, the semantic properties of an individual's propositional attitudes are *non-local* properties of the individual's brain. Unlike a symbol's syntactic properties, they do not supervene upon physical properties of the individual's brain. If they are non-local properties of an individual's brain, how can semantic properties of the individual's propositional attitudes be causally efficacious, given that causal processes *are* local?[3]

I think that each epiphenomenalist threat deserves a separate treatment. In the present chapter, I will restrict myself to the preemption threat and will postpone examination of the threat of externalism until the next one. In the present chapter, I will fictitiously assume that semantic properties of an individual's propositional attitudes supervene upon the physical properties of the individual's brain, just as a symbol's syntactic properties supervene upon the symbol's physical properties. In the process, I hope to throw light on what, in chapter 5, I called the asymmetry between the syntactic and the semantic properties of hypothetical mental symbols.

7.2 ARE MENTAL PROCESSES PSEUDO-PROCESSES?

In chapter 5, I claimed that what makes what I called CRTM (the computational representational theory of mind) attractive is that it provides a theory of mental processes. The picture was that the semantic properties of propositional attitudes reduce to the semantic properties of mental symbols (of Mentalese). Semantic properties of

---

[3] All of my discussion is predicated on the assumption that causal processes are local processes.

mental symbols enter (are referred to or quantified over by) intentional psychological generalizations. Mental symbols have not only semantic properties; they have syntactic properties too. Now, according to the computational assumption, mental processes are computational processes, i.e., formal operations upon symbols which, according to the Formality condition, are responsive to (or detect) only the syntactic properties of symbols. Computational processes take a symbol (or formula) as input and yield a new symbol (or formula) as output after performing some operation upon the form (or shape) of the input. Furthermore, intentional psychological generalizations are grounded in computational mechanisms. So, just as intentional psychological generalizations are grounded in computational mechanisms, the causal role of semantic properties of mental symbols (hence, of propositional attitudes) is indirectly secured (by proxy, as it were) via the causal role of syntactic properties of mental symbols. But now, as I emphasized earlier, a symbol's syntactic properties are not basic physical properties of the symbol. If, on physicalistic assumptions, basic physical properties of a symbol are supposed to have causal efficacy, then the question arises: how can the causal efficacy of a symbol's syntactic property not be preempted (or screened off) by the causal efficacy of the (more basic) physical properties of the symbol? But now, if the causal efficacy of the syntactic properties of symbols is preempted by the causal efficacy of their physical properties, then the suspicion arises that, even on the computational assumption, the alleged mental processes turn out to be what Salmon (1984) calls pseudo-processes.

To see what the difference is between a genuine physical process and a pseudo-process, consider the following example from Salmon (1984). A white pulse travels from a spotlight to a wall. The travelling pulse of light is a paradigmatic physical process. Suppose we place a red filter at any point on the path between the spotlight and the wall. From the instant the light pulse interacts with the filter, it becomes red and remains so until it reaches the wall. So before interacting with the filter, the light pulse was white. After interacting with the filter, it is red. If the wall is white, the spot of light projected on the wall will be red. On Salmon's view (following Hans Reichenbach's lead), a genuine physical process is one which can transmit a mark. To quote Salmon (1984: 142):

A single intervention at one point in the process transforms it in a way that persists from that point on . . . If we do intervene locally at a single place, we can produce a change that is transmitted from the point of intervention onward . . . The light pulse is a causal process whether it is modified or not, since in either case it is capable of transmitting a mark.

So a genuine causal process can transmit or preserve a change introduced locally in a single step.

Now, imagine a spotlight attached to the center of the ceiling of a circular otherwise dark room. When the light is turned on for a brief instant, it casts a spot of light on a particular point of the wall. Call this point A. Suppose now that the spotlight is mounted on a rotating device. If the light is turned on and the rotating device is set in motion, the spot of light which is cast upon the wall will turn in a regular fashion around the wall – or it will be perceived to do so by a human observer at the appropriate speed of rotation of the rotating device. Whereas each emission from the spotlight to a point on the wall is a genuine causal process, the succession of revolving spots of light on the circular wall is what Salmon takes to be a paradigmatic *pseudo*-process. The revolution of the spot of light can be taken to be the product of two genuine processes: the emission of light from the spotlight and the rotation of the spotlight.

Suppose we place a red filter at any point on the path of the light pulse from the spotlight onto the wall. Let the red filter be at A. Then the spot of light on the wall at A will be red. Now, as the spotlight revolves and emits a spot of light onto point B (distinct from A) on the wall, the spot of light on the wall at B will not be red any more. The succession of spots of light on the wall does *not* preserve the mark locally produced in one step. We could install a red lens in the spotlight but this would not constitute a local intervention. Placing many different red filters in several different places along the wall or having a red filter revolving around the wall at the same speed as the spot of light would involve several local interventions at several different points, not a single intervention at a single point in the process.

Now, imagine that we extend the radius of the circular room or the distance between the revolving spotlight and the circular wall. If the spotlight rotates at a constant speed, then the revolving spot of light on the wall may well reach a speed greater than the speed of light. As

Salmon (1984: 143) says, "there is no upper limit on the speed of pseudo-processes."

For other examples of pseudo-processes in Salmon's sense, we can think of the succession of shadows projected by a moving object – for example, a car in motion – on the ground. The motion of the car is a genuine process. But the succession of shadows projected on the ground is a pseudo-process. Kim (1984: 93–94) has mentioned other examples of pseudo-processes such as the succession of reflections of an object in a mirror and the succession of symptoms produced by a disease: neither are two successive reflections of an object in a mirror causally related to each other, nor are two successive symptoms of a disease.

Consider the putative causal relation between two of my beliefs: my belief c that there is orange juice in the ice-box causes me to acquire the belief e that there is something to drink in the kitchen. By virtue of token physicalism, c and e are two brain-state tokens. On the computational story (reviewed in chapter 5), the intentional psychological law which is instantiated by the individual causal relation between c and e is in turn implemented by (or grounded in) the computational process which turns the mental symbol to which I am related in virtue of having belief c into another mental symbol to which I am related in virtue of having belief e. This computational process turns one formula into another formula by application of some formal operation. Now, the suspicion arises that such mental processes are just so many pseudo-processes. The genuine process whereby one brain-state token c brings about a different brain-state token e would be a biological, chemical, and physical process through and through. The computational process connecting two mental formulae would, therefore, stand to the genuine process as either of the two following pseudo-processes stands to the real process: as the motion of the car's shadow stands to the motion of the car; as the regular revolving spot of light around the wall stands to the combination of the emission of light from the spotlight onto the wall with the rotation of the spotlight. The suspicion is that the computational process which transforms one mental symbol into a new one by the application of some formal operation is just like the succession of two mirror images of an object or like the succession of two symptoms of a disease – a mere pseudo-process. To dissipate the suspicion that mental processes are pseudo-processes, I will try to respond to the

threat of preemption: I will try to justify the view that syntactic properties of a symbol (and semantic properties if there are any) which
supervene on the symbol's physical properties may enter genuine
causal explanations.

7.3 THE CAUSAL EXPLANATION OF BEHAVIOR

I now want to make explicit two sets of assumptions about the causal
explanation of behavior. I will first consider three assumptions about
intentional behavior. I will then distinguish causal explanations from
both causation (i.e., the causal relation) and non-causal explanations.

Consider the causal relation *c* causes *e*, the first relatum of which is a
propositional attitude (e.g., my belief that there is orange juice in the
ice-box) and the second relatum of which is some physical event, for
example, my bodily motions when I got up from my armchair, crossed
the living room, walked into the kitchen and opened the ice-box. I
first assume that not all of an individual's behavior is intentional
behavior. There are things I do for no reason: I inhale oxygen for
example; I hiccup and I snore, if and when I do, for no reason.
Whatever I may believe and/or desire cannot explain why I do these
things. This is non-intentional or instinctive behavior. Other things I
do, I do for reasons, as when I pick up a glass of water in front of me.
Some of my reasons for doing what I do when I have reasons for doing
them are my propositional attitudes. A person's intentional behavior
includes the things the person does which can be explained by what
he or she believes and desires. As I will argue in chapter 8, not all
intentional behavior though is voluntary behavior; some intentional
behavior is non-voluntary. Furthermore, in the present chapter, I will
make two other very widespread assumptions about an individual's
intentional behavior: I will assume that an individual's intentional
behavior is identical to some of the individual's physical bodily
motions. And I will assume that an individual's intentional behavior
can be the effect of one (or more) of his or her propositional attitudes.
Both Davidson's anomalous monism and functionalism as well are
committed to both assumptions about intentional behavior. In the
next chapter, I will question both assumptions.

In various places, Davidson (1967: 161; 1970: 215) has expressed
the view that the causal relation is an *extensional* relation between
particular events no matter how they happen to be described. Now,

Kim (1984; 1989b), Sosa (1984), Horgan (1989) and others have expressed their worry that anomalous monism (AM) makes mental properties of mental events (or semantic properties of propositional attitudes) epiphenomenal on the ground that SNCC (the strict nomological character of causality) and MA (mental anomalism) conspire to make *only* physical properties of mental events causally efficacious and to deprive mental properties of mental events of causal efficacy. They have expressed their worry that, on AM, the mental *qua* mental is doing no causal work in strongly intensional terms of a four-place causal relation, which Horgan (1989) has nick-named *quausation*, and which holds between the fact that event *c* has property *F* and the fact that event *e* has property *G*. Not only does *quausation* threaten to turn a relation between events into a relation between facts; it also turns what is, according to Davidson, a purely extensional relation into an intensional one. In response, Davidson (1993: 6) has pointed out that, on his view, "there is no room for a concept of 'cause as' which would make causality a relation among three or four entities rather than between two." But, as I am about to argue, Davidson's dismissal of Horgan's quausation might be a little too quick.

As I argued in chapter 5, I think it best to divide the issue of whether Davidson's AM entails the epiphenomenalism of mental properties into two separate issues: the issue of explanatory exclusion and the existence of intentional psychological laws. As I said in chapter 5, I do not think that Davidson's AM is committed to the assumption of explanatory exclusion according to which *only* strict physical laws can ground individual causal relations. However, I do think that Davidson is attracted to the view that intentional psychological generalizations are best construed as analytic truisms (stating conceptual connexions), not causal laws.

I will assume that the *relata* of an individual causal relation are events. Now, there are two well-known views of events in recent philosophy: there is Davidson's extensionalist view of the causal relation according to which events are mere individuals. And there is Kim's (1973a) view according to which an event is the instantiation of a property by an object at a time and place. Perhaps, one may reconcile the contrast between the two views by distinguishing raw events (Davidson's events) from facts, such as the fact that an object has a property at a time and place (Kim's events). In any case, whether we take Davidson's or Kim's view of events as fundamental,[4] I think we must recognize a distinction between the causal *relation* and a causal *explanation*. Furthermore, the relation between what I just called facts (or Kim's events) will play a crucial role in a causal explanation. A causal explanation will involve a relation between the fact that c is F and the fact that e is G. If Davidson's events are individuals (or "objects" of a certain sort), then facts (or Kim's events) have a propositional structure. Explanations (as recognized by Davidson) trade on the propositional character of facts. For the fact that c is F to explain the fact that e is G, the obtaining of the former must bear some causal responsibility with respect to the obtaining of the latter via the instantiation of some causal nomic dependency between properties F and G.[5] So in order to understand causal explanations, we must make room for two relations: the relation between events c and e and the relation between the fact that c is F and the fact that e is G. Given that a cause has presumably an indefinite number of properties, what is distinctive of a causal explanation is that it involves a reference to, or some kind of quantification over, some causally efficacious property or properties of the cause. Even though one might grant Davidson his claim that causal relations are extensional relations between events, still he would no doubt recognize that not any description of a cause can occur in a causal explanation of its effect. I assume that providing an explanation consists in answering some Why-question by supplying some relevant missing information.[6]

Incidentally, as I argued in chapter 5, the very fact that event c has

---

[4] Of course, unlike Davidson's view of events, Kim's is not purely extensional since it involves a reference to a property.

[5] In his dissertation, Max Kistler (1995) makes the distinction between the causal relation between individual events and the relation between facts and he elaborates the notion of the causal responsibility between facts.

[6] This latter claim puts me in the camp of what Salmon (1984) calls the epistemic conception of explanation, which he contrasts with the ontic view. Two typical epistemic views would be Hempel's view according to which explanations – both deductive and statistical – are inferences (or arguments) and Van Fraassen's erotetic view according to which explanations are answers to why-questions. On Salmon's ontic view, the explanation of particular phenomena consists in showing how they fit into causal patterns or regularities in the world. I wonder, however, whether Salmon's stark contrast between the ontic and the epistemic views of explanation is really justified. After all, as Dennett (1991a) points out, even if a causal pattern is out there in the world, it requires a particular cognitive sensitivity to detect it.

many different properties is one reason why the very notion of a strict law, to which Davidson is committed, is really controversial. Let us think of laws as nomic dependencies between properties. A law will be strict if the instantiation of the property mentioned in the antecedent guarantees the fact that the property mentioned in the consequent is bound to be instantiated. But now, we may see that the very fact that the event which instantiates the property mentioned in the antecedent instantiates also many other properties may prevent the instantiation of the property mentioned in the consequent.

Furthermore, on my view, not every correct explanation is a causal explanation. I might, for example, explain the fact that my son happens to instantiate the property of being a nephew by pointing out that he is my son and I have siblings. In thus explaining why my son is a nephew, I have made use of the definition of a nephew – of what is constitutive of being a nephew or what defines the meaning of the English word "nephew." Or consider the following question: why do I live in Paris? Two broad kinds of responses might be relevant. I may explain why I live in Paris by mentioning the fact that I decided to take a job offer there. Alternatively, I may explain the fact that I live in Paris by mentioning the fact that I live in the fifth arrondissement of Paris: I live in Paris in virtue of living in the fifth arrondissement. The former explanation is a causal explanation. The latter is not: there is no causal relation between the fact that one lives in one of a city's district and the fact that one lives in the city. So what is distinctive of a causal (as opposed to a non-causal) explanation is that it tracks some genuine process.[7]

7.4 A RESPONSE TO THE PREEMPTION THREAT

What I have, following Lepore & Loewer (1987), called the preemption threat has been called the problem of explanatory exclusion by Kim (1989a), McLaughlin (1989) and Horgan (1991). The problem arises from the assumption that semantic properties of an individual's propositional attitudes are not identical to, but supervene upon, or are multiply realized by, basic physical properties of the individual's brain, just as a symbol's syntactic properties supervene upon, or are multiply

---

[7] By assuming that not all explanations are causal explanations, I thereby also depart from Salmon's (1984) view.

realized by, the symbol's physical properties. Suppose that my belief c that there is orange juice in the ice-box is a cause of my behavior e (itself identified with my bodily motions), how could the semantic property of my belief c be causally efficacious in the production of e in the presence of the biological, chemical and physical properties of c? Does not the causal efficacy of the various biological, chemical, physical properties of my brain-state token c preempt or screen off the causal efficacy of its semantic property? Again, note the fictitious assumption made here that the semantic property of my belief supervenes upon basic physical properties of my brain, as a symbol's syntactic property supervenes upon its physical properties.

This assumption amounts to assuming a distinction I mentioned in chapter 6 and will discuss shortly between what has been called the *broad* and the *narrow* content (or semantic property) of an individual's propositional attitude. Only the latter, not the former, is supposed to supervene on the physical properties of the individual's brain. A purported solution to the preemption threat amounts, therefore, to securing a causal role for the narrow semantic properties, not for the broad semantic properties, of an individual's propositional attitudes. In the last section of the present chapter, I will examine a view I call *content-dualism* which argues that the present response to the preemption threat can be used to secure a causal role for narrow content and concedes that broad content is epiphenomenal.

I will call S the semantic property of my belief c (itself a brain-state token) and I will call P c's biological, chemical and physical properties. The assumption is that c's having S supervenes upon c's having P, just as a symbol's syntactic property supervenes upon its physical properties. In terms of the definition of supervenience provided in chapter 1 (section 5), this means that c would not be S unless some physical property P were co-instantiated by c and whenever c is P, it is S.[8] On the basis of this assumption, the semantic property S of an individual's propositional attitude can be treated as a *functional* property of the individual's brain, i.e., as a property which can be multiply realized by more basic physical properties of the individual's brain or as a higher-order property of more basic physical properties of the individual's brain (in the functionalist sense).

---

[8] Notice, as I argued in chapter 1, that the claim that property S supervenes on property P does not entail that only physical property P, not physical property P', can underlie the instantiation of S.

The following example of a functional *state* from Lewis (1966: 100) will show that functional states of a physical device are characterized by their having a certain causal role:

> Consider cylindrical combination locks for bicycle chains. The definitive characteristic of their state of being unlocked is the causal role of that state, the syndrome of its most typical causes and effects: namely, that setting the combination typically causes the lock to be unlocked and that being unlocked typically causes the lock to open when gently pulled. That is all we need to know in order to ascribe to the lock the state of being or not being unlocked. But we may learn that, as a matter of fact, the lock contains a row of slotted discs; setting the combination typically causes the slots to be aligned; and alignment of the slots typically causes the lock to open when gently pulled. So alignment of slots occupies precisely the causal role that we ascribed to being unlocked by analytic necessity, as the definitive characteristic of being unlocked (for these locks). Therefore alignment of slots is identical with being unlocked (for these locks). They are one and the same state.

Lewis then starts with the causal role of a particular state of a combination lock – the state of being unlocked. He ends up identifying that state with a physical structure – a particular alignment of slotted discs.

Consider now the following examples of typically functional *properties*: being a carburetor, being a can opener, being a corkscrew. Such functional properties, which are characterized by the having of a certain causal role, can be multiply realized by different physical devices with different physical properties. So can the property of keeping track of time, which can be realized by a sun-dial, a sandglass, a pendulum clock or a quartz watch. Now consider the property of a substance of being analgesic. Morphine and aspirin both have the functional property of being analgesic. Of course, morphine and aspirin are distinct chemical properties. Both chemical properties, however, realize the higher-order functional property of being analgesic. In fact, being analgesic is a functional property different substances may have in virtue of having several different more basic chemical properties. Following the tradition of Ramsey (1931), Carnap (1966: ch. 26) and Lewis (1972), one may define the functional property of being analgesic in terms of being a higher-order property of the more basic chemical property (of being morphine and aspirin): it is a higher-order chemical property of more basic chemical properties.[9] As noted by Yablo (1992), the conceptual relation between a higher-order functional property and the more basic physical property which realizes it is much like the traditional relation between a *determinable* property of an object (i.e., being colored) and a *determinate* property (i.e., being red). By referring to the functional higher-order chemical property (of more basic chemical properties), one thereby refers to a disjunctive class of more basic chemical properties.

Suppose that I have a migraine and I suppressed the pain by swallowing an aspirin. I want to compare two alternative causal explanations of the same fact. I may explain the suppression of my pain by mentioning the fact that I swallowed an aspirin. And I may explain the suppression of my pain by mentioning the fact that I swallowed an analgesic pill. I agree with Block (1990) and Jackson & Pettit (1988, 1990a) that the causally efficacious property of the pill in the chemical process of pain suppression was the presence of acetylsalicylic acid in the pill, not its being analgesic. Given that the chemical property of the pill was causally efficacious, does not its causal efficacy *ipso facto* preempt (or screen off) the causal efficacy of the functional property? My response to this question consists in distinguishing two kinds of causal explanation.

On my view, the threat of preemption can be mitigated by distinguishing at least two ways properties can be relevant to a causal explanation. Consider two possible explanations of the same *explanandum*: the glass broke because Anna dropped it vs. the glass broke because someone dropped it. In both cases, one and the same mechanism (or physical process) is involved; but the explanations are slightly different. The former *explanans* is a singular proposition involving reference to a particular person. The latter *explanans* is a general proposition quantifying over persons but involving reference to no one in particular. Suppose the former is true, then the latter is true in virtue of the former. Similarly, I submit, a causal explanation of the suppression of my pain may of course proceed by *referring to* (or naming) the chemical property of my pill which is causally efficacious in the chemical process of pain suppression. This is what Jackson &

---

[9] A particular pill will therefore have some basic chemical property and some higher-order chemical property. The higher-order (or functional) property is a property of property: it is a second-order property of the pill's chemical property.

Pettit (1988, 1990a, 1990b) call a *process* explanation. It may also proceed by mentioning the functional property of the pill of being analgesic. In this case, by virtue of the fact that the pill's functional property is a higher-order property of the pill's chemical property, the latter explanation proceeds by *quantifying over* a set of chemical properties which pills may have and which, by assumption, are causally efficacious in the process of pain suppression. Again, in this case, the latter functional explanation is true in virtue of the truth of the former chemical explanation. What I will call a *functional* explanation Jackson & Pettit (1988, 1990a, 1990b) call a *program* explanation.

To illustrate the fact that a property can be relevant to a causal explanation without being directly causally efficacious, I will briefly apply Jackson's & Pettit's program explanation model to the case of mental causation. We assume that semantic property S of an individual's propositional attitude supervenes on some more basic physical property P of the individual's brain. Given that S is a higher-order property than P and given that S and P are both properties of one and the same brain-state, the instantiation of S does not contribute to bringing about the instantiation of P. The instantiation of S with respect to the individual's behavior e is not a sequentially more remote causal factor which produced the instantiation of P which in turn produced e. Nor does the instantiation of S collaborate with the instantiation of P to produce e. On Jackson & Pettit's model, although inefficacious in bringing about e, the instantiation of S none the less is relevant to explaining the production of e by *programming* the existence of a more basic property P which in turn is causally efficacious in the production of e, as shown in figure 7.

Notice that, as expected on functionalist assumptions, the *program* relation between the instantiation of S by c and the instantiation of P by c is a conceptual, logical or inductive, not a causal, relation: S and P are co-instantiated by c; the instantiation of S by c can be thought of as evidence that some more basic property P is thereby co-instantiated by c.

As I mentioned above, I take it that the program relation between the instantiation of S by c and the instantiation of P by c has close affinities with Yablo's (1992) view (expressed in traditional terminology) that the mental property of an individual's propositional attitude stands to the physical property of the individual's brain which realizes it in the same relation as a *determinable* stands to its *determinate*, i.e., as

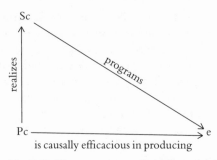

Figure 7 The program explanation model

something's being colored stands to something's being red; or as something's being red stands to something's being scarlet. With Jacob (1991), consider a device – a color-detector – designed to track red objects: a red object's being red will therefore play a causal role in its being detected by a color-detector. I agree with Yablo's (1992) claim that the determinable property of the object of being colored will not thereby be deprived of causal role. The object's being colored does play a causal role since the machine is a color-detector, not a shape-detector. By mentioning the property of a red object of being colored, we do provide a causal explanation of the machine's behavior since we rule out other possible causal explanations such as the machine is a shape-detector. The difference between the explanation based on the hypothesis that the machine is a color-detector and the hypothesis that the machine detects red objects is that the latter is more fine-grained than the former. Or consider a machine whose task it is to detect shapes. Suppose the machine is programed to detect squares, but you do not know the program. If your first guess is that the machine is a polygon-detector, then you have made a first step in the causal explanation of the machine's behavior. For you have ruled out other possible competing causal explanations, such as the machine is a circle-detector. Again, the hypothesis that the machine detects squares is more fine-grained than the hypothesis that it detects rectangles which is more fine-grained than the hypothesis that it detects polygons which in turn is more fine-grained than the hypothesis that it is a shape-detector.

My claim, then, is that by mentioning the functional (programming or determinable) property of the pill of being analgesic, I do provide a causal explanation of the suppression of my pain. First of all, such an explanation is indeed causal since it rules out alternative competing causal explanations of the suppression of my pain such as that a nerve might have been severed. The first part of my claim, then, is that by mentioning the functional (programing or determinable) property of the pill, I do track a causal process (of pain suppression): I track one causal process among other possible though competing causal processes. Secondly, as noticed by Putnam (1973a, 1975a), the reason why a causal explanation which refers to a causally efficacious determinate property does not screen off or make superfluous a causal explanation which refers to a determinable functional property and thereby quantifies over a set of more basic causally efficacious properties is that they do not supply the same information about the process involved. The second part of my claim, then, is that different causal explanations, tracking one and the same causal process, may deliver different pieces of information about the causal process which they track.[10]

By referring to the causally efficacious chemical property of the pill, the chemical explanation reveals the actual process of pain suppression. By mentioning the pill's functional property of being analgesic, the functional explanation supplies information about a class of possible unrealized chemical processes. Just as the latter does not distinguish the actual chemical process among various possible processes, the former says nothing about the existence of possible alternatives to the actual chemical process. In fact, one may imagine a chemist who knows the chemical composition of acetylsalicylic acid. He thereby is in possession of very detailed and fine-grained information about the particular chemical process of pain suppression involving the absorption of aspirin. But let us suppose that he does not possess the concept of analgesic. He would thereby be deprived of the possibility of acquiring more general (possibly relevant) information about a whole class of chemical processes – information which could be stated by quantifying over many different individual chemical processes. Upon acquiring the concept of analgesic, he would then be in a position of learning something new about this class of chemical processes.

[10] Notice that since I am taking an epistemic (non-ontic) view of explanation, I am presently using the notion of information conveyed by an explanation in a cognitive (or epistemic) sense, not in the information-theoretic sense (of chapter 2).

So the suspicion was that mental computational processes may turn out to be mere peudo-processes. In response to this suspicion, I want to emphasize the fact that in saying that a causal explanation supplies information about a class of *possible* physical processes one is not thereby saying that the processes involved are *pseudo*-processes (in Salmon's sense). The functional explanation supplies more general, less specific, information about the actual process than the chemical explanation. Only what Jackson & Pettit (1990c) have called "the fine grain preference," i.e., the assumption that information about the details of a causal process should always be favored over more general information, could justify the claim that the chemical explanation makes the functional explanation superfluous. But, as I just tried to illustrate, I do not think that the fine grain preference is itself justified. Relative to some explanatory goals, an explanation supplying less specific information might in fact be better than an explanation supplying more specific information. The explanatory value of the concept of an analgesic substance, for example, resides in the very fact that it abstracts away from the details of different chemical properties.

7.5 CONTENT-DUALISM

As I said at the beginning of the present chapter, semantic properties of an individual's propositional attitudes have (or lack) two features: they are neither basic nor local physical properties of the individual's brain. To say that the semantic properties of an individual's propositional attitudes are not local properties of the individual's brain is to say that they do not supervene on the physical (chemical and biological) properties of the individual's brain. The first feature generates the threat of preemption. The second generates the threat of externalism. Externalism has gained acceptance from reflection on the fact that the semantic properties of an individual's propositional attitudes are open to Twin Earth thought experiments of the kind invented by Putnam (1974). Given an individual's thought about a natural kind (e.g., gold or water), it is possible to imagine a counterfactual situation in which the following holds: the internal physical and functional condition of the individual's brain is held constant in the actual and in the counterfactual situation while the content (or semantic property) which it is natural to ascribe to either his utterance or his mental state in the actual situation differs from the content of his utterance or mental state in the counterfactual situation. Now, if externalism is so defined, then it is by no means obvious that it applies to the contents of all of an individual's thoughts: it is not clear that, for example, an individual's arithmetical thought that $2 + 5 = 7$ is open to a Twin Earth thought experiment.[11] All an externalist needs, however, is that some – not all – of an individual's thoughts be open to Twin Earth thought experiments.

In the rest of this chapter, I want to argue that the response I provided above to the threat of preemption cannot be appealed to in order to respond to the threat of externalism. In order to do this, I will succinctly examine a widespread reaction to externalism which I will call content-dualism. Content-dualism is the view that one may distinguish the *narrow* from the *broad* (or *wide*) content (or semantic property) of an individual's propositional attitude. As I said in chapter 6, on this view, the broad content of an individual's belief is its truth-condition; the narrow content is its inferential role.[12] I will argue that a content-dualist's appeal to something like the above response to the preemption threat in order to secure a causal role for the narrow semantic property of an individual's propositional attitude ultimately fails. On the one hand, if the content-dualist did succeed in securing a causal role for the narrow contents of an individual's propositional attitudes, he would still have to concede that broad content is epiphenomenal. On the other hand, it fails because the content-dualist faces the dilemma: either narrow content is not narrow enough or it is not content at all.

If externalism is correct, then two microphysical twins whose brain-states are physically indistinguishable can none the less have distinct semantic properties. So, for example, consider two such microphysical twins: Bill and Bob. Bill believes that cup c_1 in front of him contains coffee. He wants a sip of coffee. His belief and desire explain (causally explain) why he picks up c_1 with the fingers of his left hand, raises the cup up to his lips and drinks coffee from it. Bob believes that cup c_2 in front of him contains coffee. He too wants coffee. This is why he performs the same bodily motions as Bill. Now, suppose that cups c_1 and c_2 are perceptually indistinguishable. There is a sense in which

---

[11] See McGinn (1989).

[12] Good representatives of the content-dualist strategy are Block (1986; 1987), Dennett (1982b), Fodor (1987b), Loar (1982), McGinn (1982).

Bill and Bob believe different things since Bill's belief is true iff c_1, not c_2, contains coffee. Bob's belief is true iff c_2, not c_1, contains coffee. So Bill's and Bob's beliefs have distinct *broad* contents (or semantic properties). But, given that c_1 and c_2 are perceptually indistinguishable, there is a sense in which they believe the same thing: they both believe that the cup in front of them contains coffee; each believes that the cup in front of him contains coffee. Could this be the common *narrow* content (or semantic property) of their belief? There are reasons for skepticism.

Undoubtedly, the content of Bill's and Bob's beliefs that the cup in front of each of them contains coffee is *narrower* than the contents of their beliefs that c_1 contains coffee and that c_2 contains coffee. But could the content of either Bill's or Bob's belief that the cup in front of him contains coffee supervene on the physical properties of Bill's or Bob's brain? As will appear shortly, the content-dualist badly needs the assumption that the narrow semantic property of an individual's propositional attitude does indeed supervene on the physical properties of the individual's brain. And this assumption is indeed controversial. The shared content of Bill's and Bob's beliefs has just been expressed by an English sentence containing the word "coffee." It is easy to imagine that, though perceptually indistinguishable by Bill and Bob, the liquid contained in Bill's cup and the liquid contained in Bob's cup differ: imagine that only the liquid contained in Bill's cup is genuine (caffeinated) coffee; the liquid contained in Bob's cup is not. If so, then the content of Bill's belief and the content of Bob's belief when they both believe that the cup in front of them contains coffee cannot supervene on the physical properties of their respective brains. One semantic question is whether we can maintain the assumption that there exists a narrow content of Bill's and Bob's belief which does supervene on the physical properties of their brain even though we might not be able to express it by means of a sentence of English or, for that matter, of any natural language.

In fact, content-dualism makes two claims: one claim is semantic; the other claim is causal explanatory. The semantic claim is that the narrow content of an individual's thought may both be genuine content and supervene upon the physical properties of his or her brain. The causal explanatory claim is that *only* the explanation of narrow behavior by narrow content is genuine causal explanation. The content-dualist strategy raises, therefore, two basic problems.

One is that, as I said, the assumption that some genuinely semantic property of an individual's propositional attitude can be narrow enough to supervene upon the physical properties of his or her brain is deeply controversial. The other problem is that, even granting that the narrow content of an individual's belief supervenes on the physical properties of the individual's brain, I do not think that the content-dualist has really succeeded in establishing that explanation of broad behavior by broad content is not causal explanation. Let us take the two problems in reversed order: the causal explanatory problem first, the semantic problem second.

In order to consider the causal explanatory claim made by content-dualism, I will assume that there is a suitable notion of content which is both appropriately narrow and genuinely semantic. I shall examine this very assumption when I consider the content-dualist semantic claim. Even though it presumably does not supervene on the physical properties of their respective brain, what is interesting about the narrower content of Bill's and Bob's belief that the cup in front of each of them contains coffee is that it seems perfectly suited to explain Bill's and Bob's behavior when we think of what they do as the same thing: namely, each of them simultaneously picks up the cup in front of him with the fingers of his left hand, raises it to his lips, and drinks coffee from it. Let us waive temporarily the fundamental problem of whether we can express the putative narrow content by a sentence of a natural language. I will come back to it at the end of the present section. Whatever causal explanatory job can be done by the above narrower content will *a fortiori* be done by the putative absolutely narrow content of Bill's and Bob's belief.[13] Call the *explanandum* narrow behavior. I want to contrast narrow behavior with broad behavior: Bill's broad behavior involves the fact that he picks up c_1; Bob's broad behavior involves the fact that he picks up c_2. The very ingredient which distinguishes the broad content of their respective thoughts from the common narrower content distinguishes broad behavior from narrow behavior. Given that the narrower content seems ideally suited for the causal explanation of narrow behavior, the question then naturally arises: is the explanation of narrow behavior by narrow content the *only* genuine form of causal psychological

---

[13] By "putative absolutely narrow content," I mean content which supervenes on the physical properties of Bill's and Bob's brains.

explanation? Is the explanation of broad behavior by broad behavior non-causal?

Behavior can be intentional or non-intentional. Non-intentional behavior is instinctive (or reflex) behavior. Propositional attitudes are irrelevant to the explanation of non-intentional behavior. An agent's cup-related behavior counts as intentional if the agent's behavior is to be explained by some of the agent's cup-related internal representation. Narrow content is too narrow to explain broad behavior and broad content is unnecessarily broad for the explanation of narrow behavior. The broad content of Bill's belief involves a reference to cup c_1; the broad content of Bob's belief involves a reference to cup c_2. Each belief content is a singular proposition. The common narrow content of Bill's and Bob's belief involves an existential quantification over cups. So both the broad content of Bill's belief and the broad content of Bob's belief logically entail their common narrow content, as either of two singular propositions may entail one and the same existentially quantified proposition. The same contextual item from the environment is required to turn (existentially quantified) narrow content into (singular) broad content and narrow behavior into broad behavior.

Now, the strategy of content-dualism is to argue that, unlike the explanation of narrow behavior by narrow content, the explanation of broad behavior by broad content is *not* causal explanation. If only the explanation of narrow behavior by narrow content were causal explanation, then the content-dualist might appeal to the response to the preemption threat to secure a causal role for the only kind of semantic property which may play a role in causal explanation, i.e., narrow content.

The reasoning seems to be the following. The content-dualist starts with the assumption that narrow content can explain narrow behavior. This assumption, I take it, is uncontroversial. What is controversial is whether the narrow content of an individual's propositional attitude does supervene upon the physical properties of the individual's brain. As I see it, Putnam's (1988) view that no semantic property of an individual's propositional attitude – narrow or otherwise – can supervene on the physical properties of the individual's brain plays a major role in his rejection of functionalism.[14] Now, the reason why

---

[14] However, as I pointed out in chapter 6, Harman's (1982) version of functionalism is a "long armed" version consistent with externalism.

the assumption that narrow content can explain narrow behavior is not controversial is the following: neither can narrow content explain broad behavior; nor is broad content required to explain narrow behavior. The content-dualist further assumes that the explanation of narrow behavior by narrow content is causal explanation. Finally, he assumes that *only* the explanation of narrow behavior by narrow content is a genuine causal explanation. The content-dualist's intuition here is that all the causal work is done, as it were, by narrow content. What makes broad content broad is the additional relation between a mental state with narrow content and an item from the environment – the very same relation which makes broad behavior broad. Now, the content-dualist takes this relation to be causally spurious. This assumption needs justification.

The assumption that *only* the explanation of narrow behavior by narrow content is genuinely causal explanation has been defended by Kim (1982) and Fodor (1989b, 1991) on the ground that only if they supervene on the physical properties of an individual's brain can semantic properties have causal efficacy in the production of intentional behavior. This principle has been defended by Stich (1978a, 1983: 161–64) and by Kim (1982: 183). Stich calls it the principle of psychological autonomy. But he concludes from it that semantic properties are not suited to causal psychological explanation. Kim splits it into two sub-principles which he calls the supervenience thesis and the explanatory thesis: according to the former, "every internal psychological state of an organism is supervenient on its synchronous internal physical state." According to the latter, "internal psychological states are the only psychological states psychological theory needs to invoke in explaining human behavior." Stich's principle of autonomy and the combination of Kim's supervenience and explanatory theses are equivalent to Fodor's (1989b: 138) premise of the supervenience of causal powers according to which "the causal powers of an event are entirely determined by its physical properties" (where the determination relation is just the converse of supervenience).

As noted by Stich (1983: 161–64), there is some affinity between his principle of autonomy (or equivalently Kim's supervenience and explanatory theses) and what, following Putnam (1974), Fodor (1980) called methodological solipsism. However, as I pointed out above and in chapter 5, according to Fodor's methodological solipsism, what Fodor calls the Formality condition applies to mental processes, not to psychological intentional laws. It is, therefore, unlike Stich's own syntactic theory of the mind (STM), a version of the representational theory of the mind (RTM) in that according to CRTM (i.e., the computational RTM), intentional psychological laws do refer to semantic properties of mental symbols; and they are implemented by purely formal computational mechanisms. In so far as he subscribes to content-dualism, the advocate of CRTM must assume that the narrow semantic properties of an individual's mental symbols, like their syntactic properties and unlike their broad semantic properties, do supervene on basic physical properties of the individual's brain. As noted above, this is a controversial assumption. Recently, Fodor (1994) has rejected content-dualism and the appeal to narrow content in intentional psychological laws because reference to narrow semantic properties threatens the possibility of intentional psychological laws. On his recent picture, intentional psychological laws refer only to broad content. However, broad content intentional psychological laws are still implemented by purely formal (non-semantic) computational mechanisms.[15]

The principle of autonomy has been questioned by Evans (1982: 203–4) and Peacocke (1981) on the ground that there is no such thing as narrow behavior: what Bill does is to pick up c_1, not c_2, and what Bob does is to pick up c_2, not c_1. I agree that we may want to explain why Bill picks up c_1, not c_2, whereas Bob picks up c_2, not c_1. It seems to me, however, equally uncontroversial that we may want to explain why Bill and Bob pick up the cup in front of them. So I do not agree that there is no such *explanandum* as narrow behavior. If what we want to explain is why Bill and Bob respectively pick up c_1 and c_2, and not vice-versa, i.e., their broad behavior, then the relevant *explanantia* are the broad contents of their respective beliefs. If what we want to explain is their narrow behavior, i.e., why they do the same thing, then the relevant *explanans* is the common narrow content of their beliefs.

To accept, however, that there is room for the explanation of narrow behavior by narrow content is a far cry from the much stronger claim

---

[15] In chapter 6, I have argued that one can avoid the clash between narrow content holism and the possibility of intentional psychological laws by assuming that such laws do not refer to, but quantify over, the semantic properties of individuals' mental states.

(made by the autonomy theorist) that *only* the explanation of narrow behavior by narrow content is genuinely causal. In order to argue that only explanation of narrow behavior by narrow content is causal explanation, the content-dualist will be tempted to appeal to the analyticity of such principles as "If Bill wants a sip of coffee and if he believes that cup c_1 contains coffee, then Bill will seize c_1." If such a principle were analytic, then presumably the explanation of broad behavior by broad content would be some kind of conceptual, not causal, explanation. What is distinctive of the explanation of broad behavior by broad content would count as conceptual, not causal, explanation. However, as I argued in chapter 5, although the connection between the broad content of Bill's belief and his broad behavior seems purely conceptual (and hence, not causal), it is not. What happens is that we take it for granted that particular cups of coffee do not miraculously come and go. However, unbeknownst to Bill, cup c_1 might be replaced by indistinguishable cup c_2. Given Bill's desire, he might well believe that c_1 contains coffee and seize cup c_2 while believing that he is seizing c_1. So the connection between the broad content of Bill's broad belief and Bill's broad behavior is not conceptual after all.

So the content-dualist has no firm grounds for claiming that *only* the explanation of narrow behavior by narrow content is causal explanation. If so, then the content-dualist could at best appeal to the response to the preemption threat to secure a causal role for narrow content. Notwithstanding the above doubts (to the examination of which I will shortly turn) that narrow content of an individual's thought is either too narrow to be content or it will fail to supervene on the physical properties of the individual's brain, the content-dualist still faces the externalist threat, i.e., the threat that broad content be epiphenomenal.

Let us now consider the semantic claim. There is, as I indicated above, room for different degrees of semantic narrowness: Bill and Bob may both believe that the cup in front of each of them contains coffee. The content of this belief is narrower than the content of their respective belief that c_1 contains coffee and that c_2 contains coffee. If they were to believe, for example, that the cup in front of each of them contains a brown liquid, then the content of this belief would be narrower than the content of their belief that the cup in front of them contains coffee. Semantic narrowness is a comparative, not a classificatory concept, relative to a given semantic broadness.

Now, Evans (1982: 202) has argued that "it is of the essence of a representational state that it be capable of assessment as true or as false." This amounts to the claim that a genuine semantic property must at least – as noted in chapter 3 – have strongly intensional and misrepresentational powers. A content-dualist might grant that a fully representational state must be truth-evaluable and still stick to the view that one component or ingredient of the full broad semantic property of a representational state may be narrow content. Following the pioneering work of Kaplan (1989), Perry (1977; 1979), and then Block (1986), Recanati (1993) and others have argued that one may distinguish the linguistic meaning (what Kaplan calls "the character") of an indexical (or demonstrative) linguistic utterance from its full truth-conditional content.

Consider, for example, an utterance of (σ) "I am hungry." Different persons might utter different tokens of σ and thereby express different propositions with distinct truth-conditions: different states of affairs must obtain for the thought expressed and/or the utterance to be true. Although each utterance of σ may express a proposition different from any other utterance of σ, all utterances of σ, being utterances of the same sentence-type, have one and the same linguistic meaning (or character). The linguistic meaning of σ is the semantic property all utterances of σ have in common, something like the meaning of the open sentence "x is hungry" together with a rule for determining x to the effect that x is the speaker who uttered σ. To determine the proposition expressed by, or the truth-condition of, a particular utterance of σ, the hearer must fill the slot occupied by the free variable (i.e., instantiate the free variable) and determine which individual is said to have the property expressed by the predicate "hungry." Consider a particular utterance u of σ by Clinton. Then u is true iff Clinton was hungry at t. The character or linguistic meaning of an indexical utterance can, therefore, be taken to be a component of the utterance's full truth-conditional content. Understanding the linguistic meaning of an indexical utterance is not grasping the proposition expressed. But it is understanding something. Not knowing, for example, who uttered u, a hearer knowing English still knows that u is true iff somebody uttered σ at t and he or she was hungry at t. So the content-dualist proposal would be that the narrow content of a thought is to its broad content what the linguistic meaning of an utterance of σ is to its truth-condition.

Furthermore, according to inferential role semantics, the narrow content of a thought just is its inferential role, i.e., its role in deliberation and the planning of action. So the content-dualist would be happy to accept Perry's (1977; 1979) suggestion that a thought's inferential role (i.e., narrow content) can be captured in terms of the linguistic meaning of the utterance used to express it. To see this, consider a famous example of Perry's (1977: 23). Suppose I am about to be attacked by a bear. I entertain a thought I would express in English by the utterance "I'm about to be attacked by a bear." You, as a witness, entertain a thought you would express by uttering "He's about to be attacked by a bear." In this situation, we are likely to behave differently: I roll up in a ball; you run away for help. Of course, the linguistic meaning (or character) of the first-person pronoun "I" and the linguistic meaning (or character) of the third-person pronoun "he" are different. The two utterances, therefore, have distinct linguistic meanings. Let us agree that they have the same truth-condition: they are both true iff Pierre Jacob is about to be attacked by a salient bear. What this example encourages us to do is to see the correlation between linguistic meaning and behavior: different linguistic meanings are paired with different behaviors. Given the link between the narrow content of an individual's thought and his or her behavior, this example gives us reasons for identifying a thought's narrow content with the linguistic meaning of the utterance expressing it. The idea, then, would be that a belief's conceptual (or inferential) role is to the belief's truth-conditional broad content what an utterance's linguistic meaning is to the utterance's truth-conditional content, i.e., an ingredient of the belief's truth-condition.

There are two problems with this suggestion. One problem is whether an utterance's linguistic meaning can capture the narrow content of the thought expressed. Consider the thought expressed by an utterance containing the English first-person pronoun "I." Loewer & Lepore (1986), Recanati (1993), Wettstein (1986) and others have argued that the narrow content of a first-person thought expressible by a use of the pronoun "I" cannot be identified with the linguistic meaning (or character) of "I." In virtue of its linguistic meaning, "I" presents its referent as the speaker to both speaker and hearer of the utterance. But arguably, the speaker thinks of himself or herself in a first-person way, not under the third-personal description *the person who uttered this token of "I."* Nor does the speaker presumably think of himself or herself in the same way as the hearer thinks of the speaker since, unlike the speaker, the hearer might think of the speaker as the speaker. If so, then the narrow thought constituent expressible by "I" cannot be identical to the linguistic meaning of "I."

Waiving this important objection, the second problem can take the form of a dilemma: the semantic dilemma of the content-dualist. Accepting the possibility that a belief's conceptual role be an ingredient of the belief's full-blown truth-condition, then the question arises whether the belief's inferential role may have all the properties assigned to a belief's narrow content by a content-dualist. In particular, the narrow content of an individual's thought is supposed to supervene on the physical properties of the individual's brain. Could the inferential role of an individual's belief supervene on the physical properties of his or her brain? Rather, how could it?

One ingredient of the truth-conditional content of an indexical utterance expressing a first-person thought is its linguistic meaning. If, however, the thought's narrow content is not identical with the utterance's linguistic meaning, the former threatens to be ineffable. Fodor (1987b: 50), when he still subscribed to content-dualism, in effect did embrace this view:

> Narrow content is radically inexpressible, because it's only content *potentially*; it's only what gets to be content when – and only when – it gets to be anchored. We can't – to put it in a nutshell – *say* what Twin thoughts have in common. This is because what can be said is ipso facto semantically evaluable; and what Twin-thoughts have in common is ipso facto not.

Narrow content, then, is whatever you plug into a context and which yields a truth-conditional broad content. In the case of linguistic meaning, we have a grasp on what we would plug in. If a thought's narrow content differs from linguistic meaning, then we lose our handle. An intentional realist will gladly admit that not all content need be linguistic content. However, the suspicion arises that genuinely narrow content is not content at all. In the words of McDowell (1984: 103), the suspicion is that the alleged (narrow) semantic ingredient of a thought turns out to be "a putative *bearer* or *vehicle* of content," not a genuine "*aspect* or *ingredient* of content."

If narrow content does turn out to be inexpressible by any sentence of a natural language, then the suspicion is, as I said, that the content-

dualist faces a dilemma: either the content of an individual's propositional attitude is appropriately narrow enough to supervene on the
physical properties of his or her brain or it is not. If it is, then the suspicion is that it is a mere carrier or vehicle of content, not genuine
content. If it is genuinely semantic, then the suspicion is that it is not
narrow enough to supervene on the physical properties of the individual's brain.

The content-dualist is, therefore, in the following uncomfortable
position: he badly needs the assumption that the narrow semantic
properties of an individual's propositional attitudes supervene on the
physical properties of individual's brain in order to apply the response
to the preemption threat and secure a causal role for narrow content.
However, on the one hand, this assumption is shaky. On the other
hand, even if we grant the content-dualist this dubious assumption, he
still has to concede that the broad semantic property of an individual's
propositional attitude is epiphenomenal. Nor can the content-dualist
retort that he does not have to concede that the broad semantic property of an individual's propositional attitude is epiphenomenal on the
ground that explanation of broad behavior by broad content is not
causal explanation. As I have argued above, his claim that only the
explanation of narrow behavior by narrow content is causal explanation is unjustified. In other words, he still has to face the threat of
externalism to which I will turn in chapter 8. As will emerge, the
strategy envisaged for securing a causal explanatory role for the broad
semantic properties of an individual's propositional attitudes bypasses
the requirement that they supervene upon the physical properties of
the individual's brain.

8

Explaining intentional behavior

In the previous chapter, I have tried to defuse the threat of preemption. It is now time to meet the challenge of externalism. The threat of preemption arose from the fact that the semantic properties of an individual's propositional attitudes are higher-order physical properties, not basic physical properties, of his or her brain. The challenge of externalism arises from the fact that genuinely semantic properties of an individual's propositional attitudes are not local properties of his or her brain. If externalism is correct, then the semantic properties of a pair of beliefs simultaneously entertained by a pair of microphysical duplicates may differ from each other as a genuine $100 bill differs from a counterfeit or a genuine Picasso painting differs from a forgery. The authenticity of either a genuine $100 bill or a Picasso painting seems to be an extrinsic property of either a piece of paper or a canvas. In one case, the piece of paper bears a special historical relation to the authoritative governmental agency who impressed a stamp on it. In the other case, the canvas bears a special historical relation to Picasso's intentions and hands. But it seems, a genuine $100 bill and a counterfeit may have the same causal properties, just as a forgery may have the same causal properties as a genuine Picasso painting. They may reflect photons in the same way and react to chemical tests indistinguishably.

The preemption threat, I claimed above, generates the suspicion that mental processes relating either two propositional attitudes or a pair of propositional attitudes and an individual's bodily movement turn out to be pseudo-processes in Salmon's (1984) sense. The threat of externalism, I now want to argue, can be seen as the suspicion that the semantic properties of an individual's propositional attitude turn out to be *Cambridge* properties of the individual's brain in Geach's (1969) sense.

The notion of a Cambridge *property* can be derived from the notion of a Cambridge *change*. Geach (1969: 72, 99) has called mere Cambridge changes the change undergone by Socrates when he became shorter than Theaetetus as a result of Theaetetus' physical growth and the change posthumously undergone by Socrates "every time a fresh schoolboy [comes] to admire him." Of course, Theaetetus' growth is a biological process, as a result of which – let us suppose – Socrates became shorter than Theaetetus. We may assume that every time a boy comes to admire Socrates, some physical process of belief-formation occurs in the boy's brain, as a result of which Socrates becomes the object of the boy's admiration. Being shorter than Theaetetus may be called one of Socrates' Cambridge properties. So may the property of being (posthumously or not) admired by a schoolboy.

Consider Fodor's (1987b: 33–34) example of a Cambridge change. The coin in my pocket can occupy one of the two following states: being heads up or being tails up. Let us conventionally stipulate that "being an H-particle" applies to any particle in the universe just in case the coin in my pocket happens to be heads up and "being a T-particle" applies to any particle in the universe just in case the coin in my pocket happens to be tails up. By turning my coin upside down, I can change all particles in the universe from H-particles to T-particles, and vice-versa. The change from being an H-particle to being a T-particle (or conversely) is a Cambridge change. The properties of being H-particles and/or T-particles are Cambridge properties of physical particles.

The prototypical instances of putative Cambridge properties I now want to consider are an individual's *legal* properties. Interestingly, several philosophers have assumed that the explanatory role of an individual's legal properties seems to be a revealing model for the explanatory role of the semantic properties of an individual's propositional attitudes. An individual's legal properties no more supervene on the individual's physical properties (let alone on the physical properties of the individual's brain) than the property of a canvas of being a genuine Picasso painting supervenes upon the physical properties of the canvas. The claim that an individual's legal properties are not causally efficacious has been exploited by Kim (1982) and Stich (1983) together with the conditional premiss that, if the semantic properties of an individual's propositional attitudes are, then so are an individual's legal properties, in order to argue (by *modus tollens*) that semantic properties are *not* causally efficacious. The claim that an individual's legal properties are causally efficacious has been recently exploited by Baker (1991a) together with the conditional premiss that if an individual's legal properties are causally efficacious, then so are the semantic properties of an individual's propositional attitudes, in order to argue (by *modus ponens*) that semantic properties *are* causally efficacious.

Now, it seems to me, ordinary social life abounds in Cambridge changes. Consider the change whereby Xantippe, who was Socrates' wife, became a widow upon Socrates' death. Didn't Xantippe undergo a genuine change at time *t*, the time of Socrates' death, since at *t* she turned into a widow, which she was not before *t*? Notice that such a change, if it occurred, did not supervene upon any physical change affecting Xantippe. Xantippe has acquired a new legal property – the property of being a widow. But her new legal property does not supervene upon any new underlying or subvening intrinsic physical property. No physical change or process underlies or subserves her change in legal status. My claim is that her acquiring her new legal status is a Cambridge change. Her new legal property is one of Xantippe's Cambridge properties.

Before I justify this claim, I want to consider Stich's (1983: 165–66) *replacement* argument in favor of his autonomy principle (see also Davidson 1987 who, however, does not accept the autonomy principle). Suppose I am kidnapped and replaced by an exact physical copy down to the last molecule. Although we are physically and chemically indistinguishable, there are many things which I could do (or could have done, if I did not actually do them) which my physical replica cannot (or could not) do, such as divorce my wife or sell my car. What gives me, not my replica, the power to sell my car or divorce my wife is that I bought my car and I married my wife. My replica did not. By assumption then, the facts that I can sell my car and divorce my wife do not supervene upon any of my physical (chemical and biological) intrinsic properties which I share with my replica. Now, I want to ask the following question: don't we provide a causal explanation of the fact that I, unlike my replica, can sell my car or divorce my wife by mentioning respectively the fact that I, not my replica, am the owner of my car and the fact that I, not my replica, stand in the marriage relation to my wife? The issue is delicate, but I am going to argue for a negative response to this question.

Consider what my standing in the marriage relation to my wife explains. It does not explain why I divorced her, since I did not. What it contributes to explaining is why I, unlike my replica, *can* (or could) divorce her. Granted, the fact that I can divorce my wife implies or presupposes that I married her – which is a physical process of some sort. Still, the fact that I can divorce my wife is *not* an *explanandum* for a causal explanation since, on my view, until I divorce her, there is no process standing in need of a causal explanation. Similarly, my being the owner of my car explains not why I sold it, but why I *can* (or could) sell it. I may have the right to sell it and never sell it. In which case, there is no *explanandum* for a causal explanation.

Before going back to Xantippe, consider a similar example of Baker's (1991a). In the US, there is a "marriage penalty" law (quite surprising, I must say, to a French person): under the American law, and assuming fixity of income, Bonnie and Clyde owe more taxes, say for the year 1991, the year they got married, than for the year 1990, when they lived together and were still unmarried. Unlike Stich (1983) and Kim (1982), Baker (1991a) holds that we provide a causal explanation of why Bonnie and Clyde owe more taxes for 1991 than for 1990 by mentioning their property of standing in the marriage relation. Now, I want to deny that *owing* more taxes in 1992 than in 1991 is an *explanandum* for a causal explanation for the same reason that I deny that my having the right to divorce my wife is an *explanandum* for a causal explanation. If Bonnie and Clyde owe more taxes for 1991 than for 1990, then they owe taxes for 1991. They may, therefore, owe taxes in 1992, but if neither they nor anybody else in the Internal Revenue Service *believe* that they owe taxes, then they may never pay taxes. If they do not, then there is no *explanandum* for a causal explanation. For purposes of computing the taxes that they owe, people are divided into classes of tax payers under which they fall in virtue of their incomes and family situations. However, there is no physical process mapping the combination of a person's income and family situation onto the number of dollars the person owes to the IRS in the US.

Now back to Xantippe's widowhood again. How could Socrates' death cause Xantippe to acquire the property of being a widow? Notice that there is no time delay between the time of Socrates' death and the instant at which Xantippe becomes a widow. Xantippe could be in or out of the Milky Way, arbitrarily far away from Socrates' body at the time of his death and still acquire this property upon Socrates' death. How could such a process or causal influence take place at a speed greater than the speed of light?

Socrates' death, I submit, did not cause Xantippe's widowhood. There is no causal process from the former to the latter. In fact, there is no process at all because, unlike Kim (1973a; 1974), I would like to claim that Socrates' death and Xantippe's widowhood are not two distinct events. So *a fortiori* they cannot be linked by a causal relation or process at all. I want to claim that there is a single event – Socrates' death – which is also Xantippe's widowhood. Xantippe's widowhood is *conceptually* more complex than Socrates' death since the latter, unlike the former, is independent of the legal relation between Socrates and Xantippe. Socrates' death is a constituent of Xantippe's widowhood; but the former does not cause the latter.

We are often, it seems to me, prone to confuse causal and conceptual relations or dependencies. As Kim (1973b) has noticed, my writing "r" in succession twice, for example, is a constituent of the process of my writing "Larry." I did the latter *by* doing the former, but the former (or my doing the former) is not a cause of the latter (or of my doing the latter). Or consider the following example from Menzies (1988: 565–66):

> Fred runs 100 meters in a foot-race in 10 seconds and in doing so outruns the competitor on his left, but is outrun by the competitor on his right. Here his outrunning the competitor on his left and his being outrun by the competitor on his right circumstantially supervene on his running the race in 10 seconds in virtue of different circumstantial facts about the running times of the other two competitors. Yet we might say the cause of his losing the race was his being outrun by his competitor on the right, not his outrunning the competitor on his left.

I want, however, to object that Fred's losing the race is constituted, not caused, by his being outrun by the competitor on his right. He lost the race by being outrun: being outrun is part of losing. The relation between being outrun and losing is conceptual (or mereological), not causal.[1]

---

[1] Note that I am not denying that by mentioning the fact that Fred was outrun by the competitor on his right, one may provide an explanation of his losing the race. I am merely denying that the explanation would be purely causal.

So I suggest that the truth of propositions P_1 that Socrates and Xantippe were married at t and P_2 that Socrates died at t *entail* the truth of proposition P_3 that Xantippe became a widow at t. As noticed by Kim (1974), conversely the truth of propositions P_2 that Socrates died at t and P_3 that Xantippe became a widow at t entail that the truth of proposition P_1 that Socrates and Xantippe were married at t. I do agree that the former entailment has some explanatory force which the latter lacks. Whether or not, however, the latter entailment counts as a genuine explanation, I do want to deny that the former explanation is a genuine (or pure) causal explanation. I would even go so far as denying that, by mentioning the cause of Socrates' death, we provide a purely causal explanation of Xantippe's widowhood. Event c, Socrates' drinking the hemlock, caused event e, Socrates' death. But explanation holds between propositions, not events. In referring to an event, a proposition must refer to some property or other of the event referred to. Not any property of c can be causally efficacious in bringing e about. Socrates may have drunk the hemlock in a red cup. But the fact that he did, if he did, was not causally efficacious in the process. Nor can every property of effect e be explained by the properties of its cause which were causally efficacious in the process whereby c caused e. Here, I appeal to the distinction drawn in chapter VII between causal and non-causal explanations. Granted, Xantippe's widowhood must have been caused by Socrates' drinking the hemlock if Socrates' death was, since on my view they are one and the same event. Granted, by mentioning the fact that Socrates drank the hemlock at t, we supply a causal explanation of the fact that he died at $t + 1$. However, proposition P3 that Xantippe became a widow at $t + 1$ is *entailed* by propositions P1 that Socrates died at $t + 1$ and P2 that Xantippe was Socrates' wife at t. This is why when we explain that Xantippe became a widow at $t + 1$ by mentioning that Socrates drank the hemlock at t, we provide a *hybrid* explanation one component of which is causal and one component of which is conceptual, not causal.

The threat of externalism is potentially more damaging to mental causation than the preemption threat. The very possibility of mental causation presupposes at least the existence of a process – i.e., a change or a sequence of events – linking an individual's propositional attitudes to his or her behavior. The threat of preemption generates the possibility that mental processes are pseudo-processes. But a Cambridge change is no process at all. When Socrates became shorter than Theaetetus, Theaetetus did change, but Socrates did not. Every time Socrates is posthumously the object of a schoolboy's admiration, he undergoes no change at all. The threat of externalism generates the possibility that the semantic properties of an individual's propositional attitudes are Cambridge properties of the individual's brain. If Cambridge properties explain Cambridge changes, and if the semantic properties of an individual's propositional attitudes are Cambridge properties of the individual's brain, then it is a mistake to assume that the semantic properties of an individual's propositional attitudes can play a role in the causal explanation of the individual's behavior. If so, then intentional realism is wrong to assume that the semantic properties of an individual's propositional attitudes are causally efficacious.

8.2 ARE THERE SEMANTIC ENGINES?

According to common sense, my belief c that there is coffee in the cup in front of me is one of the causes of my intentional behavior e, which consists of my extending my right arm, picking up the cup with the fingers of my right hand, bringing the cup up to my lips and drinking coffee from it. Since we are assuming the truth of token physicalism, my belief c is one of my brain-state tokens. As such, it has different physical (chemical and biological) properties and it has a semantic property in virtue of which my belief c represents the fact that the cup in front of me contains coffee. According to externalism, this semantic property is not a local property of my brain. If this property is a Cambridge property of my brain, then it stands no chance of contributing to the causal explanation of my behavior e. If the semantic property of my belief is not a local property of my brain, and given that my brain has several local physical (chemical and biological) properties, how could the semantic property of my belief be causally efficacious in triggering the eminently local process of propagation of electrical and chemical signals from my brain to my muscles through my nerve fibers?

The possibility that genuinely semantic properties be radically epiphenomenal arises from the four following assumptions: (1) that token physicalism is true; (2) that an individual's behavior is a local physical process; (3) that the local physical (chemical and biological) properties of an individual's brain are causally efficacious in the production of the individual's behavior; (4) that externalism is true of the semantic properties of an individual's propositional attitudes. Unless we make some adjustment within this set of assumptions, then, I believe, the view that genuinely semantic properties of an individual's propositional attitudes are indeed epiphenomenal is inescapable.

As Dennett (1981a: 61) has famously said, the brain is a syntactic, not a semantic engine. In Dennett's (1991b: 119) words, "a semantic engine . . . is a mechanical impossibility – like a perpetual motion machine." Presumably, a semantic engine would be a physical mechanism having both physical and semantic properties. It would be capable of producing physical effects – such as moving gears. And futhermore, it ought to be capable of producing physical effects in virtue of having the semantic properties that it has. Dennett is denying that anything can meet these three conditions. Now, it seems to me, this is a point on which Stich (1983), who defends STM (the syntactic theory of mind), and Fodor (1987b, 1994), who defends CRTM (the computational representational theory of mind), agree with Dennett. The disagreement between STM and CRTM (as I argued in chapter 5) consists in that the latter, unlike the former, posits intentional psychological laws in which reference is made to the semantic properties of mental symbols. Stich's STM explicitly rejects the possibility of semantic engines. The reason, however, why arguably Fodor's CRTM is committed to denying the possibility of semantic engines is that, according to CRTM, semantic properties of mental symbols are causally efficacious only by proxy – via the sytactic properties of mental symbols.

Although I do not agree with every detail of his views (as will appear at the end of the present chapter), I think Dretske (1988) has the general shape of a response to the challenge of externalism, i.e., a solution to the problem of the causal efficacy of the semantic properties of an individual's propositional attitudes. What I propose to do first is to scrutinize and put the burden upon (2) by examining two underlying assumptions which, as I said in chapter 7 (section 3), are very widespread, and which I will call assumptions (2a) and (2b). After I provide an alternative to assumptions (2a) and (2b) based on Dretske's *componential* view of behavior, I will then discuss Dretske's dual *explanandum* strategy. One of the most remarkable features of the Dretskean solution which I will ultimately recommend is that, while it corroborates in a certain way the *strong* intentional realist causal thesis, it paradoxically forces the intentional realist to revise the *weak* causal thesis, i.e., the thesis that an individual's propositional attitudes are causes of his or her behavior. As I will explain, on the componential view of behavior, an individual's propositional attitudes ought rather to be seen as causes of his or her bodily motions (which are *components* of his or her behavior). The componential view of behavior is consistent with the assumption that an individual's propositional attitudes can be causes; but what they cause is the individual's bodily motion, not his or her behavior. It remains to be seen whether a view which accommodates the intentional realist strong causal thesis better than the intentional realist weak causal thesis can be said to vindicate the thesis of the possibility of semantic engines.

8.3 THE COMPONENTIAL VIEW OF BEHAVIOR

According to what I will call assumption (2a), behavior *is* physical motion: an individual's behavior is just some of his or her physical (or bodily) motion. According to what I will call assumption (2b), an individual's propositional attitude is a cause of the individual's intentional behavior. In chapter 7 (section 3), I already referred to the distinction between an individual's intentional behavior and his or her instinctive behavior: the former, unlike the latter, is what an individual does because of what he believes and desires – what he or she does because he or she has reasons for so doing. Notice that (2b) just is the intentional realist weak causal thesis. As I already said in chapter 7 (section 3), I think that both assumptions (2a) and (2b) underlie Davidson's first premiss for anomalous monism (AM).[2] They also underlie the functionalist views that an individual's behavior is the observable output of an input-output device and that an individual's propositional attitudes are brain-state tokens of the individual characterized by their causal relations to sensory inputs, other propositional attitudes, and behavioral outputs. From the fact that behavior is physical motion, it does not follow that physical (chemical or physiological) predicates are appropriate for the description of each and every behavior – in particular, intentional behavior. So from the fact that an individual's intentional behavior is identical to some of

---

[2] As I said in chapter 5 (section 5), Davidson's first premiss for anomalous monism (which is a version of the weak causal thesis) is that mental events (tokens of propositional attitudes) can enter singular causal relations.

the individual's bodily motion, it does not follow that intentional behavior can be given a physical or physiological description, let alone a physical or physiological explanation. It does not follow that the concept of intentional behavior can be reduced to some physiological concept of bodily motion. Neither functionalists nor Davidson were tempted to think so. None the less, behavior (intentional or not) is supposed to be nothing but physical motion. Now, if my belief c (that the cup in front of me contains coffee) is a cause of my behavior e, and if my behavior e is the physical motion of my right arm, hand and fingers, then, I think, the physical (chemical and biological) properties of c alone are causally efficacious in the process. c's semantic property is not.

Assumptions (2a) and (2b), however, are not inevitable. Dretske's (1988: ch. 1–2) impressive treatment of behavior suggests an alternative view of behavior which, following Adams (1991: 138), I will call the *componential* view of behavior. On the componential view, the physical motion of my right arm, hand and fingers when I pick up the cup of coffee in front of me is *not* my behavior: it is a *constituent* (or component) of my behavior e. My behavior e is the extended *process* whereby some internal state of my brain (my belief c that the cup in front of me contains coffee)[3] causes or produces m, the physical motions of my right arm, hand and fingers. In general, behavior is the process of production (or retention) of physical motion m by some internal state c of a physical system. The reason I say that behavior may involve a process of retention of bodily motion is that the best strategy of a predator on the lookout for its prey may be to remain temporarily still, and so may be that of a prey hiding from its predator. On the componential view, my behavior e, which is a process, involves the ordered pair of events composed of my belief and my bodily motions – the former causing the latter – together with the causal relation which holds between them.[4] On the componential view, then, two

---

[3] This whole discussion presupposes, as I said, token physicalism, i.e., the thesis that my belief c is one of my brain-state tokens.

[4] Perhaps I should say that my behavior e is the ordered triple $<c, m, R>$ consisting of my belief c, my physical motion m, and the causal relation R holding between c and m, however the causal relation is captured. As I pointed out in chapter 7, section 3, this may depend on how we construe the relata of the causal relation. On Davidson's view, the causal relation is a purely extensional relation between events; but on Kim's view, an event itself is the instantiation of a property by an object at a time and a place.

physically indistinguishable bodily motions may be components of two distinct behaviors: my left hand may follow twice the same path in space; the first time, it so moved as a result of *my* intention to raise it; so it was part of *my* behavior. The second time, it so moved as a result of *your* intention to raise it; so it was part of *your* behavior.[5] Of course, the process of my moving my left hand and the process of your moving my left hand are two distinct processes, since the former includes my intention to raise it while the latter includes your intention to raise it.

Now, if the componential view is right, then both assumptions (2a) and (2b) are false: not only does it follow that behavior is not mere physical bodily motion, but propositional attitudes do not cause behavior. My belief c that the cup in front of me contains coffee does not cause e, my behavior. Rather, both my belief c and the physical motion of my right arm, hand and fingers, m, are components of my behavior e. What my belief c causes is m, the physical motion of my right arm, hand and fingers, not e. My behavior e is the process via which c causes m. Of course, the componential view of behavior involves an ontological commitment to processes which are entities involving events (however conceived) together with the causal relation.[6] In favor of the componential conception, Dretske (1991b: 198–99) has argued that it accommodates the autonomy of intentional behavior better than its orthodox alternative (based on (2a) and (2b)). On the orthodox view, any cause of my belief c is, by transitivity of the causal relation, a cause of my behavior e. So intentional behavior is not autonomous. On the componential view, the cause of belief c cannot cause behavior e since c does not cause behavior e in the first place.

Embracing the componential view of behavior provides one with one more degree of freedom in vindicating the claim that the semantic properties of an individual's beliefs are causally efficacious. Arguably, the semantic property of my belief c (that there is coffee in front of me) could be causally efficacious in the production of my physical motion m. Alternatively, although not causally efficacious in the production of m – the output of the behavioral process – it could

---

[5] The two physically indistinguishable bodily motions in my example will of course take place at distinct instants of time.

[6] In any case, my discussion of the distinction between genuine processes and pseudo-processes (which I borrowed from Salmon 1984) in chapter 7 already committed me to an ontology of processes.

still, however, be causally efficacious in playing a role in the production of the whole behavioral process one constituent of which is
output *m*. Most philosophers in either the tradition of anomalous
monism or functionalism have assumed that the semantic properties
of an individual's propositional attitudes ought to be causally efficacious in the production of the individual's physical motions because
they identified an individual's behavior with his or her bodily
motions. The componential conception of behavior allows us to see
how the semantic properties of an individual's propositional attitudes
could achieve causal efficacy otherwise. If it turns out that the semantic properties of an individual's propositional attitudes play a role, not
in the production of bodily motion, but in accounting for the process
of behavior, how much of a concession would this be to the claim that
semantic properties are epiphenomenal? This is a delicate issue. For
the view that it is an intolerable concession, see Horgan (1990; 1991:
88–99). Horgan (1990: 233) claims for example that on the componential view of behavior, we cannot satisfy the requirement that my
belief that there is beer in the fridge is "explanatorily relevant to the
action" of going to the fridge. What is true is that, on the componential view of behavior, my belief cannot be a cause of my behavior
(since it is one of its components and components do not cause what
they are components of). But my belief can still perfectly well be a
cause of my bodily motions involved (as components) in my behavior.

8.4 THE DUAL EXPLANANDUM STRATEGY

The second ingredient of Dretske's solution, which Kim (1991) has
labelled the "dual *explanandum* strategy," consists of a twofold distinction. First, following the lead of the componential view of behavior,
we may distinguish the causal explanation of behavior (a process)
from the causal explanation of bodily motion (an event which is part
of the behavioral process). Secondly, we may distinguish what Dretske
(1988, 1993a) calls *triggering* causes from what he calls *structuring*
causes. The distinction between triggering and structuring causes can
be exhibited in response to what Dretske (1972) earlier called *contrastive* explanatory contexts (or demands). Hot water flows from the
faucet in my bath tub. The triggering cause is my turning the faucet
for hot water in my bath tub. Among the structuring causes of the
same process are what the plumber did when he connected the water

pipes of the bath tub to the water pipes of the rest of the apartment, to the pipes of the building and to the city pipes, and what the electrician did when he connected the electrical water-heater to the electrical circuit of the apartment and to the rest of the building. The cursor of my lap-top moves to the right. The triggering cause of this process is my pressing the key on the keyboard of my lap-top. Among the structuring causes are the activities of the computer scientists who designed the word processing program which I am using and the activities of the engineers who designed the hardware of my computer.

What Dretske calls "structuring causes" are just causes of background or standing conditions which are necessary for triggering causes to do their job. They are conditions which must obtain if my turning the faucet for hot water is to make hot water flow from the faucet. They are conditions which must obtain if my pressing the key on the keyboard of my lap-top is to make the cursor move to the right.[7] As any other event, a bodily motion has of course a great number of different causes. The distinction between structuring causes and triggering causes, however, applies to processes or to sequences of events, not to individual events. I will now exploit the above twofold distinction in an argument designed to show that the semantic properties of a physical system may be causally efficacious in a structuring causal sense, i.e., in accounting for the structure of the system's behavioral process.[8]

Remember that, in chapters 3 and 4, the semantic property of state c of physical device S was defined as c's indicator function, i.e., as the information which c has the function to carry. To see how the informational properties of state c of some physical device relate to its

---

[7] While Horgan (1990; 1991) is worried that the componential view of behavior may deprive propositional attitudes of their causal role *hic et nunc*, Garcia-Carpintero (1994) seems worried that mental causes be robbed of their causal efficacy if they are not triggering causes of behavior.

[8] Interestingly, in the context of a discussion of the causal explanation of the ontogenetic development of cognitive structures generally (and language acquisition in particular), Chomsky (1980b: 2) makes a roughly similar distinction between what he calls "the unfolding of an internally controlled process" and the "triggering effect" of "external conditions" which are "necessary for" or "facilitate" the unfolding process. Chomsky there talks of learning as "the growth of cognitive structures along an internally directed course under the triggering and partially shaping effect of the environment."

causal properties, I will consider first an artefact and then an organism.

Consider first the bimetallic strip in Dretske's (1988) favorite artefact: the thermostat. The thermostat involves a bimetallic strip which, like any thermometer, carries information about (or nomically covaries with) room temperature. However, unlike a thermometer, the thermostat also does something: it turns the furnace on. Furthermore, it turns the furnace on when the room temperature drops to, for example, 15°C. So what the thermostat does is based on the information about room temperature which is carried by a particular state of its bimetallic strip. When room temperature drops to 15°C, the bimetallic strip bends and, in so doing, it closes an electrical circuit to which the furnace is connected. So the bimetallic strip acts as a switch in the electrical circuit: this is its causal property. Its causal property is in turn correlated to its informational property – the fact that it covaries nomically with room temperature.

Call c the curvature of the bimetallic strip carrying the information that room temperature is 15°C. Call m the flow of electrons in the wires to the furnace prompted by the closing of the electrical circuit. One thing is to explain the production of m by c. Another thing is to explain the internal structure (or shape) of behavior: why does c cause m rather than something else, for example, m'? Why is c coordinated to m and not m'? In explaining the production of m by c, we are in effect revealing the diagram of the electrical wiring between the bimetallic strip in the thermostat and the furnace. In explaining the structure of thermostat behavior (i.e., in explaining the c–m coordination), we are in effect explaining what a thermostat typically does: the fact that the thermostat has a bimetallic strip which is both a thermometer and a switch which can turn a furnace on. The point is that, in explaining the production of m by c, we need not, as in the explanation of thermostat behavior, refer to the informational property of the bimetallic strip. Part of the contrast between the two explanations is that the former, unlike the latter, is bound to be an electrical explanation. The explanation of the production of m by c mentions the flow of electrons through the wires. The explanation of thermostat behavior, by contrast, mentions the property of the device of carrying information about temperature, not its being made of wires in which electrons flow. Even if it is hard to imagine how a hydraulic device could be a thermostat (harder than to imagine a hydraulic computer), it is quite clear that by mentioning the informational property of a thermostat, we ascend to a level of description in which we abstract away from the fact that it is electrons which are flowing through its wires.[9]

Now, consider the contrast between triggering and structuring causes of behavior. The triggering cause of the thermostat's behavior is the drop in room temperature to 15°C. The triggering cause emerges in response to the question: why did the thermostat turn the furnace on at time t? The causal response to this question involves a reference to the triggering cause of the process: the thermostat turned the furnace on at t because the temperature dropped to 15°C at t. The drop of temperature at t caused the bimetallic strip to bend at t. The curvature of the bimetallic strip at t in turn acted as a switch in the electrical circuit to which the furnace is connected. Notice that when a triggering cause is relevant, we are interested in the *tokening* of c at t.

The structuring cause of the same process, by contrast, emerges in response to a question about the structure of the process (or about the c-m coordination): why does the thermostat turn on the furnace, rather than something else? Why does state c of the bimetallic strip cause m (rather than something else, for example, m')? Why is the thermostat's behavior constituted by a c-m coordination, not a c-m' coordination? Notice that when a structuring cause is relevant, we are interested in a *type* of process, not in any particular instantiation of this type of process: why does c cause m, not at t, but on each and every occasion in which the temperature drops to 15°C? What we want to explain is the regular coordination between c and m in certain repeatable circumstances. If we want to supply a causal explanation to this question, we must refer to the intentional activities of the electrician who wired the bimetallic strip so that it would act automatically as a switch in the electrical circuit to which the furnace is connected each time the room temperature would drop to 15°C. Now, in order to turn the furnace on automatically each and every time room temperature drops to 15°C, the thermostat must have some internal state sensitive (or responsive) to room temperature. Given that the thermostat does have such an internal thermometer, the electrician might have, if he had so wished, wired the bimetallic strip to an electrical circuit to which the dishwasher, not the furnace, is connected. In which case,

---

[9] Though hard to imagine, a hydraulic thermostat would be a system in which water, not electrons, would flow through pipes, not wires. The hard part is to imagine how such a hydraulic device could involve a component sensitive to, and carrying information about, temperature.

every time the room temperature would drop to 15°C, the thermostat would turn on the dishwasher, not the furnace. The thermostat would then produce output *m*', not *m*. The point is that, if we want to explain the *c-m* coordination in the thermostat's behavior, we need to advert to a selectional process which, in the case of the thermostat, is an intentional process. A device without a *c-m* coordination would not have been *selected* by an electrician to do the job of a thermostat.

I shall now consider an example of a *c-m* coordination system in animals, i.e., in noctuid moths which are favored meals of bats.[10] The bat emits ultra-sounds. The noctuid moth has a very simple system for detecting the bats' ultra-sounds. It has one ear on each side of its thorax. Each ear has two auditory receptor neurons, the A1 cell and the A2 cell, each connected to the thoracic ganglion which is the moth's decision center. A1 neurons are sensitive to sounds of lower intensity than A2 neurons. The rate of firing is proportional to the loudness of the sound. The A1 neurons allow the moth to detect a bat at a distance of about 100 feet away (long before the bat can detect the moth via echolocation). If the A1 neuron on the left is more active than the A1 neuron on the right, then this indicates the presence of a bat 100 feet away on the left. Detection of a bat 100 feet away triggers a movement away from the source. As the bat gets closer and the sound it emits gets louder, activity of the A1 neuron is replaced by the activity of the A2 neuron. When the bat is 8 feet away, the A2 neuron picks up the sound and prompts erratic flight maneuvers involving wild loops and power dives. "As a result," writes Alcock (1975: 127), "the insect does not know where it is going but neither does the pursuing bat, whose inability to plot the path of its prey may permit the insect to escape."

So consider a prey, *O*, whose behavior is to run away from its predator, *P*. The question is: why did *O* run away? One thing is to explain the production of *O*'s particular flight motions *m* at *t*. How are *O*'s flight evasion motions controlled by the transmission of electrical signals from the A1 cells to the thoracic ganglion? Another thing is to explain the *c-m* coordination in *O*. Why does a tokening of *c* in *O* control *m*, a flight motion, rather than *m*', a fight motion? Suppose *O* flew as a result of predator *P*'s approach at *t*. *O*'s state *c* registered *P*'s

[10] I borrow the example from Alcock (1975: 124–27); see also Ridley (1995: 56–58; 152–53). It is mentioned in Dretske (1988: 91–92).

presence at t. So P's approach triggered c's detection of P and c in turn caused m. P's approach is the triggering cause of O's behavior. Explaining why O's perceptual state in turn caused m (O's flight movements) rather than something else – why c caused predator-flight movements m rather than predator-fight movements m' or no movement at all – involves providing a structuring cause of O's behavior. So, besides distinguishing triggering and structuring causes of O's behavior, we may distinguish two *explananda*: one thing is explaining the muscular contraction and the propagation of electrical pulses within nerve fibers in O which make possible the production of motions m by c; another thing is explaining why, upon perceiving predator P, O executes flight motions m. The former explanation might refer to physical, chemical and biological properties of c only. The latter explanation – the explanation of the coordination between O's perceptual state c and O's flight motions m – involves reference to c's semantic property. The idea here is that an organism without a coordination between perceptual state c and predator-flight movement m would not have been selected by evolution, i.e., would not have survived.

Reference to internal state c is, therefore, systematically ambiguous. When we focus either on the production of m by c or on the triggering cause of the process which prompted c (the drop of temperature in the thermostat or the predator's approach for the prey's internal state),[11] we are in effect referring to a particular *token* of c. Only tokens enter individual causal relations. When we are focussing on the structuring cause of behavior – the c-m coordination – then we are referring to the *type* of internal c – which may have many different instantiations in the lifetime of either the thermostat or the prey. Types are involved in regular nomic connections.

Notice that one feature shared by the explanation of the production of m by c and the explanation of the system's behavior by reference to its triggering cause is that no role is given to the informational property of internal state c of the system.[12] By contrast, the explanation of the system's behavior by reference to its structuring causes does refer to the informational property of internal state c of the system – be it the bimetallic strip in the thermostat or some perceptual state in the prey.

[11] In effect, the cause of c.

[12] This is true in both the case of the thermostat and of the prey.

In the case of the thermostat, this last point is illustrated by the fact that the electrician who wired the bimetallic strip to the furnace via the electrical circuit relied on and used its informational property, namely the fact that the bimetallic strip has a determinate curvature when and only when the temperature drops to 15°C. So the fact that there is in the thermostat an internal thermometer whose shape covaries with, and carries information about, room temperature is a fact about the thermostat which helps explain – in the structuring causal sense of 'explain' – the structure of the thermostat's behavior or the coordination between c and m. Calling F the room temperature, c the curvature of the bimetallic strip, and m the ignition of the furnace via the flow of electrons through the wires, we can, following Dretske (1988: 84), diagram the explanatory situation as in figure 8.

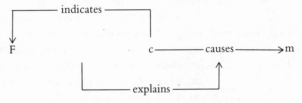

Figure 8 From Dretske (1988: 84)

For simplicity, like Dretske, in this diagram, I call "F" a state of affairs, a fact or an instantiated property – something which, in the terminology of chapters 2–4, I would call s's being F or the fact that the temperature dropped to 15°C. This diagram instantiates the systematic ambiguity between types and tokens mentioned above: a particular token of c may cause m; but (as I said in chapter 2) the informational (or indication) relation is a relation between types; *a fortiori*, in the higher-order explanation relation holding between the fact that c indicates F and the fact that c causes m, c occurs *qua* type.[13]

Although the informational property of c's curvature can be said to play a role in bringing m (furnace ignition) about, still c's electrical wiring to the furnace in turn came about as a result of the design of an

---

[13] Assuming that the causal relation is neither intentional nor epistemic, and to alleviate the worry that the explanation relation in the diagram may reintroduce intentionality by the back door, one may construe the explanation relation as a higher-order causal relation. The diagram would then read as follows: the fact that c indicates F causes c to cause m.

intentional agent with propositional attitudes. Our task, then, is to find instantiations of the above diagram with the following two features: c's informational property must be replaced by (or converted into) a genuinely semantic property; reference to the activities of an intentional agent with propositional attitudes is altogether to be dispensed with. Now, each feature raises its own peculiar difficulty.

8.5 THE CHARGE OF CIRCULARITY

In fact, in Dretske's own (1988: 86–87) treatment of the case, the explanation of the thermostat's behavior by reference to its structuring causes involves a reference, not just to the informational property of the bimetallic strip, but to its *representational* (i.e., semantic) property as well. On Dretske's view of the matter, the bimetallic strip has its informational property merely in virtue of being composed of metal. Metal bars nomically covary with, and therefore carry information about, temperature. And they do so as a matter of objective fact. On Dretske's teleosemantic view, the semantic (or representational) property of state c of the thermostat's bimetallic strip is its indicator *function*: the information which it is its function to carry. The function of the bimetallic strip is – what else? – to carry information about temperature. How has state c of the bimetallic strip acquired its indicator function? On Dretske's view, c has acquired its indicator function by virtue of the fact that an electrician recruited it as an electrical switch, i.e., as a cause of m, the flow of electrons in the wires prompting furnace ignition. The informational property is thus converted into a representational (or semantic) property by being made into a cause of motion.

Notice the important fact that, on this view, the fact that c causes m is a causal property of c; but causing m is not c's function; c's function is to carry information about temperature. In the informationally based teleosemantic view I espouse here, and unlike in the pure psycho-functionalist view (discussed in chapter 6), beliefs do not have behavioral (or motor) functions; they have indicator (or informational) functions.[14] On the one hand, an individual's belief may of course be a cause of some of the individual's physical motion. But neither can

---

[14] This distinction is blurred in Garcia-Carpintero's (1994) discussion of structuring causes. See Dretske (1994b).

the belief cause the individual's behavior (of which it is a part); nor is it the function of the belief to cause some motion: not all of a belief's effects need be its function. On the other hand, I am not here repudiating the functional role semantic view that some of the semantic properties of an individual's belief may derive from the interactions between it and other beliefs of the individual. I am, however, combining this insight from functional role semantics with an informationally based teleosemantics.

This view of the indicator function of the bimetallic strip fits in with Wright's (1973, 1976) etiological theory of function which I described in chapter 4. The electrician's recruitment of c as a switch is a selection process. Again, the process of recruitment of state c (the curvature of the bimetallic strip) as a cause of motion is an intentional process involving an agent with propositional attitudes. Importantly, the view is not that the function of the bimetallic strip is to cause anything such as the flow of electrons to the wires. We have here a model of how some internal state of a physical system having informational property can acquire a genuine semantic property by being recruited by an intentional process as a cause of motion. But since the recruitment process is an intentional process, we shall have to find some non-intentional process capable of recruiting an organism's internal state having an informational property as a cause of the organism's motion.

Now, as Baker (1991b) and Cummins (1991) have noticed, Dretske's account of the causal structuring role of c's semantic property runs the risk of being circular. c possesses its informational property objectively: c's particular curvature indicates that room temperature is 15°C independently of the fact that c has been turned by an electrician into an electrical switch. However, c's particular curvature does not possess any genuinely semantic property until it is so converted into a cause of motion. It represents the fact that room temperature is 15°C only after and because it has been recruited as a cause of furnace ignition. So the question is: if, on Dretske's account, c acquires its semantic property by being recruited as a cause of motion m, how can Dretske concomitantly claim that c's semantic property explains (in the structuring causal sense) the thermostat's behavior, i.e., the fact that c causes m?

At this point, two strategies seem open to Dretske, one of which is to abandon the project of conferring a causal explanatory role to genuinely *semantic* properties. The claim was that c's semantic property –

the fact that it represents, even if derivatively,[15] room temperature (as being 15°C) – explains why *c* causes *m*. The first strategy consists in weakening the original claim into the weaker claim that *c*'s informational property – the fact that it carries information about room temperature – plays a role in explaining why *c* causes *m*. This in fact is what Cummins (1991: 106) says Dretske's account commits him to: "it is . . . *natural meaning* that does the explaining, that has been given a job to do in the explanation of behavior. Non-natural meaning is, by definition, just the fact that the correlative *natural meaning* explains behavior." But on the one hand, I do not think that Dretske is so committed. What, I think, Dretske is committed to is the view that one condition for *c*'s semantic property to play a role in explaining why *c* causes *m* is that past tokens of *c* (prior to the *c-m* coordination) had indicator properties – that they indicated room temperature before the electrician wired the bimetallic strip to the furnace. But to assume that, prior to the *c-m* coordination, tokens of *c* had (or must have had) indicator properties does not thereby deprive semantic properties of tokens of *c* occurring after the *c-m* coordination from playing a role in explaining why *c* causes *m* after the *c-m* coordination has been established.[16] On the other hand, Dretske ought not to adopt this strategy since it would preempt the very possibility of explaining (in the structuring causal sense) how *false* representations can cause motions and thereby enter the explanation of behavior. And to do so would be to give up on the idea that genuine semantic properties of genuine representations can be causally efficacious.

The second strategy consists in a modification of Dretske's formula for converting *c*'s informational property into a genuine semantic (or representational) property. We may put the burden of circularity on the appeal to motion *m*. In Dretske's formula, *m* has a dual role: on the one hand, in virtue of the fact that *c* causes *m*, *c*'s informational property is thereby converted into a semantic property; on the other hand, *c*'s semantic property explains why *c* causes *m*. According to the second strategy, what is responsible for the circularity of the account is the

---

[15] I mean that whatever meaning state *c* of the thermostat has, it is not original (underived) or primitive intentionality, but derived meaning (see chapter 1 for discussion).

[16] As indicated above, in the *explanandum* "why *c* causes *m*," reference is made to a token of *c*. In the explanation in which reference is made to past tokens of *c* (prior to the *c-m* coordination), it is *c qua* type which has indicator properties.

fact that *m* is referred to both in the condition via which *c* acquires its indicator function and as part of what *c*'s semantic property is supposed to explain (in the structuring causal sense). The second strategy consists in dissociating the two causal relations one relatum of which is *c*: it consists in divorcing the causal relation responsible for conferring upon *c* its semantic property from the causal relation which *c*'s possession of its semantic property must explain. Instead of *referring* (rigidly so to speak) to *m* twice, the idea is to weaken the condition via which *c*'s informational property is converted into a semantic property by quantifying over physical motions. Instead of assuming that *c*'s informational property is converted into a semantic property by the fact that *c* is recruited as a cause of (particular motion) *m*, let us merely assume that *c* acquires its indicator function (hence its semantic property) by being recruited as a cause of *some* physical motion or other. If there is some physical motion or other which *c* can cause, then this is a sufficient condition for *c*'s acquiring a semantic property. We thereby weaken reference to a specific motion by *quantifying* over physical motions in the condition whereby *c* acquires its indicator function. We may in turn refer to particular motion, *m*, as what *c*'s semantic property must contribute to explain. On the modified view, *c* acquires its indicator function (or its semantic property) by virtue of causing some physical motion or other. The fact that it possesses its semantic property can, then, without circularity, explain why *c* causes a particular physical motion, *m*.

This is, I think, a welcome modification – one recommended by Fodor (1990e), which Dretske ought to accept and which he (1991c) seems to accept. For two reasons, the example of the thermostat may be misleading. First of all, given that the curvature of the bimetallic strip *c* acts as an electrical switch, the range of physical motions which *c* can be expected to cause seems restricted to the flow of electrons in the wires and the subsequent ignition of whatever device happens to be connected to the wires. If we think of the process of conversion of the thermostat's informational property into a semantic property as a model for the conversion of the informational property of some internal state of an organism into a semantic property, we do not, I think, want to assume that the organism's internal state (having informational property) will derive its semantic property from its being recruited via some non-intentional process as the cause of *one* particular physical motion. Being recruited to cause a *range* (or an equivalence class) of distinct physical motions (e.g., a motion of the left hand or a motion of the right hand) will confer a semantic property upon some information-carrying internal state of an organism.

Secondly, in the case of an artefact like the thermostat, as in some cases of learning (based on teaching), we may identify the representational content of the state having semantic property – what it is its job to indicate – with the circumstances in which it is beneficial to produce physical motion *m*. In the case of the thermostat, we may identify the state of affairs represented by the curvature of the bimetallic strip – i.e., room temperature being 15°C – with the condition under which the electrician judges that the furnace ought to be ignited. But, as I argued in chapter 4, in the case of instinctive behaviors of organisms, there might be a divergence between the property represented – i.e., the stimulus – and the property which contributes to enhancing the organism's fitness – i.e., the benefit. For example, what might be beneficial respectively to a frog and to a bacterium is to ingest a fly and to detect the presence of anaerobic water conditions. What the former detects, however, are small dark moving dots; the latter's magnetosome detects the direction of geomagnetic north. This is why, in chapter 4, I suggested two modifications in Dretske's (1988) formulation of the Design Problem.

8.6 ONTOGENETIC VERSUS PHYLOGENETIC ORIGINS OF REPRESENTATIONS

As I have made clear, the fact that the curvature of the bimetallic strip *c* of a thermostat carries information about room temperature is an objective fact about it. Bimetallic strip *c*, however, acquires its semantic property derivatively in virtue of the fact that it has been recruited by an electrician with propositional attitudes as a cause of furnace ignition. *c*'s semantic property helps in turn explain the structure of thermostat behavior, i.e., why *c* causes *m* (furnace ignition). As I said above, the electrician's recruitment of the thermostat's bimetallic strip is an instance of the kind of selection process, which, according to the etiological theory of functions, can yield functions. An organism's information-carrying state too can acquire semantic properties by being recruited as a cause of the organism's physical motions. There are basically two non-intentional recruitment processes which can turn the informational property of an organism's internal state into a semantic property: natural selection and learning. Indicator functions (in Dretske's sense) can arise from both natural selection and learning.

Unlike individual learning, natural selection is a process at work in the biological or phylogenetic evolution of the species to which the organism belongs. As I said in chapter 4, the objection that only cognitive mechanisms, not particular cognitive states, arise from natural selection can, I think, be met by distinguishing the primary proper function of the state-producing mechanism from the derived function of the state produced. So representational states can indirectly derive their indicator function from the function of a producing mechanism which results directly from natural selection. Learning is a selective process at work in the ontogenetic or individual development of the organism. Both natural selection and individual learning, therefore, are non-intentional processes via which an information-carrying state *c* of an organism can acquire an indicator function by being recruited as a cause of some motion or other of the organism.

Among an individual's representations, however, there are many interesting differences between those which derive from natural selection (which have a phylogenetic origin) and those which derive from the individual's learning (which have an ontogenetic origin). As I pointed out in chapter 2, on the informational semantic picture elaborated by Dretske (1981), what distinguishes a conceptual structure from a sensory experience is the way the information is coded. What accounts for the difference between the visual *experience* of, for example, a daffodil and the *concept* of a daffodil is that, in the visual experience of *s*'s being *F*, the fact that *s* (a particular flower) is *F* (a daffodil) is coded analogically, whereas the conceptual recognition that *s* is *F* carries the same information digitally. Now, the conceptual recognition (or identification) of a flower as a daffodil just is the *belief* that *s* (the flower) is *F* (a daffodil). So we may say that the experiential state is a sensory representation, and the belief a conceptual representation, of the fact that *s* is *F*. The transition from the experiential state to the belief state was then described as a (Lockean) process of *digitalization*, i.e., of abstraction, extraction or elimination of information. Now, Dretske (1981) assumed that the Lockean process of digitalization was a case of individual (ontogenetic) learning. Dretske (1995) identifies sensory experiences with states having what he calls *systemic* indicator functions: they are representations with a phylogenetic origin which derive their semantic properties from natural selection. The reason their indicator functions are called systemic is that they derive their indicator functions from the producing mechanisms (or system) which give rise to them and whose own functions derive from natural selection. Dretske (1995) identifies beliefs or conceptual representations with states having what he calls *acquired* indicator functions: they are representations with an ontogenetic origin in the individual whose representations they are. We might say that the former are innate representations; the latter are acquired representations.

There are two sides to the informational picture of the difference between beliefs and sensory representations. On the one hand, the view is that all states worthy of the name belief owe their semantic properties to an ontogenetic process of learning: all of an individual's beliefs are states whose contents have been fixed by a recruitment process in which they have been hired as causes of physical motions within the lifetime of the individual. On the other hand, no experiential state can owe its semantic property to learning: all of an individual's experiences are states whose contents have been determined by being recruited as causes of physical motions in the individual's ancestors and inherited by the individual from his or her ancestors via genetic transmission.

Take the latter consequence first: how plausible is it that the content of an experience cannot depend on individual learning? This is a delicate issue. Consider, for example, my gustatory and olfactory experience of wine. Arguably, I have learnt to appreciate differences between different wines through my individual career as a wine drinker. Now, how much does this tell against the view that the contents of experiences are fixed by the phylogenetic evolution of the species and inherited genetically? Surely, it is open to someone like Dretske (who claims that the content of experience is determined by phylogenetic evolution and genetic transmission) to argue that it would be a mistake to confuse an experience of a wine with the appreciation of a difference between two wines. The latter, he might retort, unlike the former, is a conceptual representation of the fact that there is a difference between two experiences.

Now, consider the former consequence. How plausible is it that no belief is innate? Again, this is a delicate issue. Cummins (1991: 105–7) has emphasized what he takes to be the inconsistency between the informational view of the difference between beliefs and innate representations and what he calls "a central empirical claim of most cognitive science of the past twenty years, namely the claim that a great deal of learning is based on innate knowledge." Now, I think, probably like Cummins, that the view that all beliefs are acquired representations has a distinctively *empiricist* flavor. What, I think, is right in Cummins' charge is that the above picture is incompatible with the view that there might exist *innate concepts*. True, many cognitive scientists (e.g., Fodor 1975) assume the existence of innate concepts. Now, unlike "belief," "concept" is a relatively technical term in both philosophy and psychology. What of innate beliefs? No doubt, many cognitive scientists (e.g., Chomsky 1975, 1980a,b) refer to innate knowledge of, for example, the principles of universal grammar. It is, however, controversial whether or not we want to assimilate a child's *tacit* knowledge of the principles of universal grammar – or for that matter, a mature native English speaker's *tacit* knowledge of the grammar of English – to other cases of conscious knowledge and (justified) beliefs. Arguably, the very fact that many cognitive scientists call such cases of linguistic knowledge *tacit* (or implicit) knowledge, states of *cognizing* (Chomsky's 1975, 1980a,b terminology), *subpersonal* states (Dennett's 1969 terminology) or *subdoxastic* states (Stich's 1978 terminology) suggests reasons not to confuse innate knowledge and ordinary cases of knowledge based on ontogenetically acquired beliefs. Besides, the view that an individual's belief state derives its semantic property from an ontogenetic process of recruitment as a cause of some of the individual's motions is of course compatible with the innateness of the belief-forming mechanism. Furthermore, the view that learning is a process of extraction, selection or elimination of information seems quite plausible and independently supported by much work in the cognitive science tradition to which Cummins refers. It is, therefore, far from clear that Dretske's distinction between innate representations and beliefs is at odds with anything in cognitive science.

On the informationally based teleosemantic picture which Dretske defends, and which I accept, for state-*type c* of organism *O* to acquire the semantic property that *s* is *F* (as it might be), past tokens of *c* may have carried the information that *s* is *F* to begin with, i.e., prior to the *c-m* coordination (where *m* is some physical motion performed by *O*). Now, one important difference between innate representations whose semantic properties derive from natural selection and acquired representations whose semantic properties derive from learning is that, if c's semantic property derives from O's ontogenetic learning, then *all* past information-carrying tokens of c may have occurred *within* O. If c's semantic property derives from natural selection, then *not* all past information-carrying tokens of c have occurred within O: they must have occurred in many ancestors of O too.[17] Now, Dretske (1990a: 829; 1991b: 207) wants to derive from this difference the further difference that *only* beliefs – only ontogenetically based representations – are "internal states whose meaning explains the behavior of the system of which they are a part . . . whose meaning makes a difference to the behavior of the system of which they are a part." Phylogenetically based innate representations have semantic properties and they may well cause physical motions, but the semantic properties of innate representations do not explain behavior. Only beliefs are, on his view, semantic engines: only their semantic properties causally explain behavior. I'll call this thesis the Asymmetry thesis. According to the Asymmetry thesis, the conceptualized semantic properties of an individual's beliefs can play a causal role in the causal explanation of the individual's intentional behavior; the non-conceptual semantic properties of an individual's innate (sensory) representations cannot play a role in the explanation of the individual's behavior.

With Dretske, I fully accept the distinction between ontogenetically based representations and phylogenetically based representations. The former – propositional attitudes – have conceptual content, the latter – sensory representations – have non-conceptual content. Dretske (1991b: 201–2) argues that the meaning conferred upon an individual's mental state by learning has special causal efficacy which meaning shaped by evolution by natural selection lacks. The contents of an individual's beliefs and desires causally explain his intentional *voluntary* behavior: they causally explain what the individual does when he has reasons for doing what he does. I fully concur. Some of what an individual does – as when he perspires, shivers, salivates, or blushes – is not explainable by the contents of his beliefs and desires. Perspiring, shivering, salivating, and blushing are not so explainable because they are instances of instinctive, not intentional, behavior. They are not explainable by reference to any of the individual's mental representations (innate or acquired).

[17] The fact that all past tokens of c did or did not occur within a single organism depends on whether c derived its indicator function from individual learning or from evolution, as emphasized by Laurier (1994).

However, I want to claim, not all of an individual's intentional behavior is explainable by the contents of his propositional attitudes. Some of what humans and non-human animals do they do not because they have beliefs and desires, but because they have sensory representations with non-conceptual contents. This is intentional behavior because it is behavior based on mental representations. But it is not intentional voluntary behavior based on the contents of an individual's propositional attitudes. It is intentional *non-voluntary* behavior based on innate sensory representations with non-conceptual contents. As an example of intentional non-voluntary behavior, reconsider my example from chapter 2 (section 5): upon hearing the sound produced by my wife when she pressed the C of the third octave on a piano, I turned my head rightwards. I claim that my turning my head rightwards was intentional non-voluntary behavior: I turned my head rightwards because I had a sensory non-conceptual representation of the sound as coming from my right hand side.

As I make clear in figure 9, I think we need not just a twofold distinction between intentional and non-intentional instinctive behavior; we need in addition a distinction between intentional voluntary behavior and intentional non-voluntary behavior.

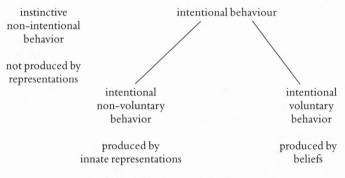

Figure 9 Taxonomy of behavior

So I think Dretske's twofold contrast between intentional voluntary behavior and instinctive behavior misses one important distinction between two kinds of intentional behaviors. This omission is, I think, one reason why Dretske subscribes to the Asymmetry thesis. Now, I can state the Symmetry thesis, for which I want to argue: just as the semantic properties of an individual's beliefs and desires may be causally efficacious in the causal explanation of the individual's intentional voluntary behavior, the semantic properties of an individual's sensory representations may be causally efficacious in the causal explanation of the individual's intentional non-voluntary behavior.

From the fact that not all tokens of an information-carrying state-type, prior to its acquiring semantic properties, did not occur in a single organism, how could it follow that the semantic properties of an individual's innate representations do *not* explain his or her intentional non-voluntary behavior? Obviously, in order to justify the denial that the semantic properties of an individual's innate representations can explain his or her intentional non-voluntary behavior, as Millikan (1990c: 809) has observed, Dretske needs a further premiss.

On several occasions, Dretske (1988: 47, 92; 1990a: 826–30) flatly denies that what Lewontin (1983) and Sober (1984a: 147–52) call a *variational* or *selectional* (evolutionary or phylogenetic) explanation of behavior is a causal explanation of an individual's intentional non-voluntary behavior. Unless it refers to the triggering cause of behavior, a causal explanation of an individual's behavior must refer to some of its structuring causes. Unlike a causal explanation of an individual's behavior, a selectional explanation of behavior does *not* make reference to structuring causes of behavior, and since it does not either mention the triggering cause of behavior, it does not, therefore, explain an *individual's* intentional non-voluntary behavior at all. If it does not, then, what does a selectional explanation explain? On Dretske's view, a selectional explanation explains not an individual's intentional non-voluntary behavior, but the *distribution* of behavioral traits in a population (species, group, or collection). It explains why organisms with a certain *c-m* coordination survived and proliferated better than organisms without.

Consider Sober's (1984a: 149) contrast between two explanations of the same fact: the fact that all children in a class can read. We can provide a *developmental* explanation of this fact by explaining why each child in the class can read. A developmental explanation accounts for how each and every individual separately learned to read: how and why each child's reading ability arose within the individual. We might then aggregate every developmental explanation to explain why all children in the class can read. We can also provide a *selectional* explanation of this fact by disclosing an admission procedure (or an entry condition) in the class such that only children who could read were admitted in the class.

Or consider Sober's (*ibid.*: 150) contrast between a Lamarckian developmental explanation and a Darwinian selectional explanation of the fact that giraffes have long necks. The former account would invoke "a progressive tendency" showing "how individual ancestral giraffes were modified, thereby producing a change in the giraffe population." According to Sober, the Darwinian turn consisted in giving the question an "irreducibly population-level" twist. The new question became that of why the giraffe population is composed of long-necked individuals rather than not.

Dretske (1988: 92–93, 95) has added nicely crafted examples of his own to justify his claim that selectional explanations do not refer either to triggering or to structuring causes of behavior and are not, therefore, causal explanations of an individual's behavior at all. Facts such as that Clyde's wife has red hair or that all of Dretske's friends are martini drinkers can similarly be provided contrastive explanations: a developmental explanation would respectively refer to psychological features of Dretske's friends or to genotypical properties of Clyde's wife; a selectional explanation would refer respectively to Dretske's friendly preferences for martini drinkers and to Clyde's preference for red-headed partners. For a last illustration, consider Dretske's (1990a: 827–28) example of a clock collector, Clyde, who collects only clocks which run slow. Let Ben be such a slow-running clock. From the fact that we know that Ben is one of Clyde's clocks and from the fact that we know that Clyde collects only slow-running clocks, do we know why Ben runs slow? Obviously not: we still do not know what mechanism makes Ben run slow. Clyde chose Ben because it runs slow, not vice-versa. The fact that Ben runs slow explains why Clyde chose it. The fact that Clyde chose it may be evidence for thinking that Ben runs slow: if we know that Clyde collects slow-running clocks and that Ben is among Clyde's collected clocks, we may infer (or predict) that Ben runs slow – without being even acquainted with Ben. But the fact that Clyde chose Ben because it runs slow does not explain why Ben runs slow. After all, had Clyde failed to notice it, Ben would not run any faster. As philosophers of science have been fond of pointing out, sometimes predicting is one thing; explaining is another.

Sober's and Dretske's examples are indeed suggestive of an important contrast. While selectional explanations are pitched at the population level, developmental explanations are pitched at the individual level. *Prima facie*, what a selectional explanation can explain is neither why an individual has property P nor why he does anything.[18] The intuitive idea is that selection (natural or otherwise) can only weed out, trim, sieve or prune what is there to be weeded out, trimmed, sieved or pruned. It can't create what is to be trimmed. Similarly, a selectional explanation cannot explain why an individual happens to have property P. Only a developmental explanation can do this. A selectional explanation can only explain why a population of individuals has a particular composition, for example, why a given property is prevalent among members of a given population today. A selectional explanation of, for example, intentional non-voluntary behavior will explain why today's population contains organisms with a given c-m coordination: in this explanation, c's semantic properties in ancestors will contribute to explaining why ancestors with a c-m coordination survived better than organisms without the c-m coordination. Now, Dretske assumes that the only alternative to a selectional explanation of intentional non-voluntary behavior – the only genuinely causal explanation of an individual's intentional non-voluntary behavior – can only refer to the *genotypical* properties which the organism has inherited from his ancestors.

Given his overall ambition – to show that there are semantic engines and that semantic properties are not epiphenomenal – Dretske's view that the semantic properties of phylogenetically based innate representations lack causal efficacy in the explanation of intentional non-voluntary behavior seems to me like the wrong way to go. After all, according to intentional realism, if innate representations have genuine semantic properties – something Dretske does not doubt – then their having semantic properties must make a causal difference. But if semantic properties of innate representations contribute to selectional explanations, and if selectional explanations are not causal explanations of intentional non-voluntary behavior,

---

[18] Thus Dretske (1988: 95) writes: "A selectional explanation of behavior is no more an explanation of an individual organism's behavior . . . than is a selectional account of the antisocial behavior of prison inmates an explanation of why Lefty forges checks, Harry robs banks, and Moe steals cars. The fact that we imprison people who forge checks, steal cars, and rob banks does not explain why the people in prison do these things."

then what good does it do an animal to have innate representations with semantic properties?

Dretske's thesis that the semantic properties of innate representations, unlike the semantic properties of beliefs, do *not* play a causal role in the explanation of an individual's (intentional non-voluntary) behavior, depends, therefore, upon his claim that *selectional* explanations are *not* causal explanations. In a causal explanation of an individual's behavior, reference is made either to the triggering cause or to one of its structuring causes. If the behavior is intentional, among the structuring causes are the semantic properties of a propositional attitude – an indicator which acquired its indicator function by being recruited via individual learning as a cause of one of the individual's physical motions. If the individual's behavior is intentional non-voluntary, then among the structuring causes of behavior are the genotypical properties responsible for the c-m coordination in the individual. Because the individual cannot modify them or adjust them to his or her environment during his or her lifetime, the semantic properties of the individual's innate representations involved are disqualified from the causal explanation of the individual's intentional non-voluntary behavior.

I, however, see three complementary reasons for weakening Dretske's sharp distinction between the semantic properties respectively of innate and acquired representations and for rescuing semantic properties of innate representations from causal impotence. I said earlier that the major difference between innate representations and beliefs is that all past tokens of an individual's belief-type may have carried information within the lifetime of the individual, whereas past tokens of an innate representation-type cannot all have carried information within the lifetime of a single organism. This difference should not, however, lead us to downplay an important common feature between innate representations and beliefs. According to the etiological theory of functions, for natural selection (indirectly) to convert the informational property of some internal state c of some organism's ancestor into a semantic property, not only must c have had its informational property; c must also have been able to cause m: it was in virtue of being recruited as a cause of m that c acquired its semantic property in the organism's ancestors. Furthermore, presumably, natural selection still operates on present organisms, so that it is still a sieving force upon today's organisms.

My first reason for weakening Dretske's sharp distinction between the semantic properties of an individual's innate representations and the semantic properties of an individual's beliefs, therefore, is that, in spite of the role of genetic coding in the transmission of innate representations, the informational and causal properties of tokens of an innate type of representation c which promoted the c-m coordination in past organisms are presumably still at work on present organisms. So the only remaining difference between innate and acquired types of representations seems to be that all relevant tokens of the former, unlike all tokens of the latter, did not lie within a single organism. It does seem like an empiricist prejudice to disqualify on this ground only the semantic properties of innate representations from playing a causal role in explaining an individual's intentional non-voluntary behavior.

My second reason for weakening Dretske's claim that selectional explanations are not causal explanations of the possession of phenotypical trait P by an individual is that it seems to me quite easy to imagine that natural selection could promote individuals having P by destroying individuals lacking the selected trait, P. To go back to Clyde's proclivity for slow-running clocks, imagine that not only does Clyde collect slow-running clocks, he also destroys clocks which run fast or on time. If so, then Clyde's selective-cum-destructive activities do contribute to causally explaining why, in his environment, there are only slow-running clocks. Clyde's activities do not merely select those individual clocks which happen to have the property of running slow. They directly contribute to eradicating out of existence all clocks not having this property: having the property of running fast or on time. Selection, then, would certainly be a factor in the causal explanation of why certain individual items happen to have property P: it played a causal role in driving out of existence all individuals lacking P.

My third reason for weakening Dretske's claim that selectional explanations are not causal explanations is that, as Neander (1988) has pointed out, what Dretske takes to be a genuine causal explanation of intentional non-voluntary behavior actually needs supplementation by a selectional explanation. What Dretske takes to be a genuine causal explanation of an individual's intentional non-voluntary behavior is explanation based on the individual's genotype. The individual whose intentional non-voluntary behavior we want to explain has inherited his genotype from his ancestors. But in Neander's (1988: 425) terms, "somewhere back along the line . . . there were occasional mutations or significant genetic recombinations." Some, not all, of these genetic mutations had adaptive (or advantageous) consequences. Those with adaptive consequences were favored by natural selection. Granted, the organism has genetically inherited this *c-m* coordination from its ancestors. Part, therefore, of the explanation for why an organism has a given *c-m* coordination is that this *c-m* coordination is coded in its genetic program. But part of the explanation for why its ancestors had genes coding for this *c-m* coordination must have been that having this coordination was advantageous or adaptive, i.e., organisms in the past having such a coordination survived and proliferated better than organisms without. But now, it is, as Dretske concedes, the job of a selectional explanation to explain why adaptive consequences of genetic mutations gave rise to genomes which in turn were expressed into (behavioral) phenotypes with adaptive traits. So it turns out that the genetic explanation of why an individual has inherited a *c-m* coordination must be supplemented by a selectional explanation. So Dretske's dilemma is that either full developmental explanations are not purely causal explanations of an individual's intentional non-voluntary behavior; or selectional explanations after all are causal or at least are part of causal explanations, contrary to Dretske's assumption.

The reason, I think, Dretske was misled into thinking otherwise is that his well-crafted examples of contrasts between developmental and selectional explanations, however suggestive, misrepresent one important feature of the role of natural selection in biological evolution: unlike the choice of a spouse, the admission procedure of a child into a class, or the choice of a slow-running clock, the process of natural selection is *not* what Dawkins (1986: 45ff) calls a *single-step* selection process; it is what he calls a *cumulative* selection process, i.e., a selection process repeated over and over again over many generations (and presumably still active today).

To see what is the difference between a cumulative selection process and a single-step selection process, let us assume that a selection process of either kind is what Neander (1995b) calls a random/select (or R/S) sequence involving two steps: the first step consists of the random generation of variations which are then submitted to a selection procedure. In a single-step selection process, no

R/S sequence can alter the probability of the outcome of any other. But in a cumulative selection process, an R/S sequence can alter the probability of the outcome of the next R/S sequence. For an example of a single-step selection process, consider the random spinning of the wheels of Dawkins' (1986: 7) combination lock where anyone of the 4,096 possible positions is equally likely or unlikely to turn up. Suppose combination 1,207 opens the lock. No matter how many times you have already spinned the wheels, the probability of your hitting 1,207 is always the same and is not affected by prior trials. Similarly, in a typical lottery situation, earlier R/S sequences do not affect the probability of the outcome of the next one. This probabilistic independence is what is violated by the gambler's fallacy. But now with Neander (1995b), imagine a machine with three holes A, B and C, tossing 10 balls with a different integer on it. In order to win, you have to predict which ball with which number fills respectively holes A, B, and C. If the ball filling A is the one with the number you predicted, then you don't have to predict which ball will fill A and you only check holes B and C. Before the first trial, the probability of winning the game was $1/10^3$. If your prediction about A has been borne out, then before the second trial, the probability of winning becomes $1/10^2$. So the probability of the outcome of the second R/S sequence has been affected by the result of the first R/S sequence. This is a typical cumulative selection process of the kind instantiated by natural selection.

I earlier claimed that a full genetic (developmental) explanation of why an individual has inherited a c-m coordination must be supplemented by a selectional explanation. This applies in particular to cumulative selection processes. My own view, therefore, is that natural selection as it is appealed to in selectional explanations may contribute to explaining why individuals have the phenotypical and genotypical properties which they have. As I pointed out above, when we ask why prey O executes flight motions m we may be asking at least three different explanatory questions. We may be asking: why did O execute flight movement m at t? To answer this question, we refer to the cause of internal state c in O at t: the approach of predator P was registered by c at t. c in turn caused m in O. The approach of predator P is then the triggering cause of O's behavior. Or we may want to understand how neurons' firing in O's nervous system produce muscle contraction involved in O's executing m. Finally, we may want to know why state type c in O is coordinated to flight motions m rather fight motions m'. Why is there a c-m coordination in Os? Part of the answer is that organisms which were preys of predator Ps without c-m coordination in the past did not survive natural selection. Part of the answer is that today's Os have inherited their coordination from their ancestors by genetic transmission. If what I have said above about cumulative selection processes is on the right track, then selectional explanations and causal explanations of individuals' intentional non-voluntary behavior are intertwined. Although Sober's and Dretske's contrast between developmental and selectional explanations fully applies to single-step selection processes, it must, I think, be weak-ened as it applies to cumulative selection processes. This is why, it seems to me, a selectional explanation may contribute to explaining why an individual possesses some property by explaining a change in the population to which the individual belongs.

If so, then the only ground left for the strong asymmetry between the semantic properties of innate and acquired representations is that genetic transmission of innate representations prevents their mod-ification by individual experience. Although this feature of innate representations may strike an empiricist chord, I do not think it bears enough weight to disqualify the semantic properties of an individual's innate representations from playing a structuring causal role in the explanation of the individual's intentional non-voluntary behavior.

It is time to sum up what I think I have achieved in this chapter. I have borrowed two major ingredients from Dretske (1988): the com-ponential view of behavior and the distinction between structuring and triggering causal explanations. Combining these ingredients, I have tried to show that the semantic properties of an individual's propositional attitudes can explain (in the structuring causal sense) the individual's intentional voluntary behavior. I have also tried to show, contrary to Dretske, that the semantic properties of an individual's innate representations can explain (in the structuring causal sense) the individual's intentional non-voluntary behavior. The main advantage of this construction, I take it, is that it allows us to vindicate the causal explanatory role of the semantic properties of an individual's states of mind without being committed to the condition that the semantic properties of an individual's mental states must supervene on the physical properties of his or her brain.

9

Conclusion: a postlude on semantics and psychology

As I recognized in chapter 1, the intentional realist who subscribes to token physicalism takes out, in Dennett's (1971) terms, a loan of intentionality. I have now discharged some of what I take to be the debt incurred by the intentional realist.

In part I, I have argued that semanticity has two primary non-semantic sources: it arises out of the nomic dependencies between properties of an individual's mental states and properties instantiated in his or her environment; and it arises out of the selective processes shaping both the phylogenetic evolution of the species of which the individual is a member and the individual's ontogenetic development. My own approach to the naturalization of intentionality has, therefore, been a mixed or impure informationally based teleosemantic approach. As I remarked several times, it contrasts with both a pure teleosemantic approach and a pure informational approach.

In part II, I have tried to show that the semantic properties of an individual's propositional attitudes are causally efficacious in the production of his or her intentional voluntary behavior. In fact, I have argued that not only do the semantic properties of an individual's beliefs contribute to the explanation of his or her intentional voluntary behavior, but also that the semantic properties of an individual's innate representations explain his or her intentional non-voluntary behavior. In arguing this, I have borrowed two ideas from Dretske (1988): one is the componential conception of behavior; the other is the idea that semantic properties of an individual's representations explain his or her behavior in a causal structuring sense.[1]

Clearly, what the intentional realist is striving for is a unified

---

[1] Structuring causes are to be contrasted with triggering causes. See chapter 8.

account of the origins and the explanatory role of content. For an intentional realist, it better be the case that the view of content which emerges in response to the first task – the task of naturalizing intentionality – be sensitive to the second task – the task of showing how intentionality can play a psychological role in the causal explanation of behavior. The two tasks may pull in opposite directions: content must arise from non-semantic conditions and it must play a role in psychological explanation. The kind of content which may be grounded in non-semantic conditions will presumably lack some of the semantic subtleties required by psychological explanation. The interface between the two tasks of the intentional realist (and the two parts of this book), then, is the connection between semantics and psychology.

In the last (and shortest) chapter of this book, I want to devote a few pages to compare my overall picture of this interface with Jerry Fodor's (1994) current picture of what I called in chapter 5 the computational representational theory of mind (CRTM). The basic difference between Fodor's older picture and his new picture is that the latter drops the content-dualist distinction between broad and narrow content. To dramatize the contrast between it and its ancestor, and following Loewer & Rey (1991: xxvii), I will call this new version of CRTM minus the distinction between broad and narrow content "the pure locking theory." Calling it so draws attention to the fact that it is a version of pure informational semantics. In Fodor's (1994: 38, 87) own terms, the slogan of pure locking theory is that semantics is not part of psychology.

Pure locking theory can be captured by means of three basic theses: (i) all there is to representational content is information. More precisely, a primitive (undefinable) vehicle (or bearer) of content derives its semantic property from Fodor's (1987b; 1990a,b) Asymmetrical Nomic Dependency Condition.[2] (ii) Psychological laws involved in the causal explanation of intentional behavior are intentional in the sense that they refer to the semantic properties of individuals' mental states. (iii) Psychological laws are implemented by computational mechanisms. In other words, mental processes are computational

---

[2] Strictly speaking, the "pure locking theory" should be restricted to assumption (i). But I call the collection of assumptions (i)–(iii) the "pure locking theory" to call attention to the fact that what is distinctive of the new version of CRTM is the slogan that semantics is not part of psychology.

processes. As I argued in chapter 5, assumptions (ii) and (iii) were already part of the earlier version of the computational representational theory of mind. The pure locking theory goes one step further in divorcing semantics from psychology.

On this picture, semantics tells us how things having physical properties can have semantic properties too.[3] According to (i), symbol *r* means *horses*, if the nomic dependency between instantiations of property G of *r* and instantiations of, for example, donkeyhood asymmetrically depends on the nomic dependency between instantiations of G and instantiations of horses. Assuming that meaning *horses* is the primitive (undefinable and original, underived) content of *r*'s being G, then there is nothing else to the meaning of *r*'s being G than this higher-order asymmetric dependency between lower-order nomic dependencies between properties. Pure locking theory is a kind of radical nomic externalism. Only *external* nomic relations, i.e., (nomic) relations between a symbol and the world can confer content onto a symbol. Internal relations among symbols cannot. The archenemy of the pure locking theory is what Fodor (1994) dubbs "structuralism" and Fodor & Lepore (1991) dubbed "New Testament semantics."[4]

By seeing how assumption (ii) links assumptions (i) and (iii) together, one can understand the slogan of the pure locking theory according to which semantics is not part of psychology. According to assumption (ii), psychological laws are intentional and they refer to the contents of individuals' mental states. Assumption (i) is expected to account for the semanticity involved in intentional psychological laws. Semantics, on the pure locking theory, is metaphysics, not psychology: the job of semantics is to tell us how symbols hook up onto properties in the world. So the fact that psychological laws are intentional is taken care of by semantics and assumption (i). But psychological laws are not only intentional laws; they are also causal laws; they are *ceteris paribus* (or hedged) causal laws. And *ceteris paribus* causal laws hold in virtue of underlying causal mechanisms. In particular, intentional causal laws hold in virtue of non-semantic mechanisms. According to (iii), mental processes are computational (i.e., non-semantic) processes. So it is the job of psychology to account for the

---

[3] In this discussion, unless I specify it, by "semantic property," I mean a primitive, non-complex semantic property.

[4] See chapter 6.

fact that intentional psychological laws are causal laws by supplying a theory of the underlying non-semantic mechanisms. Now, mental processes turn thoughts into other thoughts and map thoughts onto behavior. So, given the language of thought hypothesis, mental processes relate symbols to one another. So, unlike semantics, psychology does deal with relations among symbols; but it deals with computational or syntactic, not semantic, relations among symbols.

The pure locking theory then is pure informational semantics. There are in fact two ways one can reject pure informational semantics and embrace an impure informationally based semantics. Consider some putatively primitive mental vehicle or bearer of content. On the one hand, it may (or not) derive some of its semantic features from the function of the cognitive mechanism (e.g., the belief-forming mechanism) whose output is the mental vehicle in question. According to teleosemantic accounts, the cognitive mechanism in turn may derive its function from the selective pressures at work in biological evolution or in the ontogenetic history of the invidual. Pure informational semantics will not accept this teleosemantic element. On the other hand, a non-primitive mental vehicle may derive some of its semantic features from its interactions with other mental vehicles. Such interactions may be captured by inferential role semantics. Now inferential role semantics is intolerable to semantic atomism. A pure informational semanticist who is also a semantic atomist then cannot tolerate this second version of impure informational semantics. The latter issue of semantic atomism can in turn be seen as revolving on the choice of the basis of vehicles (or bearers) of primitive semantic properties out of which complex semantic properties can be constructed. Even as radical a semantic atomist as Fodor will grant that BROWN HORSE has a complex semantic property which is a function of the semantic properties of BROWN and HORSE.

I am not a pure locking theorist because I am not a pure informational semanticist. And, as I made clear earlier, I am not a pure informational semanticist for two reasons. On the one hand, I believe that what I called in chapters 3 and 4 the problem of the transitivity of correlations can only be solved within a teleosemantic framework. On the other hand, as I explained in chapter 3, belief contents have a very strong degree of intensionality: two informationally equivalent primitive information-carrying structures may differ for a creature with inferential (or logical) abilities or sensitivities. The content of my belief that Cicero was bald differs from the content of my belief that Tully was bald. I can have the former belief without having the latter. As I argued in chapter 3, the fact that I may have the former belief without having the latter may arise from my ability to derive the belief that someone was both bald and fat from my belief that Cicero was bald and my belief that Cicero was fat. But now this very same ability will not allow me to derive the very same belief that someone was both bald and fat from my belief that Cicero was bald and from my belief that Tully was fat. In order to derive the belief that someone was both bald and fat from the belief that Cicero was bald and the belief that Tully was fat, I need the further premiss that Cicero was identical to Tully.[5] So the strongest degree of intensionality requires a sensitivity to the logical structure of information-carrying symbols. This aspect of super-strong intensionality of belief contents is what I called cognitive holism in chapters 3 and 6. It relates to the fact that an individual's belief derives some of its semantic features from its interactions with other propositional attitudes of the individual. Inferential (or conceptual role) semantics is precisely designed to capture the source of such semantic features. But pure locking theory is inimical to inferential role semantics because, according to the latter, internal relations between propositional attitudes may generate semantic features, i.e., because inferential role semantics is not consistent with pure (nomic) externalism.

So my threefold picture of semanticity could be put as follows. First, are organisms which can enter states whose properties nomically covary with properties instantiated in their environment. Perhaps *Escherichia coli* bacilli (found in the intestinal tract), which thrive in a culture based on glucose, are such creatures: they enter states which instantiate properties which are nomically dependent on glucose. In other words, *Escherichia coli* bacilli are glucose detectors: some of their states carry the information that there is glucose nearby. Assuming that they cannot either misrepresent something which is not glucose (e.g., lactose) as glucose or that they cannot hallucinate glucose in the absence of glucose, *Escherichia coli* bacilli would be examples of creatures whose states can indicate the presence of

[5] As I pointed out in chapter 3, I assume that Cicero was necessarily identical to Tully. This assumption is required for the above beliefs to be strongly intensional.

glucose without representing it. Their states can indicate the presence of glucose; but they lack the function to do so.[6] Then come creatures like cats, dogs and presumably frogs some of whose states may misrepresent a property which it is their function to carry information about. They, therefore, can enter genuinely representational states, states having underived intentionality, i.e., states with non–transitive indicator-functions. It is, I suppose, an empirical question whether they have beliefs and desires, i.e., some rudimentary inferential ability which allows them to form inferentially new beliefs and desires from older ones. Then come creatures who not only have beliefs and other propositional attitudes (i.e., states some of whose semantic properties derive from interacting with others of the creature's propositional attitudes), but also language and metarepresentational capacities, i.e., capacities to form intentions, beliefs and desires about desires, beliefs and intentions. The informationally based teleosemantic framework is designed to account for semanticity at the second level. An embryonic version of inferential role semantics might surface at the second level and fully mature at the third level enhanced by language and metarepresentational capacities.

I don't merely think that pure informational semantics is inadequate for the purpose of naturalizing intentionality, I also think that the pure locking theory, encapsulated as it is by the slogan that semantics isn't part of psychology, fails to satisfy the demands psychological explanation places upon content. The pure locking theory is tailor made for semantic atomism. Fodor not only thinks that semantic atomism is required by pure informational semantics. He also thinks that semantic holism would make intentional psychological laws impossible and he further thinks that semantic atomism is the only alternative to semantic holism. In chapter 6, I have explained why I think he is wrong on both counts. He might be right to think that the most radical version (what I called in chapter 6 the all-version) of semantic holism would destroy the possibility of intentional psychological laws if the latter required reference to the contents of individuals' mental states. But if they don't, then he is wrong. I have argued that what intentional psychological laws require is quantification over contents, not reference to contents. So I think he is wrong. I also

---

[6] This assumption makes *Escherichia coli* bacilli different from Dretske's northern marine bacteria whose magnetosomes, I granted in chapters 3 and 4, can misrepresent the direction of geomagnetic north.

happen to think that his reasons for thinking that semantic atomism is the only alternative to semantic holism are not convincing. In chapter 6, I claimed that there is a third possible position which I called meaning molecularism (or meaning anatomism).

Given that I accept what I called above cognitive holism, i.e., the fact that interactions among beliefs may be a source of semanticity, I cannot accept semantic atomism. Let me, however, emphasize the fact that, in my view, Fodor (1987b, 1994) and Fodor & Lepore (1992) should be praised for having made quite vivid the possibility that a creature possesses the concept of, for example, cow without possessing the concepts of ANIMAL, MAMMAL, HORN, HOOF, MILK, and so on. Although it may have been implicit in Kripke's (1972) and Putnam's (1974) views of natural kind terms (or concepts), not until Fodor's persistent defense of semantic atomism had this possibility been so convincingly entertained. However, it is quite a step to go from this possibility to embracing semantic atomism. The former does not justify the latter.

In chapter 7, I ascribed two theses to content-dualism: a semantic thesis and a causal explanatory thesis. The semantic thesis was the conjunctive claim that the narrow content of an individual's belief is genuine content and that it supervenes upon the physical (chemical and biological) properties of the individual's brain. The causal thesis was that only the explanation of narrow behavior by narrow content was genuinely causal explanation. In chapter 7, I rejected both theses. Because I reject both theses and because they are constitutive of content-dualism (as I understand it), I reject content-dualism. Don't I therefore agree with the pure locking theorist's rejection of narrow content? Well, I agree that what is genuinely semantic (as opposed to merely syntactic) in the content of an individual's belief cannot supervene upon the physical properties of the individual's brain. However, unlike the pure locking theorist, I do not want to conclude from my rejection of content-dualism that all there is to content is information. I think there are various degrees of finegrainedness of content: in other words, there are degrees of narrowness of content none of which satisfies the semantic constraint imposed by content-dualism. In a word, I reject content-dualism. But I welcome content-pluralism.

In chapter 8, following Dretske, I embraced the componential view of behavior and the distinction between triggering causes and structuring causes. I then argued that the semantic properties of an individual's representations (innate and acquired) play a role in the causal explanation (in the structuring causal sense) of the individual's behavior, not his or her physical motion. And I argued that an individual's behavior is not identical to his or her physical motions since the latter is a constituent of the former. I conceded that if what we want is to provide a causal explanation (in the triggering causal sense) of an individual's physical motion, then only the physical (chemical and biological) properties of the individual's brain might be causally efficacious. I therefore conceded that the semantic properties of an individual's mental states are epiphenomenal in the production of the individual's physical motion. But to concede that they are epiphenomenal in explaining (in the triggering causal sense) the individual's physical motion is not to concede that they are epiphenomenal in the explanation (in the structuring causal sense) of the individual's behavioral process.

To link the point of the last paragraph with the point made one paragraph earlier: rejecting both the semantic and the causal explanatory theses of content-dualism does not force us to concede that content is epiphenomenal after all. We may concede that the content of an individual's belief does not supervene on the physical properties of his or her brain and still maintain that content is efficacious in the causal explanation of the individual's behavior (in the causal structuring sense), not in the causal explanation of his or her physical motion (in the triggering causal sense). The mistake was in assuming that unless it does supervene upon the physical properties of an individual's brain, the content of the individual's mental state cannot be causally efficacious. It cannot be causally efficacious in explaining the individual's physical motion. But it may be causally efficacious in explaining his or her behavior. Neither should recognizing that content can't be narrow enough to satisfy content-dualism be a cause for despair about the causal role of content. Nor should the fact that inferential role semantics gives rise to semantic holism be a cause for thinking that intentional psychological laws are then impossible. Not, if all they require is quantification over contents.

Now, my main bone of contention with the pure locking theory is that it severs the connection between semantics (or the metaphysics of content) and the role of content in psychological explanation. To see exactly how the pure locking theory severs the connection between semantics and psychology, consider what Fodor (1994) calls "Frege cases": cases where two beliefs or two desires of one and the same individual may differ even though they have, according to pure informational semantics, the same content. So Oedipus had the desire to marry Jocasta, but he did not have the desire to marry his mother, even though Jocasta was Oedipus' mother. And of course the difference between the two desire-states is highly relevant to the psychological explanation of Oedipus' behavior. Frege (1892) would have said that "Jocasta" and "Mother" are two names with two distinct senses (*Sinne*) or modes of presentation of Jocasta for Oedipus.[7] Frege, therefore, posited a genuinely semantic difference between the senses of two coreferential names. So when Oedipus entertained thoughts about Jocasta under the mode of presentation of Jocasta associated with the name "Jocasta," he was prepared to behave in a certain way; when he entertained thoughts about Jocasta under the mode of presentation of Jocasta associated with the name "Mother," his behavior differed.

Assuming that Oedipus' mother is necessarily Jocasta or that "Jocasta" and "Mother" are nomically coreferential, then the Fregean theory is not quite open to an informational semanticist, neither a pure, nor an impure informational semanticist: the reason why the informational semanticist cannot directly postulate a semantic difference between "Jocasta" and "Mother" is that, on the above assumption about necessary identity, the two symbols carry the same information.

The pure locking theory can account in non-semantic terms for the difference between the two desires: Oedipus' desire to marry Jocasta involves a relation to one mental symbol standing for Jocasta, say α, whereas his desire not to marry his mother involves a relation to a different mental symbol, β, standing for the same woman, where mental symbols standing for Jocasta can be thought of as modes of presentation of Jocasta. On the one hand then, according to the pure locking theory, there may be a purely syntactic difference between two primitive informationally equivalent symbols, α and β. On the other hand, by assumption (iii), the mechanisms responsible for psychological intentional laws are purely computational. Such under-

---

[7] Of course, "Jocasta" and "Mother" belong to English and were not names of Jocasta for Oedipus who did not speak English.

lying computational mechanisms may well recognize a formal difference between α and β. According to the pure locking theory, therefore, Oedipus' desire involving the mental formula $\Phi\alpha$ and Oedipus' desire involving the mental formula $\Phi\beta$ may be distinct desires with the same content. In virtue of their non-semantic differences, they may enter different computational processes. The fact that both desire-states are part of different computational processes explains why each desire-state gives rise to two different kinds of behavior on Oedipus' part.

The problem, however, the pure locking theory faces, I think, is what Cummins (1991) has called "Stich's Challenge" or what Kim (1991) has called the problem of "Syntacticalism": isn't the pure locking theory another version of Stich's syntactic theory of mind (STM)? The pure locking theory, it seems to me, does not have the resources to adequately respond to Stich's Challenge or to Syntacticalism. In effect, it capitulates to Stich's STM.[8]

Granted, in the pure locking theory, by assumption (ii), intentional psychological laws refer to contents. Stich's STM, by contrast, prohibits all reference to content in psychological explanation. If, however, the content referred to in intentional psychological laws is broad informational content, then it is not going to help us distinguish between Oedipus' two belief-states: his belief that Jocasta is attractive and his belief that his mother is attractive. Both beliefs must have the very same content. Furthermore, on the pure locking theory, the connection between each belief and the range of behavior it leads to is purely computational, i.e., non-semantic: only the fact that mental symbol α has a different shape from mental symbol β will explain why having one belief, Oedipus does one thing, whereas having the other belief, he does something else. This is what I mean when I say that the pure locking theory severs the link between semantics and psychological explanation.

---

[8] This is a point I made earlier in chapters 5 and 8. Earlier however, I made it in the context of the older version of the computational representational theory of mind in which provision is made for the content-dualist distinction between narrow and broad content. If intentional psychological laws did refer to the narrow content of individuals' mental states, then the gap between CRTM and Stich's STM would be significant. Given the pure locking theorist's commitment to the assumption that all there is to content is information, then the new version of CRTM moves a step closer to Stich's STM.

Let us now by contrast see how on my impure informationally based approach to content, the connection between semantics and psychological explanation can be maintained. As I mentioned above (see chapter 3), unlike the pure locking theorist, I assume that two primitive informationally equivalent information-carrying structures α and β may have distinct logical potentials. From his beliefs that Jocasta is attractive and that Jocasta is brown-haired, Oedipus may infer that there is someone who is both attractive and brown-haired. But from his belief that Jocasta is attractive and that Mother is brown-haired, he cannot, without the extra-assumption that Jocasta is Mother, infer that there is someone who is both attractive and brown-haired. Now, this difference between two primitive informationally equivalent information-carrying symbols α and β is neither informational nor purely syntactic. I called it logical.

Unlike the pure locking theorist, then, I do posit a difference in the logical structure (or logical potential) of two primitive informationally equivalent information-carrying symbols α and β. This difference can only be detected by a creature logically capable of moving from singular thoughts to general thoughts, i.e., by a creature capable of forming a quantified thought by a logical process. This means that only a creature with such logical (or inferential) abilities can enter states having such fine-grained semantic properties, i.e., beliefs and desires. On this view, there is a difference between the contents of Oedipus' two beliefs: the distinction between his two belief-states is really a logical distinction. It is not only a distinction between the shape of α and the shape of β; it is a difference in the logical potential of α and β. And furthermore this logical distinction makes a difference to Oedipus' behavior. In other words, what I claim is that Oedipus couldn't act out of the contents of his beliefs and desires (as he did) and be a pure informational creature with no logical abilities.

References

Adams, F. (1991) "Causal Contents," in B. McLaughlin (ed.)(1991) *Dretske and his Critics*.

Alcock, J. (1975) *Animal Behavior, an Evolutionary Approach*, Sunderland, Mass.: Sinauer Associates, Inc.

Antony, L. (1991) "The Causal Relevance of the Mental," *Mind and Language*, 6, 4, 295–327.

Antony, L. & J. Levine (1991) "The Nomic and the Robust," in B. Loewer & G. Rey (eds.) *Meaning in Mind*.

Armstrong, D. (1973) *Belief, Truth and Knowledge*, Cambridge University Press.

Bach, K. (1987) *Thought and Reference*, Oxford: Clarendon Press.

Baker, L. R. (1988) "Cognitive Suicide," in R. H. Grimm & D. D. Merrill (eds.) *Contents of Thought*, Tucson: University of Arizona Press.

(1991a) "Belief in Explanation," mimeo.

(1991b) "Dretske on the Explanatory Role of Belief," *Philosophical Studies*, 63, 99–111.

Barwise, J. & J. Perry (1983) *Situations and Attitudes*, Cambridge, Mass.: MIT Press.

Block, N. (1980a) "Introduction: What is Functionalism?," in Block (ed.) (1980b) *Readings in the Philosophy of Psychology*.

(1980b) *Readings in the Philosophy of Psychology*, 2 volumes, Cambridge, Mass.: Harvard University Press.

(1986) "Advertisement for a Semantics for Psychology," in P. French, T. Uehling, Jr. & H. Wettstein (eds.) *Midwest Studies in Philosophy*, vol. X, Minneapolis: University of Minnesota Press.

(1987) "Functional Role and Truth-Conditions," *Proceedings of the Aristotelian Society*, 61, 157–81.

(1990) "Can the Mind Change the World," in G. Boolos (ed.) *Meaning and Method; Essays in Honor of Hilary Putnam*, Cambridge University Press.

References

(1994) "Consciousness," in Guttenplan (ed.) *A Companion to the Philosophy of Mind*.

(1995) "On a Confusion about a Function of Consciousness," *The Behavioral and Brain Sciences*, 18, 2, 227–87.

Boghossian, P. A. (1990a) "The Status of Content," *The Philosophical Review*, 69, 2, 157–84.

(1990b) "The Status of Content Revisited," *Pacific Philosophical Quarterly*, 71, 264–78.

Brownell, P. H. (1984) "Prey Detection by the Sand Scorpion," *Scientific American*, 251, 6, 94–105.

Burge, T. (1979) "Individualism and the Mental," in P. French, T. Uehling, Jr. & H.K. Wettstein (eds.) *Midwest Studies in Philosophy*, vol. IV, Minneapolis: University of Minnesota Press.

(1982) "Other Bodies," in A. Woodfield (ed.) *Thought and Object*, Oxford: Clarendon Press.

(1989) "Wherein is Language Social" in A. George (ed.) *Reflections on Chomsky*, Oxford: Blackwell.

Carnap, R. (1966) *An Introduction to the Philosophy of Science*, ed. (M. Gardner ed.), New York: Basic Books.

Carston, R. (1988) "Implicature, Explicature, and Truth-Conditional Semantics," in R. Kempson (ed.)(1988) *Mental Representations: the Interface Between Language and Reality*, Cambridge University Press.

Chomsky, N. (1975) *Reflections on Language*, New York: Pantheon Books.

(1980a) *Rules and Representations*, New York: Columbia University Press.

(1980b) "Rules and Representations," *The Behavioral and Brain Sciences*, 3, 1–15.

Churchland, P. M. (1981) "Eliminative Materialism and the Propositional Attitudes," in Churchland (1989) *A Neurocomputational Perspective, the Nature of Mind and the Structure of Science*, Cambridge, Mass.: MIT Press.

(1984) *Matter and Consciousness*, Cambridge, Mass.: MIT Press.

(1992) "Activation Vectors versus Propositional Attitudes: How the Brain Represents Reality," *Philosophy and Phenomenological Research*, 52, 2, 419–24.

Churchland, P. S. (1986) *Neurophilosophy, Toward a Unified Science of the Mind*, Cambridge, Mass.: MIT Press.

Crane, T. (ed.)(1992a) *The Contents of Experience*, Cambridge University Press.

(1992b) Introduction, in Crane (ed.)(1992a) *The Contents of Experience*.

(1992c) "The Non-Conceptual Content of Experience," in Crane (ed.)(1992a) *The Contents of Experience*.

Cummins, R. (1975) "Functional Analysis," in Sober (ed.) (1984) *Conceptual Issues in Evolutionary Biology*.

(1983) *The Nature of Psychological Explanation*, Cambridge, Mass.: MIT Press.

(1989) *Meaning and Mental Representation*, Cambridge, Mass.: MIT Press.

(1991) "The Role of Mental Meaning in Psychological Explanation," in B. McLaughlin (ed.)(1991) *Dretske and his Critics*.

Davidson, D. (1963) "Actions, Reasons and Causes," in Davidson (1980) *Essays on Actions and Events*.

(1967) "Causal Relations," in Davidson (1980) *Essays on Actions and Events*.

(1970) "Mental Events," in Davidson (1980) *Essays on Actions and Events*.

(1973) "The Material Mind," in Davidson (1980) *Essays on Actions and Events*.

(1974a) "Psychology as Philosophy," in Davidson (1980) *Essays on Actions and Events*.

(1974b) "On the Very Idea of a Conceptual Scheme," in Davidson (1984) *Inquiries into Truth and Interpretation*.

(1975) "Thought and Talk," in Davidson (1984) *Inquiries into Truth and Interpretation*.

(1977) "The Method of Truth in Metaphysics," in Davidson (1984) *Inquiry into Truth and Interpretation*.

(1980) *Essays on Actions and Events*, Oxford: Clarendon Press.

(1982) "Rational Animals," in E. Lepore & B. McLaughlin (eds.)(1985) *Actions and Events, Perspectives on the Philosophy of Donald Davidson*, Oxford: Blackwell.

(1984) *Inquiry into Truth and Interpretation*, Oxford: Clarendon Press.

(1987) "Knowing One's Own Mind," *Proceedings of the American Philosophical Association*, 60, 441–58.

(1991) "Epistemology Externalized," *Dialectica*, 45, 2–3, 191–202.

(1993) "Thinking Causes," in J. Heil & A. Mele (eds.) *Mental Causation*.

Dawkins, R. (1986) *The Blind Watchmaker*, London: Penguin.

(1995) "God's Utility Function," *Scientific American*, 273, 80–85.

Dennett, D. C. (1969) *Content and Consciousness*, London: Routledge & Kegan Paul.

(1971) "The Intentional Stance," in Dennett (1978) *Brainstorms, Philosophical Essays on Mind and Psychology*.

References

(1978) *Brainstorms, Philosophical Essays on Mind and Psychology*, Cambridge, Mass.: MIT Press.

(1981a) "True Believers," in Dennett (1987c) *The Intentional Stance*.

(1981b) "Three Kinds of Intentional Psychology," in Dennett (1987c) *The Intentional Stance*.

(1982a) "Making Sense of Ourselves," in Dennett (1987c) *The Intentional Stance*.

(1982b) "Beyond Belief," in Woodfield (ed.) *Thought and Object*.

(1983a) "Intentional Systems in Cognitive Ethology: The 'Panglossian Paradigm' Defended," in Dennett (1987c) *The Intentional Stance*.

(1983b) "Artificial Intelligence and the Strategies of Psychological Investigation – Dialogue with Daniel Dennett," in J. Miller (ed.)(1983) *States of Mind, Conversations with Psychological Investigators*, London: British Broadcasting Corporation.

(1987a) "Reflections: Interpreting Monkeys, Theorists, and Genes," in Dennett (1987c) *The Intentional Stance*.

(1987b) "Evolution, Error and Intentionality," in Dennett (1987c) *The Intentional Stance*.

(1987c) *The Intentional Stance*, Cambridge, Mass.: MIT Press.

(1988) Review of J. A. Fodor's *Psychosemantics*, *The Journal of Philosophy*, 384–89.

(1991a) "Real Patterns," *The Journal of Philosophy*, 88, 1, 27–51.

(1991b) "Ways of Establishing Harmony," in B. McLaughlin (ed.)(1991) *Dretske and his Critics*.

Devitt, M. (1989) "A Narrow Representational Theory of the Mind," in S. Silvers (ed.)(1989) *Rerepresentation, Readings in the Philosophy of Mental Representation*, Dordrecht: Kluwer Academic Publishers.

(1990) "Transcendentalism about Content," *Pacific Philosophical Quarterly*, 71, 247–63.

Devitt, M. & G. Rey (1991) "Transcending Transcendentalism: a Response to Boghossian," *Pacific Philosophical Quarterly*, 72, 87–100.

Dretske, F. (1969) *Seeing and Knowing*, Chicago University Press.

(1972) "Contrastive Statements," *Philosophical Review*, 81, 4, 411–37.

(1981) *Knowledge and the Flow of Information*, Cambridge, Mass.: MIT Press.

(1986) "Misrepresentation," in R. Bogdan (ed.) *Belief*, Oxford: Clarendon Press.

(1988) *Explaining Behavior*, Cambridge, Mass.: MIT Press.

(1990a) "Reply to Reviewers," *Philosophy and Phenomenological Research*, 1, 4, 819–39.

(1990b) "Does Meaning Matter?," in E. Villanueva (ed.) (1990) *Information, Semantics and Epistemology.*

(1991a) "Two Conceptions of Knowledge: Rational vs. Reliable Belief," in J. Brandl, W. L. Gombocz & C. Piller (eds.) *Metamind, Knowledge and Coherence, Essays on the Philosophy of Keith Lehrer, Grazer Philosophische Studien*, vol. 40.

(1991b) "Dretske's Replies," in B. McLaughlin (ed.) *Dretske and his Critics.*

(1991c) "How Beliefs Explain: Reply to Baker," *Philosophical Studies*, 63, 113–17.

(1993a) "Mental Events as Structuring Causes," in J. Heil & A. Mele (eds.) *Mental Causation.*

(1993b) "The Nature of Thought," *Philosophical Studies*, 70, 185–99.

(1994a) "Naturalizing the Mind or If You Can't Make One, You Don't Understand How it Works," lecture delivered in Lyon, 16 May 1994.

(1994b) "Reply to Slater and Garcia-Carpintero," *Mind and Language*, 9, 2, 203–8.

(1995) *Naturalizing the Mind*, Cambridge, Mass.: MIT Press.

Duhem, P. (1906; 1981) *La Théorie phyique, son object, sa structure*, Paris: Vrin.

Dummett, M. (1973) *Frege: Philosophy of Language*, New York: Harper & Row.

(1975) "Can Analytical Philosophy Be Systematic and Ought it to Be?," in Dummett (1978) *Truth and Other Enigmas*, Cambridge, Mass.: Harvard University Press.

Evans, G. (1980) "Fodor Flawed," *The Behavioral and Brain Sciences*, 3, 1, 79–80.

(1981) "Reply: Semantic Theory and Tacit Knowledge," in S.H. Holtzman & C.M. Leich (eds.) *Wittgenstein: To Follow a Rule*, London: Routledge & Kegan Paul.

(1982) *The Varieties of Reference*, Oxford: Clarendon Press.

Evnine, S. (1991) *Donald Davidson*, Oxford: Polity Press.

Fauconnier, G. (1985) *Mental Spaces: Aspects of Meaning Construction in Natural Languages*, Cambridge, Mass.: MIT Press.

Feyerabend, P. K. (1963) "Mental Events and the Brain," in D. Rosenthal (ed.) (1991) *The Nature of Mind*, Oxford University Press.

(1975) *Against Method*, London, New Left Review Edition.

Field, H. (1972) "Tarski's Theory of Truth," in M . Platts (ed.)(1980) *Reference, Truth and Reality*, London: Routledge & Kegan Paul.

(1977) "Logic, Meaning, and Conceptual Role," *The Journal of Philosophy*, 74, 379–409.

References

(1978) "Mental Representation," in Block (ed.)(1980) *Readings in the Philosophy of Psychology*, vol. II.

Fodor, J. A. (1975) *The Language of Thought*, New York: Crowell.

(1980) "Methodological Solipsism Considered as a Research Programme in Cognitive Psychology," in Fodor (1981) *Representations*.

(1981) *Representations; Philosophical Essays on the Foundations of Cognitive Science*, Cambridge, Mass.: MIT Press.

(1983) *The Modularity of Mind*, Cambridge, Mass.: MIT Press.

(1984) "Semantics, Wisconsin Style," in Fodor (1990d) *A Theory of Content and Other Essays*.

(1985) "Fodor's Guide to Mental Representation," in Fodor (1990d) *A Theory of Content and Other Essays*.

(1986) "Why Paramecia Don't Have Mental Representations," in P. French, T. Uehling, Jr. & H. Wettstein (eds.) *Midwest Studies in Philosophy*, vol. X, Minneapolis: University of Minnesota Press.

(1987a) "Mental Representation: an Introduction," in N. Rescher (ed.) *Scientific Inquiry in Philosophical Perspective*, Lanham, Md.: University Press of America.

(1987b) *Psychosemantics; the Problem of Meaning in the Philosophy of Mind*, Cambridge, Mass.: MIT Press.

(1989a) "Substitution Arguments and the Individuation of Beliefs," in Fodor (1990d) *A Theory of Content and Other Essays*.

(1989b) "Making Mind Matter More," in Fodor (1990d) *A Theory of Content and Other Essays*.

(1990a) "Stephen Schiffer's Dark Night of the Soul: A Review of *Remnants of Meaning*," in Fodor (1990d) *A Theory of Content and Other Essays*.

(1990b) "A Theory of Content, I: The Problem," in Fodor (1990d) *A Theory of Content and Other Essays*.

(1990c) "A Theory of Content, II: The Theory," in Fodor (1990d) *A Theory of Content and Other Essays*.

(1990d) *A Theory of Content and Other Essays*, Cambridge, Mass.: MIT Press.

(1990e) "Reply to Dretske's 'Does Meaning Matter?'," in E. Villanueva (ed.) *Information, Semantics & Epistemology*.

(1991) "A Modal Argument for Narrow Content," *The Journal of Philosophy*, 88, 1, 5–26.

(1992) "A Theory of the Child's Theory of Mind," *Cognition*, 44, 283–96.

(1994) *The Elm and the Expert*, Cambridge, Mass.: MIT Press.

Fodor, J. A. & E. Lepore (1991) "Why Meaning (Probably) Isn't Conceptual Role," *Mind and Language*, 6, 4, 328–43.

(1992) *Holism. A Shopper's Guide*, Oxford: Blackwell.

Garcia-Carpintero, M. (1994) "Dretske on the Causal Efficacy of Meaning," *Mind and Language*, 9, 2, 181–202.

Geach, P. (1969) *God and the Soul*, London: Routledge & Kegan Paul.

Gleitman, H. (1986) *Psychology* (2nd edition), New York: Norton.

Godfrey-Smith, P. (1989) "Misinformation," *Canadian Journal of Philosophy*, 19, 4, 535–50.

(1992) "Indication and Adaptation," *Synthese*, 92, 283–312.

(1993) "Functions: Consensus Without Unity," *Pacific Philosophical Quarterly*, 74, 3, 196–208.

Goodman, N. (1955) *Fact, Fiction and Forecast*, New York: Bobbs-Merrill.

Gregory, R. L. (1966) *Eye and Brain, the Psychology of Seeing*, New York: McGraw Hill.

(1970) *The Intelligent Eye*, London: George Weidenfeld & Nicolson Ltd.

Grice, P. (1957) "Meaning," in Grice (1989) *Studies in the Way of Words*.

Grice, P. (1968) "Utterer's Meaning, Sentence Meaning and Word Meaning," in Grice (1989) *Studies in the Way of Words*.

(1969) "Utterer's Meaning and Intention," in Grice (1989) *Studies in the Way of Words*.

(1975) "Logic and Conversation," in Grice (1989) *Studies in the Way of Words*.

(1989) *Studies in the Way of Words*, Cambridge, Mass.: Harvard University Press.

Guttenplan, S. (ed.)(1994) *A Companion to the Philosophy of Mind*, Oxford: Blackwell.

Hanson, P. P. (ed.) (1990) *Information, Language and Cognition*, Oxford: Oxford University Press.

Hare, R. M. (1952) *The Language of Morals*, Oxford University Press.

Harman, G. (1982) "Conceptual Role Semantics," *Notre Dame Journal of Formal Logic*, 23, 2, 242–56.

Haugeland, J. (1981a) "Semantic Engines: an Introduction to Mind Design," in Haugeland (ed.) (1981b) *Mind Design, Philosophy, Psychology, Artificial Intelligence*.

(1981b) *Mind Design, Philosophy, Psychology, Artificial Intelligence*, Cambridge, Mass.: MIT Press.

References

Heil, J. & A. Mele (eds.) (1993) *Mental Causation*, Oxford: The Clarendon Press.

Hempel, C. G. (1965) *Aspects of Scientific Explanation and Other Essays in the Philosophy of Science*, New York: The Free Press.

Horgan, T. (1989) "Mental Quausation," in J. Tomberlin (ed.) *Philosophical Perspectives*, vol. 3.

(1990) Review of *Explaining Behavior, Mind and Language*, 5, 3, 230–34.

(1991) "Actions, Reasons, and the Explanatory Role of Content," in B. McLaughlin (ed.) (1991) *Dretske and his Critics*.

Humphrey, N. (1992) *A History of the Mind, Evolution and the Birth of Consciousness*, New York: Harper Collins.

Israel, D. & J. Perry (1990) "What is Information?," in P. P. Hanson (ed.)(1990) *Information, Language and Cognition*.

Jackson, F. & P. Pettit (1988) "Functionalism and Broad Content," *Mind*, 97, 381–400.

(1990a) "Program Explanation: a General Perspective," *Analyis*, 50, 2, 107–17.

(1990b) "Causation in the Philosophy of Mind," *Philosophy and Phenomenological Research*, 50, 195–214.

(1990c) "In Defense of Explanatory Ecumenism," mimeo.

Jacob, P. (1991) "Are Mental Properties Causally Efficacious?," *Grazer Philosophische Studien*, 39, 51–73.

(1992) "Externalism and Mental Causation," *Proceedings of the Aristotelian Society*, 92, 203–19.

Kaplan, D. (1978) "Dthat," in P. A. French, T. E. Uehling, Jr. & H. K. Wettstein (eds.) (1979) *Contemporary Perspectives in the Philosophy of Language*, Minneapolis: Minnesota University Press.

(1989) "Demonstratives," in J. Almog, H. Wettstein & J. Perry (eds.) (1989) *Themes from Kaplan*, Oxford University Press.

Katz, J. J. (1981) *Language & Other Abstract Objects*, Totowa, N.J.: Rowman & Littlefield.

Kim, J. J. (1973a) "Causation, Nomic Subsumption and the Concept of Event," in Kim (1994a) *Supervenience and Mind*.

(1973b) "Causes and Counterfactuals," in E. Sosa & M. Tooley (eds.) (1993) *Causation*, Oxford University Press.

(1974) "Noncausal Connections," in Kim (1994a) *Supervenience and Mind*.

(1982) "Psychophysical Supervenience," in Kim (1994a) *Supervenience and Mind*.

References

(1984) "Epiphenomenal and Supervenient Causation," in Kim (1994) *Supervenience and Mind*.

(1989a) "Mechanism, Purpose, and Explanatory Exclusion," in Kim (1994a) *Supervenience and Mind*.

(1989b) "The Myth of Nonreductive Materialism," in Kim (1994a) *Supervenience and Mind*.

(1991) "Dretske on How Reasons Explain Behavior," in Kim (1994a) *Supervenience and Mind*.

(1994a) *Supervenience and Mind, Selected Philosophical Essays*, Cambridge University Press.

(1994b) "Supervenience," in S. Guttenplan (ed.) *A Companion to the Philosophy of Mind*.

Kistler, M. (1995) "Causalité, loi, représentation," unpublished doctoral dissertation, Ecole des Hautes Etudes en Sciences Sociales.

Kripke, S. (1972; 1982) *Naming and Necessity*, Oxford: Blackwell.

(1979) "A Puzzle About Belief," in A. Margalit (ed.) *Meaning and Use*, Dordrecht: Reidel.

Künne, W. (1995) "Thought, Speech, and the 'Language of Thought'," mimeo.

Laurier, D. (1994) "Indication, représentation et explication," *Cahiers du département de philosophie*, université de Montréal, no 94–5.

Lehrer, K. (1991) "Reply to Fred Dretske," in *Metamind, Knowledge and Coherence, Essays on the Philosophy of Keith Lehrer*, J. Brandl, W. L. Gombocz & C. Piller (eds.) *Grazer Philosophische Studien*, vol. 40.

Lepore, E. & B. Loewer (1987) "Mind Matters," *The Journal of Philosophy*, 84, 630–42.

Lewis, D. (1966) "An Argument for the Identity Theory," in Lewis (1983) *Philosophical Papers*, vol. I, Oxford University Press.

(1972) "Psychophysical and Theoretical Identifications," in Block (ed.)(1980) *Readings in the Philosophy of Psychology*, vol. I.

Lewontin, R. (1983) "Darwin's Revolution," *New York Review of Books*, 30, 21–27.

Lindsay, P. H. & D. A. Norman (1972) *Human Information Processing*, New York: Academic Press.

Loar, B. (1982) "Conceptual Role and Truth-Conditions," *The Notre Dame Journal of Formal Logic*, 23, 3, 272–83.

Loewer, B. (1987) "From Information to Intentionality," *Synthese*, 70, 2, 287–317.

Loewer, B. & E. Lepore (1986) "Solipsistic Semantics," in P. A. French, T.

E. Uehling, Jr. & H. K. Wettstein (eds.) (1986) *Midwest Studies in Philosophy*, vol. X, Minneapolis: University of Minnesota Press.

Loewer, B. & G. Rey (eds.)(1991) *Meaning in Mind, Fodor and his Critics*, Oxford: Blackwell.

Mackie, J. L. (1977) *Ethics, Inventing Right and Wrong*, New York: Penguin.

Malcolm, N. (1972–73) "Thoughtless Brutes," in D. Rosenthal (ed.) (1991) *The Nature of Mind*, Oxford University Press.

McDowell, J. (1984) *"De Re* Senses," in C. Wright (ed.) *Frege, Tradition & Influence*, Oxford: Blackwell.

McGinn, C. (1982) "The Structure of Content," in Woodfield (ed.) *Thought and Object*.

(1983) *The Subjective View: Secondary Qualities and Indexical Thoughts*, Oxford: Clarendon Press.

(1989) *Mental Content*, Oxford: Blackwell.

(1991) *The Problem of Consciousness*, Oxford: Blackwell.

McLaughlin, B. (1989) "Type Epiphenomenalism, Type Dualism, and the Causal Priority of the Physical," in J. Tomberlin (ed.) *Philosophical Perspectives*, vol. 3.

(ed.)(1991) *Dretske and his Critics*, Oxford: Blackwell.

Menzies, P. (1988) "Against Causal Reductionism," *Mind*, 97, 551–74.

Miller, G. A. (1956) "The Magical Number Seven, Plus-or-Minus Two or Some Limits on Our Capacity for Processing Information," C. R. Evans & A. D. J. Robertson (eds.)(1966) *Key Papers in Brain Physiology and Psychology*, London: Butterworths.

Millikan (1984) *Language, Thought and Other Biological Categories*, Cambridge, Mass.: MIT Press.

(1986) "Thoughts without Laws," in Millikan (1993) *White Queen Psychology*.

(1989a) "In Defense of Proper Function," in Millikan (1993) *White Queen Psychology*.

(1989b) "Biosemantics," in Millikan (1993) *White Queen Psychology*.

(1990a) "Compare and Contrast Dretske, Fodor and Millikan," in Millikan (1993) *White Queen Psychology*.

(1990b) "Truth Rules, Hoverflies, and the Kripke-Wittgenstein Paradox," in Millikan (1993) *White Queen Psychology*.

(1990c) "Seismograph Readings for *Explaining Behavior*," *Philosophy and Phenomenological Research*, 1, 4, 807–12.

(1991) "Speaking up for Darwin," in B. Loewer & G. Rey (eds.) *Meaning in Mind*.

(1993) *White Queen Psychology and Other Essays for Alice*, Cambridge, Mass.: MIT Press.

Nagel, T. (1974) "What is it like to be a Bat," in Block (ed.)(1980) *Readings in the Philosophy of Psychology*, vol. I.

Neander, K. (1988) "What Does Natural Selection Explain? Correction to Sober," *Philosophy of Science*, 55, 422–26.

(1991) "The Teleological Notion of Function," *Australasian Journal of Philosophy*, 69, 4, 454–68.

(1994) "Dretske and the Inflation Thesis," mimeo.

(1995a) "Misrepresenting and Malfunctioning," *Philosophical Studies*, 79, 109–41.

(1995b) "Pruning the Tree of Life," *The British Journal for the Philosophy of Science*, 46, 1, 59–80.

Neisser, U. (1967) *Cognitive Psychology*, New York: Appleton-Century-Crofts.

Peacocke, C. (1981) "Demonstrative Thought and Psychological Explanation," *Synthese*, 49, 181–217.

(1983) *Sense and Content, Experience, Thought, and their Relations*, Oxford University Press.

(1989) "Perceptual Content," in J. Almog, J. Perry & H. Wettstein (eds.) *Themes from Kaplan*, New York: Oxford University Press.

(1992a) "Scenarios, Concepts and Perception," in Crane (ed.)(1992a) *The Contents of Experience*.

(1992b) *A Study of Concepts*, Cambridge, Mass.: MIT Press.

Perry, J. (1977) "Frege on Demonstratives," in Perry (1993) *The Problem of the Essential Indexical and Other Essays*.

(1979) "The Essential Indexical," in Perry (1993) *The Problem of the Essential Indexical and Other Essays*.

(1986) "Thoughts Without Representation," in Perry (1993) *The Problem of the Essential Indexical and Other Essays*.

(1993) *The Problem of the Essential Indexical and Other Essays*, Oxford University Press.

Putnam, H. (1954) "Synonymity, and the Analysis of Belief Sentences," in N. Salmon & S. Soames (eds.) (1988) *Propositions and Attitudes*, Oxford University Press.

(1960) "Minds and Machines," in Putnam (1975b) *Mind, Language and Reality, Philosophical Papers*, vol. II.

(1963) "Brains and Behavior," in Putnam (1975b) *Mind, Language and Reality, Philosophical Papers*, vol. II.

References

(1973a) "Reductionism and the Nature of Psychology," *Cognition*, 2, 1, 131–46.

(1973b) "Explanation and Reference," in Putnam (1975b) *Mind, Language and Reality, Philosophical Papers*, vol. II.

(1974) "The Meaning of 'Meaning'," in Putnam (1975b) *Mind, Language and Reality, Philosophical Papers*, vol. II.

(1975a) "Philosophy and Our Mental Life," in Putnam (1975b) *Mind, Language and Reality, Philosophical Papers*, vol. II.

(1975b) *Mind, Language and Reality, Philosophical Papers*, vol. II, Cambridge: Cambridge University Press.

(1981) *Reason, Truth and History*, Cambridge University Press.

(1983a) "Computational Psychology and Interpretation Theory," in Putnam (1983b) *Realism and Reason, Philosophical Papers*, vol. III.

(1983b) *Realism and Reason, Philosophical Papers*, vol. III, Cambridge University Press.

(1988) *Representation and Reality*, Cambridge, Mass.: MIT Press.

(1992) "Truth, Activation Vectors and Possession Conditions for Concepts," *Philosophy and Phenomenological Research*, 52, 2, 431–47.

(1994) "Putnam, Hilary," in Guttenplan (ed.)(1994) *A Companion to the Philosophy of Mind*.

Quine, W. V. O. (1951) "Two Dogmas of Empiricism," in Quine (1953b) *From a Logical Point of View*.

(1953a) "Reference and Modality," in Quine (1953b) *From a Logical Point of View*.

(1953b) *From a Logical Point of View*, Cambridge, Mass.: Harvard University Press.

(1960) *Word and Object*, Cambridge, Mass.: MIT Press.

(1977) "Facts of the Matter," in R. W. Shahan & C. Swoyer (eds.) *Essays on the Philosophy of W.V. Quine*, Brighton: Harvester Press.

Ramsey, F. P. (1929) "Theories," in Ramsey (1931) *The Foundations of Mathematics and Other Logical Essays*.

(1931) *The Foundations of Mathematics and Other Logical Essays*, London: Routledge & Kegan Paul.

Recanati, F. (1989) "The Pragmatics of What Is Said," *Mind and Language*, 4, 295–329.

(1993) *Direct Reference; from Language to Thought*, Oxford: Blackwell.

Rey, G. (forthcoming) "Dennett's Unrealistic Psychology," *Philosophical Topics*.

Richard, M. (1990) *Propositional Attitudes*, Cambridge University Press.

Ridley, M. (1995) *Animal Behavior* (2nd edition), Oxford: Blackwell.

Rosenthal, D. (1986) "Two Concepts of Consciousness," *Philosophical Studies*, 49, 329–59.

(1993a) "Thinking that One Thinks," in M. Davies & G.W. Humphreys (eds.) *Consciousness*, Oxford: Blackwell.

(1993b) "State Consciousness and Transitive Consciousness," *Consciousness and Cognition*, 2, 355–63.

Salmon, N. (1986) *Frege's Puzzle*, Cambridge, Mass.: MIT Press.

Salmon, W. (1984) *Scientific Explanation and the Causal Structure of the World*, Princeton University Press.

Schiffer, S. (1987) *Remnants of Meaning*, Cambridge, Mass.: MIT Press.

Searle, J. R. (1992) *The Rediscovery of the Mind*, Cambridge, Mass.: MIT Press.

Segal, G. & E. Sober (1991) "The Causal Efficacy of Content," *Philosophical Studies*, 63, 1–30.

Sober, E. (1984a) *The Nature of Selection*, Cambridge, Mass.: MIT Press.

(ed.) (1984b) *Conceptual Issues in Evolutionary Biology, an Anthology*, Cambridge, Mass.: MIT Press.

Sosa, E. (1984) "Mind-Body Interaction and Supervenient Causation," in P. A. French, T. E. Uehling, Jr. & H. K. Wettstein (eds.) (1984) *Midwest Studies in Philosophy*, vol. IX, "Causation and Causal Theories," Minneapolis: University of Minnesota Press.

Sperber, D. (1993) "Understanding Verbal Understanding," in J. Kalfa (ed.) *What is Intelligence?*, Cambridge University Press.

Sperber, D. & D. Wilson (1986) *Relevance, Communication and Cognition*, Cambridge, Mass.: Harvard University Press.

Sperling, G. (1960) "The Information Available in Brief Visual Presentations," *Psychological Monographs*, 74, 11.

Stalnaker, R. C. (1984) *Inquiry*, Cambridge, Mass.: MIT Press.

Stampe, D. W. (1977) "Toward a Causal Theory of Linguistic Representation," in P. A. French, T. E. Uehling, Jr. & H. K. Wettstein (eds.) *Contemporary Perspectives in the Philosophy of Language*, Minneapolis: University of Minnesota University Press.

Sterelny, K. (1990) *The Representational Theory of Mind. An Introduction*, Oxford: Blackwell.

Stich, S. (1978a) "Autonomous Psychology and the Belief-Desire Thesis," *The Monist*, 61, 573–91.

(1978b) "Beliefs and Subdoxastic States," *Philosophy of Science*, 45, 499–518.

References

(1983) *From Folk Psychology to Cognitive Science*, Cambridge, Mass.: MIT Press.

(1990a) *The Fragmentation of Reason*, Cambridge, Mass.: MIT Press.

(1990b) "Building Belief: Some Queries about Representation, Indication, and Function," *Philosophy and Phenomenological Research*, 1, 4, 783–86.

Taschek, W.W. (1995) "Belief, Substitution, and Logical Structure," *Nous*, 29, 1, 71–95.

Tomberlin, J. (ed.) (1989) *Philosophical Perspectives,* volume 3: *Philosophy of Mind and Action Theory*, Atascadero, Calif.: Ridgeview.

Travis, C. (1982) "On What Is Strictly Speaking True," *Canadian Journal of Philosophy*, 15, 187–229.

(1989) *The Uses of Sense*, Oxford: Clarendon Press.

Treisman, A. & G. Gelade (1980) "A Feature-Integration Theory of Attention," *Cognitive Psychology*, 12, 97–136.

Villanueva, E. (ed) (1990) *Information, Semantics & Epistemology*, Oxford: Blackwell.

Wettstein, H.K. (1986) "Does Semantics Rest on a Mistake?," *The Journal of Philosophy*, 83, 185–209.

Woodfield, A. (ed.)(1982) *Thought and Object*, Oxford: Clarendon Press.

Wright, C. (1986) "How Can the Theory of Meaning be a Philosophical Project?," *Mind & Language*, 1, 1, 31–44.

Wright, L. (1973) "Function," in E. Sober (ed.) (1984b) *Conceptual Issues in Evolutionary Biology*.

Wright, L. (1976) *Teleological Explanation*, Berkeley: University of California Press.

Yablo, S. (1992) "Mental Causation," *The Philosophical Review*, 101, 2, 245–80.

Index

Index

297